UNKNOWN
CAPOEIRA

Also by Mestre Ricardo Cachorro

Unknown Capoeira Vol. Two
A History of the Brazilian Martial Art

UNKNOWN CAPOEIRA

SECRET TECHNIQUES OF THE ORIGINAL BRAZILIAN MARTIAL ART

Mestre Ricardo Cachorro

Copyright © 2009 Dekel Publishing House. All rights reserved. No portion of this book, except for brief review, may be reproduced, stored in a retrieval system, or transmitted in any form or by any means – electronic, mechanical, photocopying, recording, or otherwise – without written permission of the publisher. For information contact Dekel Publishing House, Israel, or Blue Snake Books c/o North Atlantic Books.

Dekel Publishing House
P.O. Box 45094; Tel Aviv 61450, Israel
www.dekelpublishing.com
ISBN 978-965-7178-14-0

Published in North America by **Blue Snake Books**

Blue Snake Books books are distributed by North Atlantic Books
P.O. Box 12327, Berkeley, California 94712, USA

Cover and book illustration: Ingo Bertelli   **English-language editing**: Efrat Ashkenazi
Cover and book design: Gisella Narcisi   **Proof-reading**: Ilay Sofer

Printed in Israel

Unknown Capoeira: Secret Techniques of the Original Brazilian Martial Art is sponsored by the Society for the Study of Native Arts and Sciences, a nonprofit educational corporation whose goals are to develop an educational and cross-cultural perspective linking various scientific, social, and artistic fields; to nurture a holistic view of arts, sciences, humanities, and healing; and to publish and distribute literature on the relationship of mind, body, and nature.

North Atlantic Books' publications are available through most bookstores. For further information, visit our Web site at www.northatlanticbooks.com or call 800-733-3000.

PLEASE NOTE: The creators and publishers of this book disclaim any liabilities for loss in connection with following any of the practices, exercises, and advice contained herein. To reduce the chance of injury or any other harm, the reader should consult a professional before undertaking this or any other martial arts, movement, meditative arts, health, or exercise program. The instructions and advice printed in this book are not in any way intended as a substitute for medical, mental, or emotional counseling with a licensed physician or healthcare provider.

Library of Congress Cataloging-in-Publication Data:
Cachorro, Ricardo.
  Unknown Capoeira : secret techniques of the original Brazilian martial art / Ricardo Cachorro.
    p. cm.
  ISBN 978-1-58394-231-4 -- ISBN 978-965-7178-14-0
  1. Capoeira (Dance) I. Title.
  GV1796.C145C24 2009
  793.3'1981--dc22
                    2009013548
1 2 3 4 5 6 7 8 9 Dekel Productions, Tel Aviv 12 11 10 09

Testimonial of Mestre Peixinho
cofounder and Mestre of Capoeira of the Senzala Group

Ricardo and I first met in the early 1970s as Olympic Gymnastics teammates from the Fluminense Football Club in Rio de Janeiro. We are colleagues in the Floor Exercises specialization course under the great Coach Ribas.

At that time, I was cofounder and Mestre of Capoeira of the Senzala Group and was interested in the body mechanics of Floor Exercises' acrobatic moves, which helped me understand the subtle, yet important differences between the more intuitive artistic creativity and the more systematic approach of these practices.

We agree that both arts overlap in their creative elements but produce different, complex results. Capoeira has a holistic approach and a unique fluidity, and is bound to its strong historical and cultural contexts.

It was my pleasure to accept the invitation of my friend Ricardo to be the curator of his book. I hope you enjoy it.

Mestre Peixinho
Rio de Janeiro, August, 2007, Brazil

Acknowledgments

It would be impossible to write this book without the inspiration from my late friend and teacher, Mestre Adilson, from Grupo Bantus de Capoeira of Morro do Pavão e Pavãozinho, in Rio de Janeiro. His example will always be remembered as well as his wonderful stories of the great legendary old masters, whose legacy continues to inspire generations of capoeiristas around the world.

This book would not be complete without the support and generosity of my friends Mestre Camisa, Mestre Paulo Siqueira and Mestre Peixinho. Their legacy, too, will live on forever in our hearts and minds.

I owe a special debt of gratitude to Prof. Geraldo Cesar Barbosa, cofounder and sporting director of the YMCA Governors Island, for having invited me to inaugurate an teach their first capoeira classes, in Rio de Janeiro in the 1970s.

Writing this book was not only an emotional journey, but a technical challenge that would not have been met without the exceptional contribution of Efrat Ashkenzi to the final text.

During this project, I have learned very much from the long and fruitful discussions with Zvi Morik, Managing Director of Dekel Publishing House, to whom I would like to express my eternal indebtedness.

I wish to express my deepest gratitude to my wife and daughter for their unconditional love and support.

Table of Contents

Message to the Capoeira Nation xi
Introduction xiii

Techniques

Armada 1
    Armada Pulada 7
Armada Dupla 11
Aú (Classic) 15
    Aú Dobrado 19
    Aú Agulha 20
Aú Batido 22
    Aú Batido Agrupado 24
    Aú Batido Fechado 24
    Aú Batido de Cotovelo 24
Aú Chibata 27
    Aú Chibata de Chão 30
Aú Com uma Mão 32
Aú de Costas 35
    Macaco em Pé 35
    Aú de Costas Infinito 37
Aú de Frente 40
    Aú Reversão 40
    Aú Cortado 40
Aú Fechado 43
    Pião de Mão 48
Aú Giratório 48
Aú Sem Mãos 51

- **Bananeira** **55**
  - *Bananeira Giratória*...*57*
  - *Escorpião* *58*
  - *Prancha* *59*
- **Benção** **60**
  - *Benção Pulada*..*63*
- **Bloqueio** **65**
  - *Bloqueio de Dentro* *67*
  - *Tombo da Ladeira* *68*
- **Chapa** **72**
  - *Chapa Lateral* *73*
  - *Chapa Giratória* *73*
  - *Escorão* *74*
  - *Coice de Mula*...*74*
  - *Chapa Pulada*..*75*
- **Compasso**.. **77**
  - *Compasso Pulado*...*80*
- **Esquiva** **81**
  - *Esquiva Lateral* *81*
  - *Cocorinha*..*82*
  - *Resistência* *83*
  - *Esquiva de Frente*...*85*
  - *Queda de Quatro*..*86*
  - *Esquiva de Frente*...*86*
  - *Volta por Cima* *87*
- **Folha Seca**.. **89**
- **Gancho** **94**
- **Helicóptero** **96**
- **Macaco** **99**
  - *Macaco Agrupado*...*100*
  - *Macaquinho* *101*
- **Mariposa** **103**
- **Martelo**.. **108**
  - *Martelo Médio*...*112*
  - *Martelo Baixo*..*113*
  - *Martelo Pulado*..*114*
- **Martelo Preso**... **117**
- **Martelo Rodado Voador** **120**
- **Mata-borrão** **124**

Meia-lua de Chão	***126***
Meia-lua de Compasso	***131***
Meia-lua Diagonal	*134*
Meia-lua Presa	*135*
Meia-lua Solta	*137*
Meia-lua Pulada	*138*
Meia-lua Queda de Rim	*139*
Meia-lua de Frente	***144***
Gafanhoto	*144*
Meia-lua de Frente Pulada	*148*
Parafuso	*148*
Meia-lua Reversão	***150***
Mortal de Costas	***155***
Mortal de Frente	***159***
Negativa	***165***
Queda da Negativa	*168*
Negativa Derrubando	*168*
Negativa Lateral	*170*
Negativa de Frente	*171*
Troca de Negativa	*172*
Ponte	***176***
Ponteira	***178***
Ponteira Esticada	*180*
Ponteira Pulada	*181*
Ponteira Lateral	*183*
Queda	***185***
Tesoura	*186*
Alavanca de Pé	*188*
Vingativa	*188*
Arrastão	*189*
Cabeçada Baixa	*190*
Cabeçada de Chão	*190*
Vôo do Morcego	*191*
Queda de Rim	***194***
Queixada	***198***
Queixada de Trás	*200*
Rasteira	***202***
Rasteira Giratória	*206*
Relógio	*208*

- Corta-capim. 209
- Rasteira em Pé 209
- Rasteira de Costas Cruzada 213
- Banda 213
- Banda de Costas Cruzada 214
- Calcanheira 215
- Passa-pé 216
- Bloqueio de Dentro 218
- Rasteira de Mão 220
- Boca de Calça 221

Rolê 225
- Rolê Reverso 227

S-dobrado 228
- Chapéu de Couro 230

Xangô 232

Xangô de Frente 238

Unexpected Moves 241
- Arpão de Cabeça 243
- Cabeçada 243
- Escorumelo 243
- Cabeçada de Chão 244
- Telefone 245
- Dedeira 245
- Escala 245
- Galopante.. 246
- Godeme 246
- Cotovelada 247
- Cutelo 247
- Joelhada 247

Mestre Bimba's Sequences 249

Roda de Boca 254

Message to the Capoeira Nation from Mestre Camisa
cofounder and Mestre of Capoeira of the ABADÁ Group

To all fellow capoeiristas from all origins, congratulations! This is an opportunity for us to reflect once more about our role and our art.

Each day Capoeira advances in the most different societies of the world, creating a unique synergy, which is made possible due to its ludic aspect and through its diversity. Together, we build only one language, spoken by a peaceful community that is constituted of true warriors. It is integration through the art and the art of integration, all in a continuous movement.

Capoeira, per se, irradiates enthusiasm, energy, understanding, will and determination, qualities that need to be absorbed by the practitioners, whether they are students or masters; they are inherent to the body and the mind of the capoeirista.

If Capoeira is your profession or your philosophy of life, you will be able to see the world through it. If it is your recreation, though, the angles are different but the horizons are equally attractive and challenging. Remember that we are all equals, no matter our social status. Capoeira helps us overcome the hardships of our daily lives, to win and to lose; mainly to lose, because all of us are already prepared to win. You can also use discipline to help you find freedom. Freedom to act, think and develop your life, your work, your Capoeira, your hobby and your repose, in a balanced way.

Capoeira is a game of serious, cordial and polite people, of intelligent men and women. In the roda we learn how to trick, elude and mislead the other players, trying to persuade them to do what we want during the confrontation. These are tactics, which teach us to be prepared to go out on the streets. Take the malice and the illusion inside the roda and always leave with your character and your sincerity intact! Today you may overcome your opponent, tomorrow he will defeat you, but the essence of character and truth will never be defeated.

The fact that Capoeira is a multidimensional discipline, i.e., originated from the fusion of several arts and cultural expressions, suggests that it should not be practiced only in the roda. The contemporary capoeiristas must be committed to the preservation of the natural environment; they must study, research, develop themselves and try to coexist with diversity. To the Mestres, it means a continuous reflection over their responsibilities. To the students, it means the increasing perception of their new abilities.

Try to maintain contact with the old masters of Capoeira, the true owners of a kind of knowledge which is in risk of extinction. This connection of the past with the present continues to be important for the development of Capoeira.

We are a global community, as a huge tree, and what make us grow are the roots. Without them, there is no nourishment for new fruit.

Regards to all,

Mestre Camisa
Rio de Janeiro, September, 2007, Brazil

Introduction

One of the interesting things about capoeira is that millions of *capoeiristas* (the capoeira practitioners) do not aspire to learn capoeira as a martial art, such as practitioners of Japanese karate often do, to mention one example. Many capoeiristas prefer to practice capoeira as a ludic and ritualistic activity; some use capoeira for physical fitness, while others like to consider it as part of a cultural movement, or they practice it for relaxation – or to acquire motor coordination. Capoeira does focus on these activities. Nonetheless, there are many capoeiristas who use it as a martial art, which embraces history, music, dance, folklore and capoeira as a game, the jogo, demonstrated through a rhythmical dancefight, a cunning strategy sometimes replete with graceful, complex moves and gravity-defying acrobatics performed by the capoeiristas in the *roda* – a circle made of capoeiristas, within which capoeira is performed. In reality, all these features together form the realm of capoeira, and it is up to each practitioner to find his or her own purpose for learning it the best way possible.

This book focuses primarily on the beautiful, rich and efficient martial art which was born in capoeira as a means to reach all its other features. Whether fighting for life or for integration in society, the martial art of capoeira is the very reason why the art exists in the first place. History and cultural heritage are cofounders of this art, together with the need that the African and Afro-Brazilian slaves had to create it and use it to defend themselves fiercely against their oppressors, with the fighting styles which were produced from the convergence of these components.

As a result of its development in Brazil through the years, capoeira became the richest and the most spectacular and athletic martial art on the planet, while the majority of capoeiristas who focus exclusively on the ludic aspects of the game still do not know this for a fact.

Although the reader may choose to go straight to a specific chapter as an independent source of information on a given move, this book was written as a resourceful tool of *linked* information and techniques, so that the capoeirista or the researcher can reap the most benefit from reading the entire text. Each chapter was designed to approach one technique; however, reading the whole book and finding its interconnections may broaden your knowledge of capoeira as both a ludic game and a martial art.

The book was designed like a *roda* itself, i.e., there is no hierarchy of moves. A simple *negativa* can be as important as a *meia-lua reversão*; a classic *aú* can be as strategic as a *macaco* or a *folha seca*. For this reason, I do not suggest what move should be considered as a beginning or an advanced level of expertise – I prefer to leave that to your Mestre.

Although being a disciplined activity, one of the most common scenarios in a capoeira school is to see students of all levels trying to learn from their most experienced peers. Capoeira starts to play its role at this exact moment, when students show a rich diversity of techniques and interests that are immediately interchangeable among all participants of the *roda*, including the masters.

Learning capoeira is a wonderful activity; however, it should be controlled to an optimal level of performance and safety. That is also the aim of this book.

From Bimba and Pastinha to the Next Century

Capoeira is still evolving. When Manoel dos Reis Machado, the great Mestre Bimba, created his Capoeira Regional in the early twentieth century, he had no idea of the proportions and consequences his action would have in the lives of millions of people who would become capoeiristas in the twentieth and the twenty-first centuries.

When a few years later Vicente Ferreira Pastinha, the great Mestre Pastinha, established his parameters for Capoeira Angola, which emphasized the old, traditional capoeira, the two arts boosted to play a very important role in the development of the contemporary capoeira.

By establishing their differences, these two distinguished Mestres gave us a rich legacy, complete, filled with history and traditions and yet modern – capable of adapting to an ever-changing, demanding world.

INTRODUCTION

The Origins of the Name

There is some controversy among historians about the origin of the name "capoeira," which remains under dispute. The two most relevant interpretations belong to the indigenous *Tupi* language of Brazil, with *ko'pwera*, from *ko* ('scrubland') + *pwera* ('used to be'). Later the vocable was adapted by the Portuguese. The same term appears to identify the spot-winged wood-quail, whose scientific name is *odontophorus capueira*.

There is a third vocable that is said to come from the African name *Kipura*, meaning "the roosters fight," a word that is used to describe the rooster's movements in a fight, which generally took place in a circle.

A good friend of mine reminds me, which I find very interesting to note, that in Jewish tradition there is a mystical ceremony called *Kapparot*, usually performed shortly before *Yom Kippur*, the most holy day in Judaism when every adult person fasts and repents his or her sins, as it is considered to be the ultimate Judgment Day. This custom is not very ancient (dated to the Middle Ages).

His point is not only the similar sound with the vocable CAPOEIRA, but the fact that the ceremony includes a kind of ritual moves where the performer circles the "blessed" person, around his head, with the unhappy rooster (that shortly afterward ends its life on the plate as a tasteful dish), inducing him to say: "This is my *Kappara*, this is my substitute."

The Roda

Capoeira is practiced to the music of specific percussion instruments and to singing and clapping in response to the "calls" of the Mestre, who sets the rhythm, in a circle of capoeiristas called the *roda*.

The *roda de capoeira* is often reproduced in every possible setting, such as in the capoeira schools and in the streets, where it can be practiced freely amongst fellow capoeiristas (normally capoeira students), or in organized events called *vadiação*, where one or more Mestres, – or schools – invite each other for comradeship, practice and leisure.

Roda de capoeira.

The Music

Music is not only a tradition in capoeira, it is almost a religion. The more you understand its concept and engage in its context, the more you will succeed in "acquiring" capoeira rather than simply learning its techniques and mimicking its moves. Music is the poetry of capoeira and is also part of its history.

Other important cultural manifestations closely related to capoeira and worthy of attention are the *maculelê*, a Brazilian folkloric dance that uses machetes and sticks; the *samba de roda*, a specific expression of samba which is a tradition among capoeiristas; and the *puxada de rede*, a theatrical play practiced by some capoeira schools or staged in public performances. In addition, researchers find

INTRODUCTION

different degrees of contribution or traces of capoeira in *lundu, jongo, habanera, maracatú, frevo, samba enrredo* and *samba de terreiro*. These cultural expressions are analyzed in the specific second volume entitled **Unknown Capoeira: A History of the Brazilian Martial Art,** which complements this one.

The Instruments

The basic instruments in capoeira are, from left to right in the illustration below, the *berimbau* (1), the *caixixi* (2), the *vareta* (3), an old coin or small stone (4), the *atabaque* (5) and the *pandeiro* (6).

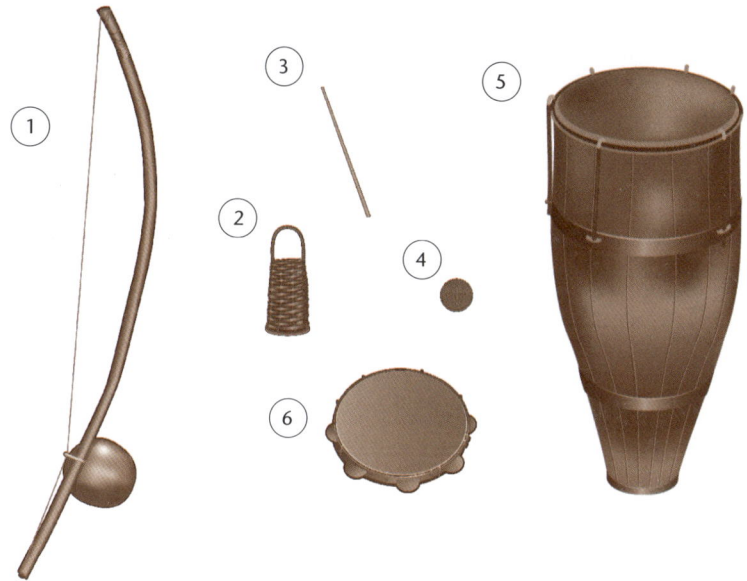

The *berimbau* is a stringed instrument that resembles a bow, made of *biriba* wood (nowadays under threat of extinction in Brazil) with a resonator called a *cabaça* made of a gourd attached to the back of the string bearer. The string is taken from tires, but before the Iron Age the old African *mbelas* used natural fibers or gut strings.

The *caixixi* is a small handbasket made of natural fiber, with rice, seeds or small shells inside, used as a rattle for percussion with the *berimbau*, which is played with the *vareta*, the *berimbau* stick, normally made of bamboo. The pitch and tune come from the coin, the metal loop or the small stone that the player uses to press the string, applying different strenghts on it. The player strikes the string with the *vareta* and presses the mouth of the *cabaça* toward the abdomen in order to muffle or release the sound at will.

The *atabaque* is the bongo drum used as percussion together with the *pandeiro*, or tambourine. In large *rodas* we can see several types of these instruments all played at the same time.

The Ecological Berimbau

A great solution for preservation of the biriba is the *ecological berimbau,* called *Berimbau Contemporâneo*, developed by Luthier Élio Moreira and Mestre Sá from Grupo Pé de Vento in São Paulo and played internationally by his son, capoeirista and musician Rodrigo Sá. I had the pleasure to spend a wonderful day with them at Mestre Camisa's farmhouse, north of Rio de Janeiro – and try out the instrument.

To my surprise, the sound was beautiful, and the sense of responsibility for the natural environment even greater. You can check it at www.berimbaubrazil.com.

The Rhythms and the Jogo

The rhythm of each performance in the *roda* is controlled by the main berimbau player, generally the master or his direct assistant. The capoeirista "dances according to the music," but make no mistake: nobody is really dancing. There is a game-fight going on, dictated by the rhythm of the music. When the Mestre starts playing Angola songs, the capoeiristas are supposed to engage immediately in a slow game, with lots

Berimbau Contemporâneo.

of ground movements, typical of Capoeira Angola, full of trickery and cunning movements. That's when the *jogo de dentro* (the closed game) shows its malice and grace. When the Mestre starts with a São Bento Grande, the two capoeiristas in the *roda* will immediately respond with a fast-paced, athletic performance, typical of Capoeira Regional. That's when the *jogo de fora* (the open game) shows its power.

Nonetheless, as capoeira became popular, the *jogo de dentro* and the *jogo de fora* were incorporated into the repertoire of patterns of most advanced capoeiristas regardless of the type of capoeira being performed, and today both patterns belong to the realm of capoeira as part of the *personal* capoeira that each capoeirista chooses to perform.

The most popular capoeira rhythms are Amazonas, Angola, Benguela, Cavalaria, Idalina, Iuna, São Bento Grande, São Bento Pequeno and Santa Maria, each with its unique characteristics. If you would like to explore these and other capoeira rhythms in greater detail, please refer to volume two: **Unknown Capoeira: A History of the Brazilian Martial Art**.

Before Playing

Before entering the *roda* to play a game, the two capoeiristas should crouch before the *pé do berimbau* to pay their ritualistic respects to the Mestre(s) and to the spirit of capoeira, which may include the Mestres themselves, the instruments, and homage to those Mestres who are no longer with us (some capoeiristas, generally of Catholic persuasion, make the sign of the cross on their foreheads out of respect for God or to their particular saints). Moments before starting the *jogo* at the sign of the Mestre, both capoeiristas should shake their right hands as a signal of respect – and, almost at the same time, get ready for a sudden attack by protecting their heads with the left hand. Normally, a *roda* is entered with slow and careful moves followed by the *ginga* – or with a faster move, according to the pace of the berimbau.

The Chamada

The ritualistic *chamada* (call) is an important aspect of the traditional capoeira (often known nowadays only as capoeira Angola). The *chamadas* are important phases of the *jogo* and should represent moments of extreme caution for the player who was *called* by the other capoeirista, as opposed to a *period of rest*, as many tourists and general capoeira audiences may believe at first. A *chamada* occurs during the *jogo* when one of the capoeiristas normally stops, smiles and opens his arms as a signal of invitation, and the capoeirista called must accept the invitation and approach his partner with caution, always suspecting that the opponent will surprise him or her with a strike. The leading capocirista chooses the time to restart the game at the *pé do berimbau* (at the foot of the berimbau). The *chamadas* are a great way to develop malice and *malandragem* – the art of trickery – in capoeiristas.

The Volta ao Mundo

The *volta ao mundo* ("around the world") is often referred to as the equivalent of the *chamada* of capoeira Angola. It is another important ritual practiced in the *roda*, generally during the game of capoeira Regional. One player can start a *volta ao mundo* (actually the capoeirista must "propose" the *volta ao mundo* to the other player) when he or she is *comprado* ("bought") by another capoeirista, who was in the Audience.

The *volta ao mundo* is done by the leading capoeirista (the one who was already playing), who will start walking counterclockwise in the *roda* followed not too closely by the capoeirista who has just "bought" (chosen) him or her to play with. During the *volta ao mundo*, only the leading capoeirista can restart the game. The *volta ao mundo* is also done when the leading capoeirista senses a change in rhythm or style proposed by his opponent in the *roda*, or simply to rest in order to restart the game, which is normally done at the *pé do berimbau* after two or three rounds in the *roda*.

The Vadiação

The *vadiação* (idleness) was first coined to mean the traditional capoeira played freely on the streets, long before the distinction of capoeira Regional and Angola was established. However, this tradition remained for some individuals and capoeira schools, and it is still possible, although more rarely nowadays, to see *vadiação* in some large urban centers of Brazil.

INTRODUCTION

The Respectful Compliment

Once the game is over, before leaving the *roda* both capoeiristas should nod their heads or shake hands, maintaining eye contact, as a sign of respect. It is also common to pay respects at the *pé do berimbau* before leaving, by quickly bending at the foot of the berimbau to touch the right hand to the floor.

The Songs

Songs are used as a prayer, a cry, a salutation or a story. The most important ones are the ladainha, used to start the *rodas*; the *quadra*, consisting of four verses; the corrido, having one or two verses normally used to control the pace of the *jogo*; and the *louvação*, in which all the capoeiristas in the *roda* respond to the verses, in unison, before the game starts.

The Batizado

Batizado literally means "baptism." It is at the *batizado* that the Mestre gives the initiate his *apelido* – the nickname which will follow him in his capoeira life – as well as his new cord and rank at the capoeira school. The *batizado* is also a graduation ceremony for advanced students, as well as a community celebration with Mestres invited from other schools gathering in comradeship and joy.

The *batizado* ceremony can be held at the capoeira school or in a public space, such as a community square or park.

The Cord System and Ranks

Unfortunately, most capoeira schools follow their own cord system of ranks. I wish this would change and that all capoeira schools around the world would use the same system, as we see in karate and judo, to mention a couple of classic examples.

Whether or not capoeira becomes an Olympic sport, and whether or not a united federation is created to gather capoeiristas from all over the world in international championships without physical contact, an "official" cord system of ranks is this author's dream for a strong capoeira for future generations. I believe this could be done with the participation of Mestres from internationally accredited schools, simply for the sake of strengthening capoeira as an organized sport, without losing the rich and unique characteristics of each school.

While this is not yet the case, here is my proposal for a cord system, which takes in consideration some of the important aspects contemplated by accredited capoeira schools in Brazil and elsewhere.

For the colors, I chose intermediate levels – a trend of most Mestres who believe a capoeirista must be experienced enough in order to become a master – and based the colors on the system used by the most popular martial arts in the world, as well as in the first systems used in Brazil in the 1960s.

The ranks include **basic**, **intermediate** and **advanced** levels.

The red cord of Mestre remains as homage to the original *Grupo Senzala*, the traditional capoeira school of Rio de Janeiro that officially introduced the red cord of Mestre used since the 1960's.

The intermediate levels are a homage to ABADÁ Capoeira, the first group to officially adopt a long-term compulsory period of experience before one can be called a Mestre (although Mestre Camisa himself was considered a Mestre at the age of 18, and this author was graduated at 20).

Capoeira has evolved since the golden days of the 60s, when everything "started up again," and nowadays there are so many schools and so many new moves that it just makes sense for a capoeira student to become a Mestre only after many years of experience – and never before the age of 30, an idea strongly advocated by Mestre Peixinho.

I am pretty sure that, at least for now, my dear friends Camisa, Peixinho and Paulo Siqueira, my colleague from the original *Grupo Bantus de Capoeira* and now at Escola de Capoeira Nzinga of Germany, would not approve my cord and rank proposal. Nevertheless, I dare to present it as a contribution to a united capoeira.

Excuses made, and – I hope – accepted, here is my proposal for the colors/ranks and minimum period of experience:

Basic Capoeira Student		Intermediate Capoeirista	
White	Six months	White and blue	Six months
White and yellow	Six months	Blue	Six months
Yellow	Six months	White and green	Six months
White and orange	Six months	Green	Six months
Orange	Six months	White and purple	Six months
		Purple	Six months

Advanced Capoeirista	
White and brown (Monitor)	Six months
Brown (Instructor)	One year
White and red (Contra-mestre or Mestrando)	Two years

Red (Mestre)	for life

Black (Grão Mestre or Honorific)
Minimum of 30 years as a Mestre of capoeira or as an honorific award.*

These periods of time between cords shall be considered a minimum, at the discretion of the Mestre. With this system, a capoeirista **could not** become a Mestre before he or she has amassed 9 years of constant practice, regardless of his or her skills.

The Uniforms

In this book, as a homage to my capoeira school, the original *Grupo Bantus de Capoeira* located in the slums of Morro do Pavão and Pavãozinho in Rio de Janeiro, all capoeiristas are wearing the traditional white capoeira pants, called *abadá*, with the traditional braided cord worn as a belt around the waist. Female capoeiristas also wear a top.

---

* The black honorific cord could be worn by a **Mestre** with 30 or more years as a graduated Mestre together with the red cord, which would distinguish him or her from the essentially honorific cord.

Traditional Pastinha Angola schools first adopted the yellow shirt with black pants, a uniform that also included shoes. Nowadays we can see students of Angola schools wearing both white pants and shirts, and often even different-colored shirts, though the yellow shirt is still widely worn with black pants and also with white pants. Tennis shoes are worn in practically all Angola schools.

Today, complete outfits are worn by the great majority of Regional capoeira schools around the world. This outfit consists of the traditional white pants or polyamide elastic pants with side stripes, a thickness 12 cotton cord belt, generally undyed (often referred to as "raw") for the beginner and colored according to each rank (and to each school), a T-shirt or top with the school logo, and sometimes tennis shoes.

Before writing this section, I discussed the issue of uniforms with Mestre Peixinho, one of the founders of *Grupo Senzala* in Rio and a capoeira legend himself. We both agree that a standard uniform should be used in the capoeira schools. However, as we were gymnastics colleagues back in the early 1970s, I felt comfortable with my opinion on the use of tennis shoes for capoeira. I argued in favor of a capoeira with no shoes at all, because once you acquire some years of experience you get used to the feel and the grip of the floor with both feet and hands in equal degree of sensation. I told him that one actually develops a special intimacy with ground maneuvers, and that he himself had learned and become a master by practicing capoeira with no shoes and no shirt.

A good and wise friend with more than 40 years of capoeira behind him answered me that he had thought the same way until he realized that the tennis shoes were a blessing for his knees when he started wearing them in international *rodas*. A great friend and a wise master.

I just wish the cords would go back to their original braided fashion and that the Mestres themselves, as a tradition and homage to their students, would go back and handcraft the cords for the sake of old times.

The Theatrical Aspects of Capoeira

The theatricality of capoeira deserves a book of its own. It is often the object of special appreciation and research. Its relation to trickery and the playful nature of the *jogo* have been the essence of capoeira since long before Capoeira Angola

INTRODUCTION

and Capoeira Regional appeared to the world. In this vein, the movie "Cordão de Ouro," where Mestre Camisa plays in the *roda* with Mestre Nestor Capoeira, is worth watching.

Religion, dramatization, fear and joy, dexterity and laziness, gestures in and out of context (actually they are always contextualized in the spirit of capoeira), joking – all are an integral part of the theatrical aspects of beautiful capoeira.

The Techniques

Good capoeiristas prefer to exhibit their techniques and fire their accurate movements, no matter how quick they are, without completing them, enforcing their superiority in the *roda* and never in real fighting. As every good capoeirista, you should not aim at hurting your partner in the *roda*, but rather on demonstrating your skills during the *jogo*. It is when the art of trickery, called *malandragem,* comes to light, bringing beautiful flourishes and a flurry of feints and fake moves built to trick your partner into responding wrongly, to your advantage.

If, on the one hand, you feel that your partner cannot evade or dodge your slowest attack, there is no reason to use your fastest. On the other hand, every attack that comes in your direction offers you chance to practice an evasive technique, giving your capoeira one of its most important characteristics – the *flow of motion*.

Intimacy with Ground and Air

Capoeira is also the only martial art in the world where the practitioner learns to deal with standing, ground and aerial performances with equivalent importance, thus allowing for hundreds of creative combinations of moves.

The Ginga

Capoeira includes a footwork movement called *ginga*, which is the main stance of capoeira. The *ginga* is a unique martial art movement and capoeira is the only fighting system in the world to provide a *continuum* during its performance, whether in an exhibition or in real fighting. Many practitioners do not realize the importance of the *ginga* to the reasoning of a capoeira fighter and to the logic of a capoeira game. Whether you want to surprise your opponent or simply escape from a difficult situation – or a combination of both, the *ginga* gives you the tools to apply grace, subterfuge, trickery, speed, balance, power and precision, all at the same time – an ingenious system of body mechanics seen in no other martial art. And that is why the *ginga* is not an easy move to learn.

The *ginga* allows the capoeirista to decide whether he or she should choose from a variety of attack or defense maneuvers from the ground, or from a standing position, including several evasion techniques that can be executed through the resourceful application of elegant and complex moves.

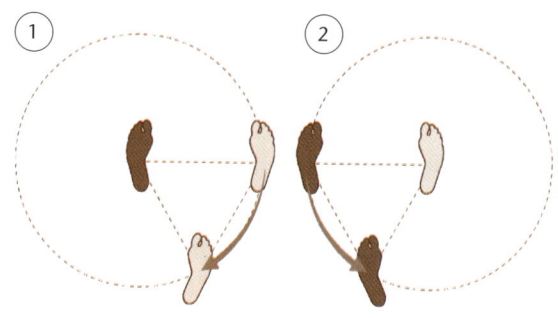

Diagram I-1: Your basic, triangular *ginga*.

This book also emphasizes the concept of the zero stance, which tries to demonstrate that the capoeirista can also use most capoeira techniques from a normal standing and motionless stance – quite useful information for those interested in capoeira as an efficient system of self-defense.

Diagrams I-1 and I-2 show the common paths of your feet during execution of a *ginga*. In Diagram I-1 number (1), your left foot is your first supporting foot and your right leg moves in a triangular fashion, seeking the perfect balance while placing your moving foot behind, forming the triangle. In (2), it is the turn of your left foot to move back. In (1), your right hand counterbalances the move by the swinging of your right arm forward; in (2), it is the other way around, and your left arm moves forward while your left leg moves back.

In Diagram I-2 your left foot is also your first supporting foot, but your right leg moves back behind your left leg, this time forming a square. You also seek the perfect balance while swinging your right arm forward to compensate for your

INTRODUCTION

weight as your right foot moves behind your left supporting foot, before you start all over again, inverting the positions of your feet.

In both cases, your legs should not be stiff – but they should not be too bent either. They should be fairly straight and flexible. Your torso also plays a very important role as a component of the *ginga*.

For instance, if you choose to use the square-shaped *ginga*, which I like to consider as a more advanced kind of *ginga*, you should compensate for the apparent unbalance (as a result of having one leg exactly behind and aligned with the other) with a more accentuated opposite move of your torso and your arms. Try it, it's fun!

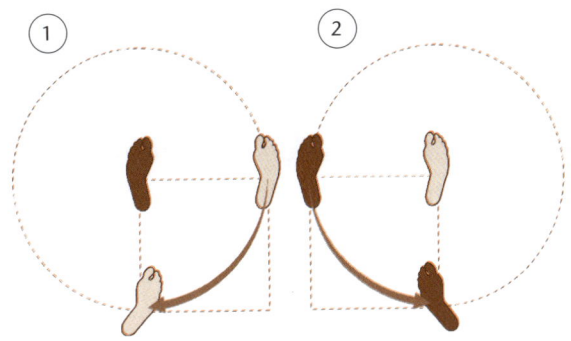

Diagram I-2: Your more advanced, squared *ginga*.

Note that you can also use a combination of the two styles in your *ginga*. You can actually make your own pattern – as long as your apply the general concept. You can find animated examples of the *ginga* at www.unknowncapoeira.com.

The Moves

Capoeira includes a variety of attack kicks and sweeps, aerials and acrobatic moves, punches, elbow strikes, knee strikes, head butts and much more. Its defense system uses evasive moves, ducks and rolls of incredible versatility. I did my best to describe all these moves in alphabetical order of each chapter, from the *armada* to the *xangô*. However, this does not mean that I have achieved my goal. Far from it, I believe. As you read these lines, chances are that a new movement is being introduced – and accepted – in a *roda* somewhere in the world.

I also did my best to come up with the terminology of the moves, from my capoeira cradle in Brazil in the 1960s and 1970s to the internationally known "contemporary capoeira." I have probably not accomplished this task to perfection level either.

For my presumptuousness, I apologize to the capoeira nation.

Practicing the Attacking Moves Alone

Many capoeira moves can be practiced alone – or outside the *roda* with a friend, once you have mastered the move and are duly qualified to practice without the direction of a master or coach. In this section, I invite those who want to practice some capoeira kicks under the focus of capoeira as a true martial art. The idea behind this strategy is simply to understand each kick in full scale, to its full potential. The more you dominate your moves, the more you will be able to avoid hurting someone during your practice. And, as a by-product, it is always good to know that you can count on yourself if you ever need capoeira for self-defense or to protect those you care for.

Using a Chair

This practice refers to the following movements, all variations of the *armada*, all variations of the *meia-lua*, the *benção*, all variations of the *martelo*, the *s-dobrado* and the *queixada*. In addition, you can always use the chair as a point of reference to practice other moves, such as the *aú*, for example.

Besides practicing at the *roda*, during a combat simulation, or with a colleague, using the hands at striker's head height, you can practice your *armadas*, *queixadas*, *bençãos*, *martelos*, *s-dobrados* and *meia-luas* by training with a chair. If the back

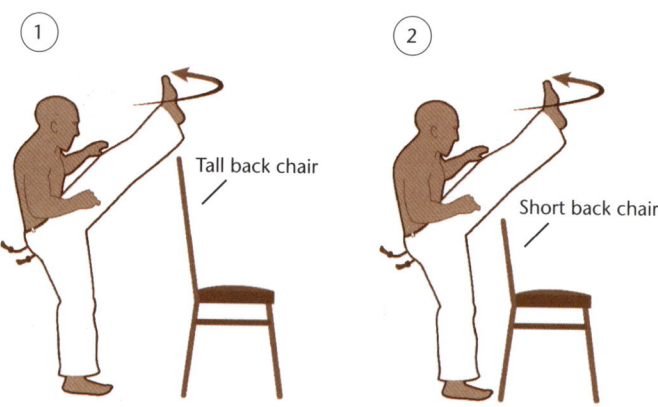

of the chair is too low, practice by passing your thigh over the back of the chair, following the instructions for each movement in this book, until you feel completely comfortable with the technique. Use your hands to simulate an imaginary aim for the strike, as discussed in the *armada* chapter. If the back of the chair is tall enough, pass your foot over it. Practice with both legs always finishing in the classical *ginga* defense position.* You must be perfectly proficient in all left and right movements.

Once you have learned these kicking techniques, you can practice them on a boxing bag, also known as a "punching bag," "heavy bag," "sandbag," or "training bag," in order to develop strength and balance. You must keep in mind that in a *roda* we seldom hit our opponent and our strikes almost always follow their full trajectory, i.e., we try to perform their often circular movements with grace and balance until they are complete, and we tend to continue launching strikes one after another while we play our game.

One of the beauties of capoeira lies in its graceful movements. Regardless of how violent or fast a capoeira fighter presents himself during a confrontation or a simulation, watching two good capoeiristas playing capoeira is a special treat for the eyes. At least it should be.

Using a Training Bag

Do not practice with a training bag without proper professional guidance! I strongly recommend obtaining your doctor's approval for this type of practice so that you do not harm your knee joints or sustain any other type of bodily injury.

Practicing with a training bag is indicated for the following techniques: all variations of the *armada*, all variations of the *meia-lua*, the *benção*, all variations of the *martelo*, the *s-dobrado* and the *queixada*, the *chibatas* from most sources, all variations of the *macaco*, the attack techniques discussed in the "Unexpected Moves" chapter plus all variations of the *chapa*.**

---

* Some movements, like the **martelo de chão** and the **s-dobrado**, require that you go back to their original stances after passing over the chair with your feet.

** For the sake of balance, these movements also require that you go back to their original stances after hitting the bag.

The training bag is also an excellent point of reference for practicing other techniques, such as variations of the *aú*. With the bag, the capoeirista can learn how to strike and how to finish the movement having to control his balance and the sudden end of trajectory caused by the resistance of the bag when hit by the athlete's foot.

With the bag, the capoeirista can learn how to strike, hit and finish the movement having to control his balance and the sudden end of trajectory provoked by the resistance of the bag when hit by the athlete's foot.

If the bag is too heavy to be displaced by your *armada*, *meia-lua* or by any of the variations included in your "training bag repertoire," no problem: simply hit as fast and strong as you have learned, and practice returning your leg to the *ginga* or to your original stance each time you hit the bag. If the bag is not too heavy, try to displace it with the strike, continuing its trajectory to reach the defense position.

I believe that the combination of these two training bag techniques, plus the constant practice at your capoeira school and in the *roda,* is the best solution for mastering a perfect capoeira strike.

When using the training bag, be sure to hit with both your feet and your legs on the bag. Gauge your efforts to your teacher's or your physician's discretion to make sure you will not hit too hard and fracture a foot or ankle bone, hurt your joints, ligaments and tendons – or rather too weakly and get no results at all from your kick. Practice safety with efficiency!

The *meia-lua de compasso* should be practiced on the training bag at what I call "the three speeds," i.e., a *meia-lua* that is slow and steady yet on a perfect trajectory, a medium-speed one and a fast, powerful one. The idea behind this strategy, which can be extended to other capoeira kicks, is to gain a complete mastery of

INTRODUCTION

the movement, and control it to perfection by actually *feeling* each *meia-lua de compasso* as a natural extension of your body movements.

The *meia-lua de compasso* should be practiced on the training bag at what I call "the three speeds," i.e., a *meia-lua* that is slow and steady yet on a perfect trajectory, a medium-speed one and a fast, powerful one. The idea behind this strategy, which can be extended to other capoeira kicks, is to gain a complete mastery of the movement, and control it to perfection by actually *feeling* each *meia-lua de compasso* as a natural extension of your body movements.

The Towel Factor

You may practice punches, kicks and head butts (not too powerful, please) on a training bag to increase the power and accuracy of your strikes.* However, what some athletes do not know is that a "solid" surface will not always help you attain your best performance.

By using a towel to train your blows, you can extend your strike to a deeper level, as though you were traversing your target, thus achieving your best impact and power.

Suppose you need to defend your life against a dangerous armed assailant. You will use a *ponteira* to quickly kick your attacker in the stomach – one of the quickest, most hazardous and easiest capoeira attacks. If your life is really at stake, you will want to make sure your kick is effective by delivering your *ponteira* "inside" his stomach, as deep as possible, to end the fight and save your life.

This technique is particularly effective if the person threatening your life is stronger than you. For instance, instead of delivering a superficial punch on the assailant's nose, by knowing the "towel factor" a woman could throw a direct

---

* Try practicing these strikes on a sideways-swinging bag.

punch deep "into" her target and avoid the risk of having to cope with the menace of a more hostile situation.

> **CAUTION: DO NOT EVER USE THESE OFFENSIVE TECHNIQUES UNLESS YOU NEED TO DEFEND YOUR LIFE OR THE LIVES OF THOSE YOU CARE FOR.**

Quick Anatomy Reference

For the purpose of accuracy, in this book I describe a few points of impact using their medical terminology. They are:

Body Region	Description
Frontal bone	the forehead and front top of the head
Mandible	the lower jaw
Maxilla	the upper jaw
Nasal bone	the rigid bone forming the upper part of the nose
Parietal bone	the top, side bone of the skull
Temporal bone	the side of the head, above the ear

Criteria for Defenses and Counterattacks

Capoeira is one of the richest martial arts in the world, and choosing among its hundreds of techniques is an art in itself. In this book, all movements I chose were presented based on my personal choice of what I consider effectively the best alternatives of action for a given defense or countermeasure both for the *roda* and, especially, with focus on the martial art aspect of capoeira.

Capoeira Is for All Genders

Unless in specific illustrations where I show female capoeiristas, for the sake of pragmatics, I chose to use the pronoun "he" or "his" to indicate a partner, an opponent, an assailant or an enemy interacting in the book.

To all my friends in capoeira, **Axé.**

Armada

A spinning outside crescent kick. The classic *armada* is a very strong and efficient capoeira move. A fast, high-rotating kick, when done appropriately, it can help you to quickly knock down an opponent or even two, with dramatic consequences. Although belonging to the class of attack moves, when followed by another *armada* or an assortment of *meia-luas* it also forms a perfect defense system of counterattacks against one or more opponents. Yet the *armada*, like most capoeira techniques, is an opportunistic move. And if you do not master the technique, you will most likely open your guard and consequently lose your battle.

Some variations of the *armada*, discussed in this chapter and the next, demonstrate the subtleness of this efficient kick and the best possible choice of the type of *armada* to be used, based on the situations presented.

For each type of *armada* there are also several specialized techniques and strategies for defense and counterattack, both for the *roda* and for actual combat, which will be explored in detail in this book. This first deals with the classic 360° style.

Objectives

In actual fighting, there are always three main objectives in a capoeira attack move, especially if you are taking a *ginga* stance. One is to keep a safe distance between your opponent and yourself. The other is to "study" your opponent, i.e., read his intentions and see what kind of reaction to your potential attack may be expected from him. However, the most important objective of the *armada*, if you have to engage in combat, is to deliver a high-speed, precise strike to your opponent's head, knocking him down and taking him, or "them," out of action.

The Point of Impact

A perfect (and lethal) attack *armada* must aim at the parietal and the temporal regions of the head. A defensive, counterattacking *armada,* the highly technical and normally surprising *armada diagonal,* can also aim at the center of your adversary's face. However, for safety reasons, do not ever try to execute an *armada diagonal* in a *roda* or on your friends, unless they are advanced capoeiristas themselves and know your intentions.

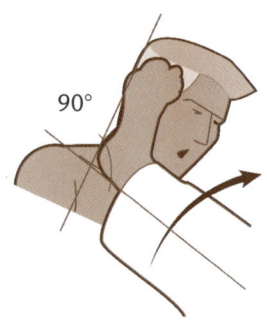

Figure 1.1: A stiff leg with foot at a forced 90° angle will prepare the right muscles for a perfect *armada*.

The Technique

For an effective *armada* you should be in an upright position when rotating and throughout the entire movement. Keep your upper body in the upright position at all times during the movement, i.e., try not to bend. Keep your supporting foot planted firmly on the ground. According to the distance from your opponent, you may step forward or back with your attacking leg in preparation for delivering your *armada*. Remember that by not "telegraphing" your move, you will manage to confuse your opponent.

ARMADA

While still looking at your target, start turning your shoulders and hips. Do not stretch your arms or let them loose during the rotation; keep them close to your guard. At the climax of the movement, your *armada* leg must be held straight and high, ideally at a 30° angle to your upright body. Keep your foot at a 90° angle to your leg, as in Figure 1.1, i.e., do not loosen your attacking leg or foot until you have conquered your objective and have struck or passed over your opponent's head in case he manages to escape down or out of your *armada* range. This will prepare the right muscles of your leg, so that your *armada* foot is hard and strong for the intended impact and ready for a second try. Give thrust to your rotation and pay attention to speed and accuracy. Refer back to the Introduction, to the section entitled *Practice the Attacking Moves Alone*, for additional help on how to deliver a powerful and accurate *armada*. For the sake of good posture, keep your arms in the classic *ginga* defense stance position when you finish your *armada*, even if you are in a motionless zero stance.

Conceptually speaking, assuming that our body has an ideal set of standard physical proportions of 7.5 heads for the whole body, and four heads being the distance from hips to toes, we can reach our adversaries with our feet before they can get to us with their hands, provided we are fast enough and have the required skills and initiative, which is a big advantage of martial arts that work with a good set of kicking variations. All the same, the perfect strike would be to launch your *armada* at half this former distance, i.e., when your adversary is two heads away from you.*

If your opponent is too far from you for your striking leg to reach, such that you are unable to hit him, you must use a forward jumping kick instead. Therefore, you need to get safely close to your rival, or enemy, when you decide to deliver an accurate *armada* to his head. Nevertheless, you also need to fire your *armada* before your adversary notices your intention and manages to evade it, counterattack you or initiate his own attack before you make your move.

This spatial reasoning must follow all your capoeira moves, according to the action chosen and the distance from your opponent.

---

* This distance may be too close if you are confronting another specialist, such as a jiu-jitsuist, a boxer or a karate fighter, but always bear in mind that the best way to practice is with a good capoeirista and that you can always surprise your opponent, whether he is a martial arts specialist or a common assailant.

Even in the friendly game of capoeira in a *roda,* it is sad to see good capoeiristas launching spinning kicks all over the place and quite far from each other. If you are already a capoeirista close to an intermediate level, or even higher, you surely know what I am saying. And you know that if your partner is also a capoeirista of the same level, the *jogo* will be more beautiful and no one needs to get hurt!

Diagram 1.1 shows the geometry behind a good *armada* strategy. Note that, ideally, the angle of your *armada* leg (example 1) should not be different when rotating, as in example 2. This requires that all moves be executed with perfection, all the way through to end of the movement – whatever its characteristics may be.

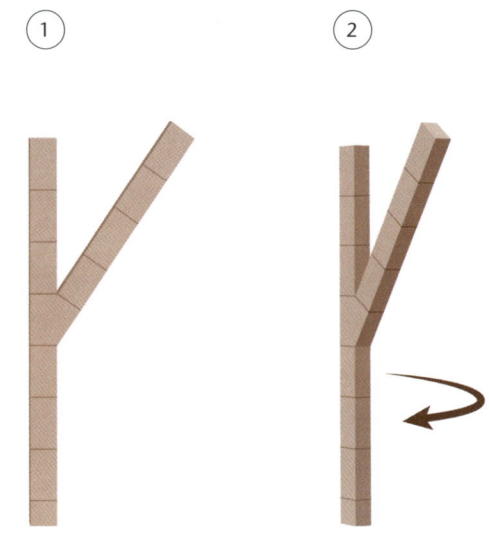

Diagram 1.1: Plan your distance before applying your *armada* techniques. Assume the correct posture and angle.

Bear in mind that once you dominate the capoeira techniques, you don't need to stick to a rigid mode of execution. Capoeira leaves you free to use your movements as you wish, as long as you know what you are doing from a professional standpoint. For instance, the descriptions of Diagram 1.1 are normally more demanding than, or at least as demanding as, their possible improvisations in the *roda*. In other words, normally there is no point in executing a 20° (angle with your head) *armada* in a *jogo*, but it would be nice to know how to do it before trying to improvise.

This means you can execute an *armada* in a different way, such as a lower one to get your opponent while he is descending into a *cocorinha,* or a slower one for whatever reason. Thus, throughout the book, with most moves you can take this freedom for granted, but I would advise you to stick to the suggested descriptions all the way through and learn to improvise in the *roda* later, once you have mastered each technique – especially if you want to learn capoeira as a martial art. Feel free to apply your own style **once you have mastered the real thing!**

Use your hands as an extra resource for aiming your *armada*. When you start rotating to begin the *armada,* be sure to pass with your last moving *ginga* hand in front of your opponent's face (if you strike with the right foot, that would be your left hand), i.e., the target, preparing to hit him with your *armada* foot in the direction of that predetermined spot. Another good use of your *ginga* hands is to apply a *cutelo* as a preventive measure, while rotating, in case you give up your *armada*. Figure 1.2 shows two fighters using their *ginga* hands as an aiming aid in preparation for their next move.*

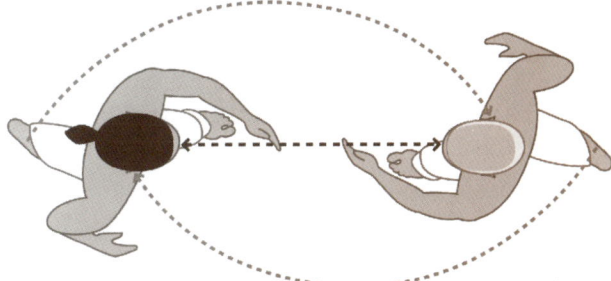

Figure 1.2: Your *ginga* hand is your aiming aid (but your opponent doesn't know that).

As an attacking kick, you can just go ahead and fire an *armada* at your opponent's head at any time during a *roda* session or in actual fighting. However, there are always some opportune ways to optimize your technique (sometimes, in capoeira, you can even "customize" your techniques). One of them is to use your *armada* when your opponent "telegraphs" a *queixada, e*specially if he places his *queixada* leg alongside your supporting *armada* leg, i.e., if he advances his left *queixada* leg the moment you have your left leg in front during your *ginga* or even at a zero stance.

This will make it easy for you to use an *esquiva* or a half-gyro spin to the right while quickly lowering your head, and then to fire your *armada* in the same direction as

---

* Even if you are not in motion with your **ginga, i.e.,** if you are at a **zero** stance, make sure to use your spinning hand as an aiming aid when you start to rotate in preparation for your **armada.**

that of his intended *queixada* immediately after having allowed his attacking leg to go by. Chances are that you will get him, as shown in Figure 1.3 (although most of the time if you just go ahead and fire your *armada* right over his *queixada*, you will succeed).

Figure 1.3: Escape from his *queixada* and fire an opportunistic *armada*.

The same can be done against a *meia-lua de frente*. Concentrate on rhythm, timing and precision, and fire your *armada* as soon as you feel that his *meia-lua de frente* has no return. You turn at the exact moment that his *meia-lua de frente* is up, but still alongside your supporting leg. As you rotate, you will evade his kick and your *armada* will get him before he completes his move (Figure 1.4).

Figure 1.4: Escape from his *meia-lua de frente* and fire an opportunistic *armada*.

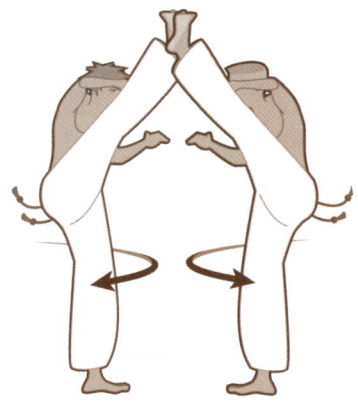

An advanced *armada* can also be fired "against" a rotating or crescent kick, if your action is precise enough in order to avoid collision. You will get him on his exposed – and most vulnerable – side. What you need, besides being accurate, is to be faster than he is, i.e., to have better reaction time. For safety reasons, do not execute this move in the *roda* with your partner, unless you are a teacher or an advanced capoeirista and you know how to avoid completing the move. This technique can also be executed with most capoeira kicks.

Figure 1.5: Be cautious with an *armada* over another *armada*, but if you time your move with your partner's, this combination can be beautiful.

ARMADA

A more advanced diagonal *armada* can always be used against other standing crescent and spinning kicks, like another *armada*, a *meia-lua de compasso* or even a *martelo*. Just watch for the speed with which some spinning kicks are delivered, while at the same time paying attention to the style of your opponent. A *meia-lua* can be hazardous if you don't have time to defend yourself. In the chapter on the *meia-lua de compasso*, see how to get the best out of the "diagonal approach."

A common application of the *armada* that we see in the *roda* is to fire a set of two or more consecutive kicks, sometimes over your partner's own *armada* (Figure 1.5). There is really no limitation, though normally a set of four *armadas* is enough, and yes, if you are precise and timely, and aware of your opponent's movements, these *armadas* can be quite surprising.

However, remember that the true essence of capoeira is the flow of motion, which allows for the production of beautiful and yet deadly moves, executed on a *continuum* from an assortment of creative and resourceful techniques, forming a respectable and unique repertoire of martial art moves.

This leads us to an almost unlimited set of combinations of moves, which can be done in many creative ways, like delivering an *armada* to an opponent who dodges down into a *cocorinha* and tries to counterattack with an *escorumelo,* but is caught by surprise with a spinning *meia-lua* done with the same original *armada* leg.

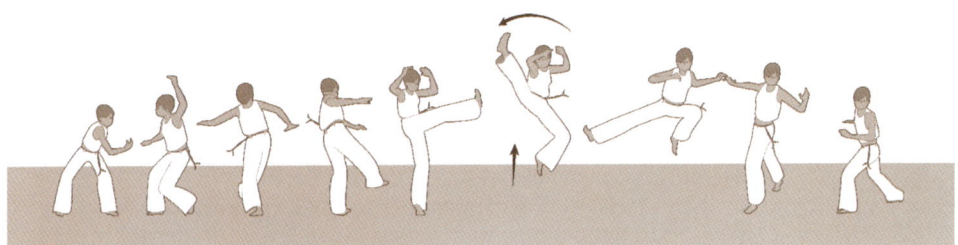

Armada pulada.

For the *armada pulada* (the jumping spinning outside crescent kick), you start rotating in almost the same way as in the classic *armada,* using your pivot leg to hop and your attacking leg as a lever to push your body upward. This technique is good if you are a quick fighter and want to avoid a *rasteira*. Additionally, you can set your first *armada* step (the first step you take with the leg you will be kicking in the air) apart from your supporting pivot leg, so that when you start rotating for the jump you will achieve greater leverage and consequently a longer jump.

There is also the sequential *armada*, something you can also call "*armada* in a roll." It is not a very easy movement, however, and as my friend Mestre Peixinho said, "anyone who has the attributes can do it." That's the problem!

In the sequential *armada*, what you do is two or three *armadas* in a roll without your *armada* leg touching the ground after each rotation.

Practicing Alone

The *armada* can be practiced effectively with an obstacle, such as a tall or short-backed chair, or a training bag. At the capoeira school, we can always practice outside the *roda* on the hands of a partner with arms outstretched and palms open. When you strike your partner's hand with your *armada* foot, he must not create resistance, but rather let his outstretched arm travel some 90° and then back for another blow.

Refer to the Introduction for more details and special tips on practicing your *armada* alone to improve your techniques.

Defenses and Counterattacks

As stated at the outset of this chapter, the *armada* is an efficient and strong capoeira move and its open guard is an invitation to all sorts of counterattacking techniques. If you know how to fire a perfect *armada*, you might as well also learn how to defend yourself against it with the greatest variation of defense and counterattack techniques from the entire repertoire of capoeira moves.

In the coming chapters, you will find an assortment of standing and ground defenses and counterattack techniques that are very useful against a good *armada*.

Some of these suggested – and quite complex – moves will require considerable timing as a result of keen reasoning because an *armada dupla*, for instance, normally takes longer to execute than a classic attacking *armada*, but that's precisely the beauty of it. You can use these moves against an *armada* if you control the flow of motion with dexterity.

ARMADA

In addition, you will note that I prefer not to suggest a hierarchy for these moves, from the easy to the more difficult ones, although this seems to be perfectly possible and is naturally done at most capoeira schools. To me, all moves are important, despite their complexity. I have seen advanced capoeiristas who didn't care to learn acrobatics and nevertheless were excellent performers. On the other hand, it is common to see a beginner perform highly complex aerial moves before mastering the essentials of capoeira.

Let me tell you this little story. When I arrived in the US to introduce capoeira in the great state of North Carolina, I was given the opportunity to work with the Afro-American community. It was fantastic. The problem was that my first pupil was a professional ballet teacher, a superb athlete who knew the fundamentals of acrobatic moves and the like. For example, it took him exactly ten minutes to learn a *meia-lua de compasso*! However, learning the *ginga*, or how to apply the *meia-lua* in the game, was a real torture.

For an immediate counterattack against a fast and high *armada*, you can dodge down into an *esquiva lateral* and a *rasteira de chão*, spin a *rasteira giratória*, or try a *banda de costas cruzada*. If you succeed in your *rasteira*, you can always come back up with the help of an *s-dobrado*, which can also come from a *negativa (escala)*, first escaping completely from the *armada*. If you are fast and efficient enough to see his quick *armada* in "slow motion," then you can even try a *tesoura*, a *rasteira de mão* or a *boca de calça*. In such scenarios you can also do an innocent *cocorinha* and come back up quickly and hard on the opponent's lower jaw with an *escorumelo*, almost sliding along his upright body all the way from your *cocorinha* to his mandible.

> **ALWAYS BE QUICK, TIMELY AND PRECISE, AND WORK FROM THE AWARENESS OF YOUR OPPONENT'S MOVES.**

Now if you are really fast and ahead of your adversary, you can try a good *rasteira em pé*, a *banda*, a *bloqueio de dentro* or a combination of *bloqueio de dentro* and *banda de costas*. Don't get too close to him if you're not certain of success. If your rival sees that you are preparing to enter his guard during his rotation, he may forgo his *armada* and surprise you with a *cutelo*, an *asfixiante* or a *cabeçada*. Your opponent is not stupid, and he, too, has a repertoire of capoeira moves!

ALWAYS RESPECT YOUR PARTNER AND YOUR OPPONENT.

For more blocking countermeasures, you can use the *chapa lateral*, the *chapa giratória* and even the *ponteira lateral*. These kicks can be used efficiently for blocking your opponent by striking his hip or his ribs before he achieves his rotation.* You can also use these kicks as "launching pads" for an evasive and providential *aú* to begin a new stance and start all over again. These, by the way, can be beautiful movements and enrich the flow of motion in a capoeira game.

The *martelo baixo* can also serve as an efficient blocking counterattack, if you strike the back of your opponent's knees. You need to be quick and powerful, though, if you really want to interrupt a good *armada*.

A *meia-lua de compasso* is another great technique against an *armada*, as long as you make sure your *armada* leg is really going to follow its course all the way through so that you can fire a high, fast *meia-lua* right over his attack. The *meia-lua presa* (the *meia-lua de compasso* with two supporting hands on the ground) is also an efficient kick, but it takes longer to execute than the ordinary *meia-lua de compasso*, so that if you need to be extra fast, stick to the latter.

You can also try the *meia-lua pulada*, as soon as your opponent starts to rotate his *armada*, but you must make sure your flying kick will go "over" his *armada* leg and inside his guard, if you really want to hit his head and avoid an unnecessary "mid-air collision" (unless you are so confident of your timing with your opponent that you can quickly fire your *meia-lua pulada* a split second after he starts his, following the attacking leg at the same height and surprising him before he completes his attack). This technique can be performed with an *armada dupla*, a *compasso pulado*, or a *meia-lua reversão*.

Examples of counterattacks against an *armada* will be shown in the coming chapters.

---

* Here you have a choice: either to hit your opponent's hip or ribs hard as in real combat, or to use enough power just to get him off balance and foil his attempt to execute the **armada**.

Armada Dupla

The double leg. The *armada dupla* is one of capoeira's greatest aerial kicks. It is a powerful kick that can be executed from a zero stance, although apparently, many practitioners do not know that and keep running to gain momentum for their jump.

The *armada dupla* is an excellent choice of attacking kick if you are in the flow of motion in a *roda* or in real combat, or as a counterattacking kick against classic crescent kicks, such as the *armada*, the *queixada* or the *meia-lua de frente*, if you are timely and try to be aware of your attacker's intentions.

Be sure to master the *armada dupla* thoroughly, so that you can launch it from a zero stance. If you need to run from a distance in order to gain speed and momentum, you might as well try another technique because by the time you've made the run, your opponent's *armada* will have been rendered useless and both fighters would have to restart combat from the beginning. Whether in a *roda* or the real thing, try to maximize your time and always respond to your opponent's or partner's moves with a counterattacking or defensive measure, in order to maintain the flow of motion.

In a *roda*, the flow of motion is one of the most important aspects of capoeira. In actual combat, this could be translated into a "unique opportunity," perhaps the only one you will have to protect yourself against your adversary.

Objectives

The *armada dupla* is primarily an attack to the opponent's head, just like the classic *armada*. In actual fighting, though, the *armada dupla* comes in handy because it produces a more "brutal" strike, even though it is highly technical. You can use it as an attack or a counterattack, from the *ginga* or from a zero stance (which is more difficult). It is effective against an *armada*, a *queixada* or a *benção* (Figure 2.1),* as a powerful overlapping move, especially in a real combat situation if your opponent is not a capoeirista.

Figure 2.1: Make no mistake: it looks awkward, but it can be highly efficient.

Just find the gap in your opponent's move, time your action and go for it. For safety reasons, don't try it for real over your partner's head in a *roda* if he is at a lower cord level, or else he might get hurt.

Landing from an *armada dupla* is not just about landing properly, but also about knowing what to do next without hurting yourself or losing control. It's also about being fit. You need to work out properly, according to professional instructions, in order to be able to live a good life without sustaining bodily injuries.

CAPOEIRA DEMANDS GOOD FITNESS!

---

* You must always consider whether you will be able to launch your ***armada dupla*** successfully against straight kicks such as a ***benção***. You may not have enough time to complete your movement in a good ***jogo***, and almost certainly will not have time to complete the move in real combat if your opponent is an advanced martial artist himself.

ARMADA DUPLA

The Point of Impact

A perfect *armada dupla* must aim at the parietal and the temporal regions of the head, just like in the classic *armada*. As with most capoeira rotating and spinning kicks, you can also execute a counterattacking diagonal *armada dupla* and take advantage of the extra time you gain to gather momentum for the jump and the turn. The move is also great for surprising an attacker using crescent kicks and upsetting his balance.

The Technique

To execute this technique, you need to be in very good shape and must have mastered at least a couple of acrobatic moves. You could start with the *compasso*, followed by the *compasso pulado*, for instance. These would be good bases from which to practice the *armada dupla*. Against a *benção*, like the one in Figure 2.1, you should add your weight to your power, so that you make sure to come down hard on his head (or on his neck, his clavicle or even his chest), assuming you are up against a real assailant!

To execute a good *armada dupla,* start by thinking of a *parafuso* or a *mariposa*. The difference is that you will use both legs from the beginning to hop into your *armada dupla*. Concentrate. The more you concentrate on what you want to do, the less distance you will need for running to gain momentum. At first, there is no problem in running a short distance to make your jump higher, but the idea is to execute the *armada dupla* from a zero stance.

Likewise the *mariposa:* use your arms to help launch you high into the air, and as soon as you lift off, twist your torso so as to pull both legs up, keeping your feet together and always at a 90° angle to your legs, turn toward the side and finally to the ground, where you will land on both feet. Think of these phases as a single, quick and accurate movement.

Figure 2.2: Find a gap and plan your distance before jumping to your *armada dupla*.

See the chapter on the *mariposa* for additional valuable information on the mechanics of capoeira's aerial movements.

Practicing Alone

The very first thing to do is to make sure you are in a gym, equipped with a soft floor exercise mat and professional guidance. **Remember that you can hurt yourself by trying capoeira moves without proper instruction.**

Defenses and Counterattacks

Your opponent is flying with a quick *armada dupla* aimed at your head. Dodge down, no matter what. Then, in a flash, remember that you are a capoeirista, so you surely have the resources to get out of this fix. Take the first resource that comes to mind, and act quickly. Your moves would probably be an *esquiva lateral*, a *resistência*, which can be followed by a *negativa* and an *s-dobrado* with *chapéu de couro* or *martelo*, or you can simply dodge down straight into the *negativa*, from which you could engage in a *queda de rim* to regain your original posture, while your opponent lands from his *armada dupla* at a moment when you could still try a *rasteira de chão* or a *rasteira giratória* (depending on your position) to catch him by surprise.

Make sure not to try crescent or spinning kicks while your opponent is up in the air and moving toward you.

Aú (Classic)

The classic cartwheel, this is one of the most beautiful and useful capoeira techniques, yet most capoeiristas are unaware of its full potential. The *aú* is the first of a system of maneuvers based on the classic cartwheel movement. It is a great simulation and evasive technique. The capoeira *aú* functions rather like the *mae-ukemi* in judo and aikido, as a defense technique when you cannot stand upright and are forced to fall down. In these Japanese martial arts, *mae-ukemi* allows you to guard your head, hitting the ground with your body, and quickly stand up again, with the least possible harm or no harm at all.

One of the beautiful and interesting tales I heard from the great Mestre Adilson (Camisa Preta) of the original *Grupo Bantus de Capoeira* is that this movement really came from the tumbleweed blowing across the deserts of Africa,* suggesting its lightness and at the same time its energy and capacity to displace itself continuously. Whether Asian monks and explorers encountered the great African

---

* I also heard that the modern name *aú* comes from the position in which we stand at the peak of the move, suggesting the letter "A" formed with our arms and head and the letter "U," formed with both outstretched legs.

warriors or various African kingdoms and exchanged knowledge with them, or whether only the African deserts are responsible for its invention, in capoeira the *aú* can do the trick quickly, gracefully and cunningly – with the advantage that you can still engage in one or more attack modes throughout the move, with little chance of getting hurt in the process.

Despite the fact that for a capoeirista it is, to a certain extent, easy to deal with most styles of the *aú* executed from a partner in a *roda*, the truth is that if you master the use of this technique to lure, feint, distract and deceive another martial artist, you will most likely take him by surprise and succeed in your mission.

Objectives

Your primary objective is to time your motion with that of your opponent in order to gauge the best time to execute an evasive *aú* to escape from him in a quick retreat, or just to deceive the adversary and lure him into a trap, while at the same time preparing yourself for a new attack or a counterattack.

This technique can be performed by means of a "long" *aú* – achieved when you travel from one point to another, or a "fixed" *aú* – achieved when you execute the complete cartwheel over practically the same spot, without traveling too far. However, you can always change objectives and fall into an *aú dobrado* or an *aú* and *queda de rim* and quickly redesign your strategy.

A common application is to execute your *aú* in the opposite direction of your partner's own *aú* (Figure 3.1). This way you will not only maintain the flow of motion, but will also restrict your "theater of war" to the space you are trying to control (rather than allow your opponent to control this space to his own advantage).

Three of the best strategic ways to *perform* an *aú* are the "diagonal *aú*," the "perpendicular *aú*," and the very close "blocking" and sometimes even scary *aú*, executed as close

Figure 3.1: A timely "counterattacking" *aú*. Retaining control over your "theater of war."

AÚ (CLASSIC)

to the opponent as possible (see Figures 3.2, 3.3 and 3.4). Many capoeiristas do not understand the richness and the – at times – usefulness of a particular technique because they only know "the move" itself. It is essential that you learn and value the performance and the "application" of each move, and understand how certain techniques can be applied in a *roda* or in a real combat situation. In capoeira you must constantly ask yourself: How can I execute this technique better?

In the diagrams of Figure 3.2, the defending capoeirista perceives his opponent's incoming *mortal de frente* (1) and begins to concentrate on his evasive diagonal escape to the left (2). He places his right foot to the right (to the reader's left), behind his back (3) and opens his arms for the *aú* while the attacker has begun his *mortal de frente*. He then quickly brings back his left leg, placing it parallel to his right leg in order to begin his diagonal *aú* while the *mortal de frente* has already taken shape with an extra "bonus" of a surprising *chibata,* a.k.a. *meia-lua solta* in some accredited capoeira schools. The defending capoeirista goes for his diagonal *aú* in the direction of the opponent's original position, thus retaining control of his "theater of war" at the same time he does away with the attack.

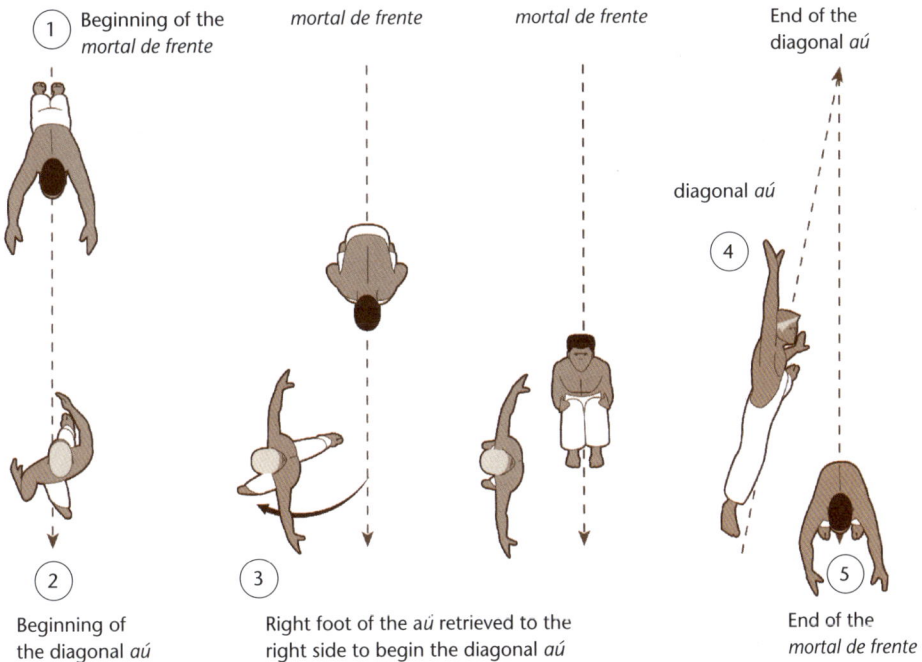

Figure 3.2: Notice the diagonal stance taken by the defending capoeirista in order to remain close to his attacker and complete his strategic *aú* on the same track. Always maintain the flow of motion.

By performing these "modes" of *aú,* the capoeirista will most likely avoid any adverse situation and be ready for new action before the adversary has had time to recover from his last move. Choose your tactic according to your best strategy. **Remember**: Time your moves with those of your opponent as much as possible, both in the *roda* and in real combat.

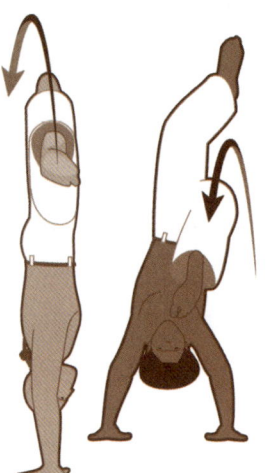

Figure 3.3: A close "perpendicular" *aú* will help you displace your opponent's attack.

Figure 3.4: A very close "blocking" *aú* will most certainly take your opponent by surprise, in or outside the *roda*.

The Point of Impact

There is no point of impact for the classic *aú* if you just do the regular evasive and misleading cartwheel. However, if you use a combination of your *aú* with one or more *chibatas,* you will have a variety of points of impact. See the chapter on *aú chibata* for many additional and exciting details.

The Technique

The classic *aú* normally starts from a standing position, from *ginga* or from zero stance. The first arm reaches the ground in the direction of movement, and the second forms an arc over the head, still in the same direction of motion. You can

AÚ (CLASSIC)

keep your supporting arms straight or slightly bent, as in the next illustration of the *aú* and *queda de rim*. The first leg to leave the ground should be the one opposite the first arm, i.e., if you start with your left arm, your first leg up will be the right leg, which should kick off and create a lever for the other leg. Your other hand then should be placed on the far side of the body. You can always bend your arms at the elbows sufficiently to support your weight while both legs pass over your fully extended body, with a 135° angle between them.* While you are upside-down, your legs should be open and fully extended. During the move, always maintain eye contact with your opponent, and don't look at your hands. To finish the movement, one foot touches the ground before the other. Your arms should always return to a defensive position.

Note that you can always freeze your cartwheel in a handstand position (see more in the chapter on *bananeira*) in order to engage in other techniques instead of concluding the *aú,* or you can finish your *aú* in a *queda de rim* or an *aú dobrado* in order to pave the way for new ground movements.

Aú and *Queda de rim.*

Aú dobrado.

Remember my first American student, the ballet teacher, whom I mentioned in the *armada* chapter? Well, he also learned the "cartwheel" in a second, but

---

* You should always be able to execute your *aú* without having to bend your arms at all, like in Olympic gymnastics.

he couldn't do the capoeira *aú* that easily. It took him a great deal of effort and instruction before he got it right.

See the chapter on *queda de rim* for more details. For the *aú dobrado,* after you start the classic *aú,* once both legs have passed over your fully extended body with a 135° angle between them, start bending the first leg, and then the second, to fall on the ground in the direction of your feet. You must hit the ground with both feet at the same time, as if you were preparing to execute a *macaco.*

For the *aú agulha,* you start as if you were going to do an *aú,* but you actually bring both legs together to land as in an *agrupado* position (see *macaco agrupado* and the "Olympic" *xangô* for more details).

Although this type of *aú* is used to deceive your partner in the *roda,* it is also used as a platform to launch a high *xangô.* Simply execute the *aú agulha* and when you land, bounce back on a *xangô* in a continuous move (Olympic gymnasts do that in floor exercises, for a series of flips).

From the *Aú agulha* you can bounce into a *Mortal* or a *Xangô.*

Practicing Alone

The best way to practice most styles of *aú* alone, to improve your skills, is in front of a mirror. Aside from the *roda,* this is the most effective way to correct your posture and improve your techniques.

The training bag is also a handy tool for practicing most styles. However, since you do not kick with the classic *aú,* you can use the bag to practice your aim and balance, using the bag as a reference point.

Refer to the Introduction for more details and special tips on practicing your *aú* alone to improve your techniques.

AÚ (CLASSIC)

Defenses and Counterattacks

There is always the possibility of descending on the *negativa*. Use a classic *rasteira* or a *rasteira giratória* to sweep your opponent's supporting hands off the ground and spin a counterattack with a *chapa giratória*, a *chapa de costas*, a *meia-lua de chão* or a low *meia-lua presa* while he is executing his moves. However, in a more complex and technical defense, if your opponent executes a classic *aú* and you need to remain fairly close to him (as could be the case in real combat), one good counteraction is to execute an *aú fechado*, a.k.a. *aú angola*, in the opposite direction. This maintains the flow of motion, which is mandatory in a *roda* and advisable elsewhere.

In this case, you can use your feet to be creative and block your opponent's attempt to change styles and use his knees or *chibatas* to reach you. You will also be closer to the ground and ready for ground maneuvers, which can be executed by converting your *aú* into an *aú dobrado*, a *macaco* or a *xangô*, depending on the distance from your opponent.

As a traditional counterattack, most common in a *roda*, if you are careful enough and aware of the threat you can knock down your adversary with a quick and cunning *cabeçada*. However, I do not recommend doing that unless your partner is a couple of cords behind you (in the cord system of your capoeira school).

If your opponent aborts his classic *aú* and falls on an *aú dobrado*, be prepared to execute a low *meia-lua presa* or to simply block him, improvising a *bloqueio de dentro* right behind his supporting *macaco* arm.

Aú Batido

A broken *aú*, a cartwheel with an overhead kick, the *aú batido* is one of several variations of the *classic aú* and is a simulation, a *floreio* and an attacking movement. A deceptive technique in principle, the *aú batido* can – and should – be used as an attacking movement in situations that require or allow for creative and spacious maneuvers. It can be executed as a dissuading or a persuading technique, i.e., as a tool to trick and deceive the opponent, drawing him into making the wrong response, thus creating the desired open guard for the decisive blow.

In the *roda*, it is common to see capoeiristas of all levels using variations of the *aú*, including the *aú batido,* for aesthetic purposes only, which is beautiful in the *roda* though pointless in actual combat.

The good thing is that all styles of the *aú* are genuinely useful in real-life situations. The serious capoeirista should be aware of that and practice with a varied flurry of feints, including these wonderful techniques in the capoeira repertoire.

Objectives

Your primary objective is to use your *ginga* motion in order to deceive your adversary with an attack aimed at one point, merely as a distraction from the real target, and create an opportunity to use the *aú batido* in order to push your opponent away from you or even knock him down with your attacking foot.

The Point of Impact

There are several points of impact – including the psychological impact – when using an *aú batido* in real fighting. In the *roda*, we normally get really close to our partner, so as to scare or warn him, but the final objective is always to surprise him and never really kick. In real-life combat, though, reaching for your opponent's head or chest will give you an important edge during a street fight, given the situation, which will probably include enough space to move around and the freedom to execute your other capoeira techniques.

The Technique

The *aú batido* should start from a classic *aú*, as a deceptive movement that suddenly turns into a blocking move or a kick, depending on the circumstances. All you have to do is go for the cartwheel, as if you were going to execute it in full. Basically, you stop your classical *aú* on one hand while forcing your kick overhead in the same direction as the original cartwheel. Your other leg should go in the opposite direction, until both stretched legs are apart, ideally with a 135° angle between them (or at least a 120° angle). Your parted legs will give you the perfect balance. If possible, the attacking leg should create a 90° angle with your supporting arm, and your other leg should be at an angle of around 45° (or, at least, an 80°/40° combination). Use your attacking kick movement as a lever to get back gracefully, undoing your original *aú*.

As shown in Figure 4.1, note that the hand on the attacking leg helps keep your balance during the movement, although you can also execute this technique without holding your leg by forcing it slightly further into the opponent's space.

Figure 4.1: An *aú batido* in action against an approaching opponent.

One variation of the *aú batido* is executed with the support of your elbow instead of your hand, as shown in Figure 4.2. I am not particularly fond of this type of movement, as it can hurt your arm if done carelessly or on a rough surface.

Figure 4.2: An *aú batido de cotovelo*.

For the *aú batido fechado* (a.k.a. *aú batido angola*), you must start with the same technique as in the classic *aú batido*, but instead of forcing your kick overhead, you take both legs with you in a not-too-stiff manner.

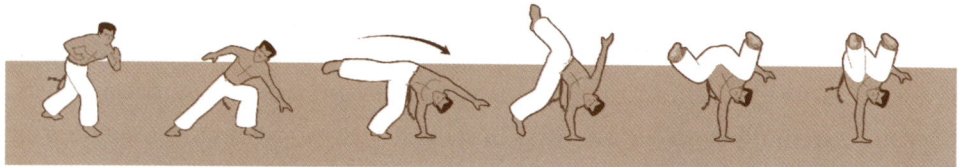

Aú batido fechado.

For the *aú batido agrupado,* you also start by using the same technique as in the other two versions, but must work your torso to achieve a good flexion and reach for your hand on the other side, from an extended arm. In this case, holding your feet or your legs, or even just touching them, is a good way to achieve a quick, balanced move.

Aú batido agrupado.

As an attack strategy, the *aú batido* must be delivered on your approaching adversary quickly and without delay. This can be done with or without the help of your free hand, as shown in Figure 4.1.

AÚ BATIDO

In the movie *Tom Yum Goong* (called *The Protector* in the US release), actor and capoeirista Lateef Crowder demonstrates the high potential of several real capoeira moves, including the *aú batido*. It is worth watching his "navigation" on the ground, as well as his intelligent use of space in trying to confuse his opponent, portrayed by actor Tony Jaa (who plays the "good guy" in this movie).

As for the other two versions of the *aú batido* – the *aú batido fechado* and the *aú batido agrupado* or *double aú batido* – you will find that their best application is in the *roda,* though you should definitely bear in mind that the most evasive and cunning capoeira moves also have their own special moments in real combat as tools for deluding and misleading a gullible adversary.

Practicing Alone

One good way to practice the *aú batido* is in front of a mirror, to correct your posture and improve your technique. As with most capoeira kicks, you should also practice it on the training bag, which will come in handy for improving your aim, power and balance.

Refer to the Introduction for more details and special tips on practicing the *aú batido* alone to improve your techniques.

Defenses and Counterattacks

If you are timing your movements with those of your opponent and don't have enough space to evade his *aú batido*, a great defense is always to descend to the *negativa* for ground maneuvers. Then you can use an *s-dobrado* and all its unfolding possibilities, so as to get your opponent while he is still trying to regain control, or if you have time, you can even use a classic *rasteira* or a *rasteira giratória* and try to sweep away your attacker's supporting hand, and then prepare to parry a counterattack with a *meia-lua de chão* or a low *meia-lua presa*.

If you don't have enough space, particularly in the *roda* with an overexcited partner, do not try to simply dodge your opponent's *aú batido,* or you will risk being struck by a sudden switch from an *aú batido* to an *aú chibata* that will eventually get you on the head or on the back.

Space is one of the challenges in capoeira practice. Think for a moment of a *roda* of Mestre Jogo de Dentro. I have seen him reduce a *roda* to a narrow circle with scarcely room for one person, and play in it. A wonderful capoeirista. Now think of bold, fast, acrobatic regional or "contemporary" capoeira done in real combat.

Usually, in real fighting one does not have a very "democratic" space. Therefore, you may need to get accustomed to quickly choosing the right move for the right occasion. Remember, you won't always have the opportunity to choose just any technique for your contest. Having said that, make sure you know how to evaluate the type of move you need according to each available situation. Again, watching other capoeiristas of all trends in action is a great help, as it allows you to study their strengths and their choices, their weaknesses and gaps – for your own benefit.

Aú Chibata

The classic cartwheel suddenly turned into an attack, using one or both legs as a whip (the *chibata*). The *aú chibata*, a.k.a. *aú com martelo*, is one of the first of a set of maneuvers based on the classic cartwheel movement in the capoeirista's repertoire of *aú* styles. Like the classic *aú*, it is a great *floreio* and an evasive technique, since you can always pretend that you are just going to whip your opponent's head, when actually you resume the classic form of the *aú* without even touching him. Alternatively, you can use your *chibata* or *martelo* and remain in the handstand position, waiting for the next move. As a subgroup, this technique offers the *joelhada*, which is done vertically on a careless opponent.

Welcome to a most versatile capoeira technique! Here you will find trickery, grace, speed and cunning, and, most of all, a wide array of possible *transitions* – a subject that is seldom discussed in capoeira.

Objectives

Your primary objective is to time your motion with that of your opponent, seeking to deceive him from your initial *aú* and whip him when he tries to approach you with his *negativa*, a *cabeçada* or a simple *giro*. You must use your *aú chibata* to "entice" your opponent into attacking you first. That's when speed is a fascinating aspect of most capoeira moves, especially those that employ supporting hands on the ground.

Then you should use your *aú chibata* to whip your opponent's head, back or chest, in which case you can kick hard, use a *joelhada* or just push him away.

Figure 5.1: Who is attacking whom?

Another way to explain the *aú chibata* is to describe it as a *chibata* done from the classic *aú* and not as a type of *aú* in its own right. You can do the *chibata* (whip kick) from the *bananeira* or the *aú fechado*, or from other types of movements, including acrobatic ones.

In Figure 5.1 the capoeirista executing the *negativa* has probably foreseen his opponent's intention to do an *aú* or has enticed him into the move. However, the opposite may also have occurred, i.e., the guy doing the *aú* may have predicted his adversary's ground navigation or lured him into his *negativa* to get him to this point.

The Point of Impact

Your target is mostly your adversary's head, when he gets too close with his *negativa* or *cabeçada*, using the top or the ball of the foot. If you let him get too close, a *joelhada* will do the trick. Sometimes you must go for his chest, using the ball of your foot only. If he closes in with a *giro,* you can whip his back hard, using the top of your foot.

The Technique

As I mentioned before, this type of *chibata* is actually a vertical kick that is normally executed from a classic *aú*. Therefore, I recommend that before trying the *aú chibata*, you first master the classic *aú*, the *aú fechado* and the *bananeira* to perfection level.

The technique for the *aú chibata* is actually the same as that of a classic *aú* mixed with the *bananeira*. During the move, never forget to maintain eye contact with your opponent. Do not look at your hands. To finish the movement in an *aú-like* manner, touch the ground first with one foot and then with the other. Your arms should return to a defensive position. However, you can engage in a *ponte* after you have used the head of your unlucky opponent as a springboard, or you can remain in a *bananeira* preparing for your next move, finish your *aú* in a *queda de rim*, or turn it into an *aú dobrado* in order to proceed to new movements.

The Other Side

In real combat we must sometimes think in terms of survival. And if this is the case, even though we are prepared to use our *chibatas* in a forward direction, since we are looking through our arms toward our adversary, there is always a chance to strike forward with a *chibata* and use this leverage to hit back at the same time on another "bad guy," with your other leg in a wide-open angle, using the heel or the bottom of your foot.

As an attack strategy, the *aú chibata* can be delivered either quickly or rather slowly. A great aesthetic resource for the *roda* and for general exhibition, it also works as a centralized system of moves that can be triggered and distributed from its peak. Its best application outside the *roda* is against a versatile opponent or against more than one opponent.

Joelhada (Aérea)

From your *aú*, whether moving or halting in a *bananeira*, if your opponent gets too close to you from a low position, such as a *cabeçada* on your upper body, you can always execute an aerial knee strike, called *joelhada* (Figure 5.2) instead of the *chibata*. It is done vertically and, preferably, onto your adversary's head.

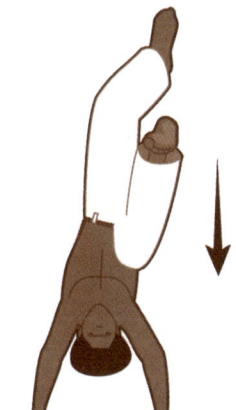

Figure 5.2: A *joelhada (aérea* as an alternative option to a *chibata).*

Versatility is your motto for the *aú chibata*. If you master the technique, you'll be able to engage in a variety of positions and motions from your *aú* and choose the perfect timing and path for your *chibatas*.

The classic *aú chibata* is a versatile combo.

Aú Chibata de Chão

From the *negativa*, you can engage in a *queda de rim* and thus turn a *chibata* back into a new *negativa* and a *rolê*. Some capoeiristas call this simply a *chibata de chão*. Others call it *aú chibata de chão*, which I prefer due to the fact that the *chibata* must be done from an existing move, no matter which one, so long as it allows for execution of a perfect *chibata*. Regardless of the terminology, this beautiful move is a trademark of capoeira and a wonderful resource for ground navigation and fighting.

Aú chibata de chão.

Practicing Alone

The training bag and the mirror are handy tools for practicing your *aú chibata* alone. Try different speeds, and always strive for a combination of precision and grace.

Defenses and Counterattacks

Normally, we would expect the same attitudes of a defense against an "attacking" *aú chibata* as the ones we may use against the classic *aú*. However, due to the more advanced prerequisites of the *aú chibata*, the opposing capoeirista must be very careful when trying to approach someone executing an *aú*. Whether you are in a *roda* or simply close to your adversary, you can perform an *aú fechado* in the opposite direction, with defensive feet together, while at the same time keeping a careful eye on your opponent's trajectory and action. In addition, I strongly recommend that you do not descend into a *negativa*, but rather use a classic *rasteira* or a *rasteira giratória* in order to sweep your opponent's supporting hands off the ground in the event that you anticipate his *aú chibata*.

One good technique to keep the motion going in the *roda* space would be to execute a "perpendicular" *aú*. You simply step back with your first *aú* leg, then take a diagonal stance and execute a classic *aú* or an *aú fechado* in a perpendicular fashion, preferably right after your opponent takes his first *aú chibata* hand off the ground. This way, you will have the advantage when he completes his move.

Note that there is no use (and it can also hurt you badly) to deliver spinning kicks against moves that are executed with both supporting hands on the ground and the legs up, such as the *aú*, the *bananeira* and the *meia-lua reversão,* among other similar techniques – unless you time your action with your opponent's, so as to catch him when he is finishing his move.

Aú Com uma Mão

The cartwheel with one hand is a faster variation of the classic *aú*. It functions sort of "in between" the *aú sem mãos* (the aerial cartwheel) and the classic *aú*. You keep your first supporting hand on the ground throughout the move. Although is a technical maneuver that also allows for simulation and evasiveness, it is not as cunning as the classical move, because of its speed. Nevertheless, the fact that it is a faster move makes it interesting for the creative capoeirista.

Objectives

The main difference is that you don't really need to worry about timing your motion with that of your opponent in order to execute an *aú com uma mão* to escape or surprise your adversary. Since this is a quick evasive movement, you should find yourself the best opportunity to move unexpectedly before his "open guard" while quickly changing your position relative to that of your opponent. You will then be ready immediately for new action. You can also take your adversary by surprise by executing two moves in a roll, not necessarily in the same direction. When done quickly, precisely and in a timely manner, this is the closest you will get to becoming a Hollywood Ninja!

The Point of Impact

There is no point of impact for the regular *aú com uma mão*. However, there is a variation of this move, an aerial wheel kick or a flying *meia-lua de compasso*, which is not really an *aú* (see *meia-lua de compasso pulada*) and is done with the help of one supporting hand on the ground for the sake of velocity and ease. In this case, you can use it with the benefits of the *meia-lua de compasso*, the *meia-lua solta*, or the *aú sem mãos*, their points of impact being the same for your *aú com uma mão*.

The Technique

The best way to start an *aú com uma mão* is from a standing position, from *ginga* or from zero stance. You should know how to easily execute a quick and perfect classic *aú* before attempting this semi-aerial. When you are ready, assuming that your left leg is your supporting leg, touch the ground with your left hand while throwing your body upward and downward, and swing your right leg back and immediately upward as hard as possible to start the move. Then launch off your left leg. If you do this with enough power, your right leg will lift you up and your left leg will follow from under you to complete the movement. Quickly synchronize the supporting arm with your right leg and your torso. Use your hip to help propel the overhead rotation, keeping your other arm ready for extra support in case you need it. This move is best done quickly. Remember to watch your opponent at all times.

Practicing Alone

The best way to practice most styles of *aú* alone is in front of a mirror, to correct your techniques. Once you feel you can perform the *aú com uma mão* well, do it in front of a reference point, using your "training chair" or the sandbag as a reference. You should try both long *aús* (when you move your first hand away from your reference point) and short ones (when you put your first hand closer to your supporting foot to stay nearer your reference point). This will give you the confidence you need to perform a perfect and effective *aú com uma mão*.

Defenses and Counterattacks

As with the classic *aú*, there is always the possibility of descending on the *negativa*, using a classic *rasteira* or a *rasteira giratória* to sweep your opponent's supporting hand off the ground – if you time your move with his. On the other hand, in contrast to the technique suggested for the classic move, it would be difficult to spin a counterattack – such as a *chapa giratória* or other spinning kicks – during your opponent's action because the *aú com uma mão* is usually a quick move, unless you are fast enough and follow his movement by twirling and executing your spinning kick to get him before he finishes his cartwheel on one hand. If this is the case, the moment he starts his *aú* twirl just like a twister, following along his move in order to deliver your *chapa giratória* or *chapa de costas* right on his thigh or torso. You can also follow along his *aú com uma mão* on a *mariposa* for the sake of aesthetics or the flow of motion in the *roda*.

Remember: If you time your movements with those of your adversary, you can execute a faster *aú sem mãos* in the opposite direction, always looking at your opponent, but don't ever even think of trying a *cabeçada* against this type of *aú*.

Another great strategy is to execute an opposing *aú fechado* instead of the *aú sem mãos*, so that you can use your feet to block your opponent's attempt to use a *chibata* to reach you. You will also be closer to the ground and ready for ground maneuvers.

Aú de Costas

The backward cartwheel, also known as *macaco em pé* (a *macaco* from a standing position). This is a back-standing walkover that can be done repeatedly over the same spot, or from one spot to another, in order to catch up to your opponent from behind. It can also be executed much like the *macaco,* a little to the side or completely straight.

The *aú de costas* functions both as an evasive and an approaching maneuver, which means that you can use it to attack your adversary. However, it is used more often as an approaching-attacking move than as an evasive one. In contrast to the *aú de frente,* once you start the movement you can complete it or control your balance in order to execute a handstand or *chibatas,* or to perform low movements.

An elegant and acrobatic move, the *aú de costas* can be both an aggressive and a tricky move, a quick move or a slow, smooth one.

Objectives

As with the classical *macaco,* the *aú de costas* is a great aesthetic and strategic tool for a good game of capoeira in the *roda,* where you can perform evasive changes of direction, approach your opponent or withdraw from him. In real combat, it is a strategic resource for duping your adversary and executing an objective *chibata* attack, striking with the tops or the balls of the feet.

There are really three subtle strategies in performing this technique. You can use a dissuading *aú de costas* just to trick your opponent into making a wrong move, or a wrong judgment, by executing at least two moves on the very same spot; you can do it as an evasive move, just like a classic *aú;* or you can do a more directional and offensive *aú de costas* right over your adversary's head (in which case the *aú de costas* is also called *macaco em pé*).

The Straight-up Style

The *aú* is an institution in capoeira. For this reason it is difficult, if not unfair, to label the style a good capoeirista prefers to use – whether a more lateral or a straight-up movement. As with the *macaco,* you can do an Olympic-style, "perfect" move or a more relaxed lateral one, and both, if done well, will be considered perfect moves. For instance, you may prefer the performance illustrated in Figure 7.1, where the capoeirista looks up on a clean, straight maneuver during the rotation. It is good as a *floreio* and it has the same strategic value. Note that the capoeirista starts as in a *ponte* or a *macaco em pé* and finishes the movement facing the original direction.

Figure 7.1: The *aú de costas.*

AÚ DE COSTAS

In the "lateral" *aú de costas,* the capoeirista begins the move looking slightly to the side. Many of the so-called "contemporary" capoeiristas believe it is done this way because the player does not know how to execute it "perfectly." In the case of inexperienced capoeiristas, this is partly true. On the other hand, many capoeira experts and Mestres simply choose to do it the lateral way for strategic reasons, some believing that the lateral *aú* and the lateral *macaco* are a more cunning form for executing the moves, which is also true. Figure 7.2 shows the more lateral approach of the *aú de costas* at the beginning of the move.

Figure 7.2: Beginning your "lateral" *aú de costas.*

The Infinite or Ferris Wheel Style

One nice *aú* that you can do, mostly in a *roda* as a *floreio,* is the "infinite" or the "Ferris wheel" style, known as the *aú infinito,* which consists of turning several *aús* over the same spot.

Figure 7.3: The *aú de costas infinito.*

The Point of Impact

Besides using the *aú de costas* as a *floreio* to scare or deceive your opponent, in real fighting you can also rain heavy *chibatas* down on his head. Watch your power, as these kicks can be true dynamite and may inflict severe injuries on your adversary. If you are trying seriously to knock him out, use the top of your feet.

Note that using your instep may cause pain or even injury to your own feet, if you hit with too much power. Be aware that using the balls of your feet for your *chibatas* may be lethal!

The Technique

Pretend you're going to walk forward, but after completing the second step, suddenly bend back as if you were going to do a *ponte,* except that you will first touch the ground with one hand, with the palm slightly open for a better grip. Thrust your first leg up hard and start the *aú de costas* to the rear, thrusting your second hand and then your second leg as if you were going to execute an *aú chibata* to the rear (which is, in fact, what you are doing). As with the *aú de frente,* your torso should be flexible enough, so as to allow you to touch the ground with your first hand while still keeping your arched supporting leg on the ground.

When you bring your other leg down to a landing position, take another step forward and start over. Your second hand travels somewhat behind your head just like in the classic *macaco,* so it is best to learn the *macaco* first to get the feel of it before trying the *aú de costas.*

To execute the *aú de costas infinito* (Figure 7.3), the "Ferris wheel" style, you don't need to travel with your cartwheel from one point to another, but rather you rotate over the very same spot, at which the movement can be done continuously. You can find this and other capoeira moves at www.unknowncapoeira.com.

The *aú de costas* is a great and efficient technique, which helps the capoeiristas keep in motion while connecting their various movements and controlling their challenging transitions. These attributes are actually one of the main differences between capoeira and all other martial arts.

If you choose to execute the "Ferris wheel" *infinito* style, walk along your *aú* line, bend back, touch the ground with the first hand, thrust your *aú de costas* back, step down, take a further step on the same *aú* track, and start all over again.

Try not to bend your first leg too much when starting your *aú de costas*. Note that if you have to bend both legs, you will be doing a *macaco* instead of an *aú*. This technique requires good body flexibility, and the less you bend your

AÚ DE COSTAS

leg while trying to touch the ground with your first hand, the better your movement will come out.

Practicing Alone

You can practice the *aú de costas* alone on the training bag, just like with the *macaco* and the *s-dobrado*. Take advantage of the different speeds you can use to execute the move, and use your *chibatas* on the bag at will. For the "infinite" style, there is no point in executing more than three moves in a row – all you will gain is dizziness.

Defenses and Counterattacks

It's possible to block an *aú de costas* right at the beginning of the move. Just use your side *bloqueio* right on your opponent's hip. Open your arms in a T-like shape over his first leg as you enter his guard. Watch out for a counterattacking *tesoura*, a *vingativa*, a *boca de calça*, an *arrastão* or a *rasteira de mão*, to name just few of the possible moves your opponent may use against your *bloqueio*.

Although it is seldom used in actual combat, pay attention to the *aú de costas infinito* done by your opponent. If you sense that he is preparing to do an *aú de costas* or a *macaco* of any type, a quick and invasive *meia-lua presa* can do the trick and block his move; and executing another one immediately can be quite devastating. Nevertheless, if you feel you are too far from your target to deliver a *meia-lua presa*, take evasive action with a timely *aú fechado* and go around your opponent in order to catch him with a *compasso pulado*, a *meia-lua de compasso* or a *meia-lua solta* when he finishes his *aú de costas*.

Aú de Frente

A forward cartwheel, also known as *aú reversão* or *aú cortado*, the *aú de frente* does not have the subtle speed variation of the *classic aú* – the *aú de frente* being faster – but it does also function as an evasive maneuver when you need to position yourself in front of or away from your target, whatever the target may be. Once you start the movement, you should complete it: there should be no "stopping" on a handstand.

The main idea behind the *aú de frente* is to use it as an escape technique, whether or not you have the intention – and the body control – to come back in a new movement.

Objectives

As with the *aú sem mãos,* you don't really need to worry about timing your motion with that of your opponent in order to execute an *aú de frente* to approach or escape from your adversary. You choose this mode mainly when you feel you need to remain standing in order to rethink your strategy.

AÚ DE FRENTE

In the "walkover" style, as shown in Figure 8.1, the capoeirista performs a "reverse" *aú de costas*, starting as in a *bananeira* and finishes facing the original direction, pretending he is going to walk away from the scene.

Figure 8.1: The "walkover" *aú de frente*.

The Point of Impact

There is no point of impact for the *aú de frente*, but keep in mind that by doing the move you will be ready to engage in a spinning kick or come back in a *xangô*, a *macaco* or a *ponte* – all of which have great kicking potential.

The Technique

After you start the classic *aú*, as soon as your second leg has passed over your fully extended body, start bending the first leg slightly, seeking the ground in a forward motion, followed by the second leg, which will execute a forward walkover starting in the second half of the movement. Your torso should be flexible, so as to allow you to touch the ground with your forward, extended leg while keeping your supporting hand on the ground. Try to keep your leg extended when your first foot touches the ground. If you don't do that and you flex your first leg, chances are that you will end up in an *aú dobrado*. After you have touched the ground with your first foot, keep your forward momentum by following through with your torso and standing up.

As with the *aú de costas*, you can execute the *aú de frente* with a lateral inclination (which some practitioners call *aú reversão*) or straight up, as shown in Figure 8.1.

Some capoeiristas do a 180° walkover, like a forward handspring on one leg, and call it *aú de frente*. I like to call it *xangô de frente*, also called *pulo do gato de frente*.

The main difference between the two techniques is that in the forward handspring you start off placing both hands on the ground at the same time, and then, with both hands still on the ground, kicking one leg up over your head. You keep your whole body arched, so as to not bend your legs all through the movement, which is done in one quick motion. Keep both palms on the ground until you feel you have both legs straight and both feet have landed on the ground.

Olympic gymnasts use all ten fingers to help push the body off the ground, as in a springboard effect, when the second leg is starting the walkover.

The *aú de frente* should be a graceful and continuous move, in whichever mode you decide to execute it.

Practicing Alone

Differently from with the classic *aú* and the *aú fechado*, you should execute the *aú de frente* at an average-to-high speed and in continuous momentum. There is no use in performing it at low and variable speeds. Remember to get professional guidance, and practice to perfection!

Defenses and Counterattacks

You don't really try to stop an *aú de frente*. You can always try the classic *aú* countermeasures where they apply, such as a *negativa*, a *rasteira* or a *rasteira giratória* to sweep your opponent's supporting hands off the ground, and spin a *chapa giratória*, a *chapa de costas*, a *meia-lua de chão* or a low *meia-lua presa* during your opponent's move. You can also spin your body in a *giro* just to follow along his movement, and when he finishes his *aú de frente* surprise him with a quick *meia-lua* right on his head, which could be really unexpected. This means you will be doing two *giros:* the first just to spin your body along his *aú de frente,* and the second to launch your *meia-lua*. Of course, you can always execute a classic *aú* or an *aú fechado* in the opposite direction, keeping watch on your opponent's movement. In this case, be decisive and fast enough to finish off your move before his or, at least, at the same time as his.

Aú Fechado

A great technical variation of the classic *aú*, replete with its own variations, the *aú fechado*, known also as *aú angola*, is an ostensibly more "negligent" type of *aú*, and is also known as *aú baixo* (low *aú*). It is not as showy as the classic open *aú*, though it can be safer and sneakier. And it is definitely richer in tactics. In my opinion, it's simply beautiful. In addition, it is definitely not a wrong or a vulgar *aú*. The *aú fechado* itself is a system of maneuvers. Like the classic *aú*, besides being a great simulation and evasive technique, this move also functions as the *mae-ukemi* used in judo and aikido, as I put it in the classic *aú* section.

Being low to the ground in an *aú fechado* gives the capoeirista a set of controls, which run from the possibility of speed variation to blocking techniques and include several types of kicks, such as the *chibatas*, kicks with the ball or top of the foot, kicks with the heels, and knee blows called *joelhada*, besides the great variation of ground strategies, which can be launched from your low stance. If you are good at it, this is the closest you can get to being a Spider-Man!

Objectives

The objectives of the *aú fechado* are to use its interesting and flexible blocking capabilities to protect yourself against an attack during the movement or to deceive your opponent, for which you have several alternatives. You can choose whether or not to time your motion with his, like in the classic *aú*. However, if you come upon an inattentive or slower adversary, you can use the varied cunning strategies available from this move's repertoire as evasive maneuvers, or in order to block and kick your adversary on several parts of his body, regardless of whether he is in a standing position or maneuvering on the ground.

Figure 9.1 shows the *aú fechado agrupado* in a defensive position, in which you group your legs and feet in order to block any attempt to kick from above, such as a *chibata,* for example.

Figure 9.1: The *aú fechado agrupado.*

Figure 9.2 shows the *aú fechado* with a *ponteira* executed with the right leg. You can get a careless opponent on a *negativa*, for instance, or attack his upper body before resuming the move. Whether you will use the balls of the feet or your heels for your attacks from the *aú fechado* depends on your opponent's position and angle.

Figure 9.2: The *aú fechado* with a *ponteira.*

As a defensive strategy, the *aú fechado agrupado* can be highly effective, especially in the *roda* where you have little space in which to escape. Moves, such as the *helicóptero* (as shown in Figure 9.3, in which the capoeirista is executing one in

AÚ FECHADO

an attacking mode against his partner), can always surprise the unsuspecting capoeirista and turn into a dangerous *chibata* without warning. In that case, you can always use the *aú fechado* to close your guard efficiently and still stick to the flow of motion.

Of course, you will not execute an *aú fechado* specifically for the sake of protecting yourself against a kick, which could hurt your tibias. The idea is to act according to the flow of motion of the game or the real combat. You can try using the soles of your feet, or the sole of one foot, against your opponent's attacking foot.

Figure 9.3: You can use your *aú fechado* with a *chibata* against a *helicóptero* in the flow of motion.

The Point of Impact

Your point of impact will vary according to your tactics. We can use the *aú* to delude our opponent into a wrong response, but if you master the *aú fechado,* you will be able to deliver some counterattacking kicks against your adversary whether or not he is executing his own *aú* (Figure 9.4), or even if he is in another stance.

Refer to all variations of the *aú* in this book for their specific points of impact.

Figure 9.4: Just for the record, a providential *aú fechado* "against" a classic *aú*.

The Technique

Place your hands slightly further apart than with the classic *aú*, and move your head a little closer to the ground. Keep your knees bent and work strongly with your hips and torso to shift your body's center of gravity over your head. Do not stiffen your legs during the move, but rather keep them flexible but nevertheless under control. You can start from a standing position, from a *ginga* or zero stance, or from a low or ground stance. You could, for instance, start with an *s-dobrado* and engage in an *aú fechado*.

Apart from the flexibility and the position of your legs and feet, the mechanics of the *aú fechado* are very similar to those of the classic *aú*. As with all other styles of *aú*, always maintain eye contact with your opponent, and don't look at your hands.

Note that as with the classic *aú*, you can also freeze your movement in a more flexible handstand position from which you can execute other techniques, instead of resuming the *aú fechado*, or you can complete the movement into a *queda de rim*, an *aú dobrado*, or an *s-dobrado*.

Use your legs and feet freely to maintain your guard and create a defensive system, while at the same time maintaining the flow of motion.

Practicing Alone

Besides the *roda*, the best way to practice most styles of *aú* is in front of a mirror, in order to improve your techniques. One thing about the *roda*, though, is to watch your partners' choices of moves as a response to your *aú fechado* and study the types of decisions they make before your move. This will give you a fantastic "database" of stratagems, from which you will be able to make a selection from the standpoint of your *aú fechado* every time you need one. This strategy is one of the secrets of the famous "trickery" that only a few Mestres know and even fewer students learn, and it works for all techniques. Therefore, when a good accredited Mestre explains to you what it takes to be a Mestre, be sure that the word "experience" is going to figure somewhere in the explanation. By "experience" I mean not only playing in a *roda*, but also studying those who perform well in it, observing how they move, their attitudes and decisions, and the gaps you find in almost every fighting context or exhibition.

The training bag provides an excellent opportunity for improving your *aú fechado*. You can use it to practice your balance, as a target reference, and of course to practice your kicks.

A good thing to do is to stop in the middle of the aú and play with your legs by touching the bag with both the sole and the ball of the foot, and then proceeding to finish the move. Do this at different speeds. Use your heels too. You should control the action from the very slow through the normal *aú* speed, and up to a faster one. Feel total control of your legs also by moving them apart and grouped together, always to the right and to the left. Make sure you feel your torso twist to either side of your movement.

Defenses and Counterattacks

If you need to defend yourself against an *aú fechado*, a good choice is to perform a classic *aú* in the opposite direction. In this case, from your classic cartwheel try to deliver a set of *chibatas* with your legs as straight as possible, in order to surprise your opponent in his *aú fechado*, and finish your move in an *aú dobrado*, so that you can come back in an *s-dobrado*, a *macaco* or a *xangô*, depending on the distance from your attacker.

You can also sweep your opponent's hands from a *negativa*, use a classic *rasteira* or a *rasteira giratória*, but be aware that if you get too close to an *aú fechado* in motion, you might get hit by the capoeirista's kick.

Note: never try to execute a *cabeçada* on a capoeirista doing an *aú fechado*!

Aú Giratório

A spinning cartwheel, sometimes known as a handspin or spinning handstand, a.k.a *pião de mão*. Actually, the first and the last are different moves, though very similar. The *aú giratório* can be executed alternating the supporting hands, as in the illustration above, or with only one supporting hand during the spin. The spinning handstand, which is really a *bananeira giratória*, is executed from the initial handstand. Both can be considered a handspin.

The main idea behind the *aú giratório* is to use it as a *floreio* and as an escape technique, whether or not you have the intention – and the body control – to come back in a new movement.

Objectives

As with all repertoires of *aú* techniques, you can use the *aú giratório* to deceive your opponent or escape from him. In the *roda*, it is a great resource for beautiful choreography. However, in real fighting, your best choice would be to execute it if you are in combat with two or more adversaries. By doing a perfect *aú giratório*, you will be able to quickly use a strategic move and at the same time choose your next action after watching your opponent's approach.

AÚ GIRATÓRIO

The Point of Impact

There is no point of impact for the *aú giratório,* but once in the handstand position, you can decide which moves should be executed next, including a set of *chibatas.*

The Technique

You can start the *aú giratório* from the *ginga* stance or the zero stance and also from links with other moves, such as the *s-dobrado,* the *martelo rodado,* the *macaco,* the classic *aú,* or from any other move that requires balance of and control over supporting arms and hands. You can also link your spinning cartwheel to other movements, such as the *pião de cabeça* (the *aú giratório* on the head, without the hands).

Begin the *aú* to your left side, as in the example shown in Figure 10.1, until you reach the handstand position, but still moving laterally, as in a cartwheel. Use your momentum to spin clockwise on your left hand, with your legs extended, and then get off that hand and spin on your right hand, continuing in a clockwise direction. There are three ways to control your balance with your supporting hand: you can stand on the lower palm, you can stand on the upper palm near the fingers, or you can use alternating arms for more spins. What you shouldn't do is let your hand "stick" to the ground while you are spinning. Always try to rotate as far as your wrist can turn, keeping your supporting arm stiff, so that it functions as a rotating axis.

Figure 10.1: Start your *aú giratório* as in a normal *aú.*

Figure 10.2: Switch hands as you spin.

As shown in Figure 10.1, first you kick up your right leg and go onto the left hand, followed immediately by your right hand kicking up your left leg. If you wish, you can also start turning before you kick up. Do as many spins as you wish and are capable of, but try to execute the move rather quickly, at regular classic cartwheel speed, so as not to leave your guard open. If you would rather do the *bananeira giratória,* put both hands down and forward at the same time and use the resultant leverage to start rotating and then alternating hands.

Most right-handed capoeiristas prefer to spin on their left hand. Practice on both hands in order to be proficient.

Practicing Alone

Besides "repetition to perfection," practicing in front of a mirror and with an imaginary target, such as your sand bag, will greatly improve your *aú giratório.* When at the *roda,* though, try not to turn your back on your partner unnecessarily. Do so only when you time your movement with his, so as to start spinning when you hold the advantage.

Defenses and Counterattacks

As with the *aú de frente,* you don't really try to stop an *aú giratório,* but rather try to go around it. As opposed to most types of *aú,* do not execute your own *aú giratório* in the opposite direction, and do not execute a *giro.* Instead, one efficient move you can execute "against" your opponent's spinning cartwheel is an *aú fechado* with your legs and feet grouped for extra protection throughout the move. This way you will be able to launch your feet outward and block your opponent's eventual *chibata,* or use your feet to try to push him down.

Aú Sem Mãos

An aerial cartwheel. It's faster than the classic *aú*, but it also functions as an evasive technique and resembles the *mae-ukemi* used in judo and aikido. It is also used in wushu, mainly known in the West as kung-fu. The main conceptual difference between the two styles is that with the *aú sem mãos* you don't have the advantage of engaging in one or more attack modes throughout the move. Once you start the movement, you have to complete it. However, as with the classic *aú*, in the *aú sem mãos* you preserve the cunning ability to surprise and distract any other martial artist, despite the fact that you must be quick and objective when executing the move in actual fighting.

Objectives

As with the one-handed *aú*, you don't really need to worry about timing your motion with that of your opponent in order to execute your *aú sem mãos* to escape or surprise your adversary. This type of cartwheel is even faster than the one done with the support of one hand. You just need to find the best opportunity to make a quick, unexpected move before your opponent's open guard, while deflecting possible moves toward you.

Do not confuse this *aú* with the floor exercise cartwheel that is done without supporting hands, as performed in Olympic gymnastics. Remember that a "perfect" move in one sport does not necessarily mean the same in another! For instance, in capoeira you can do the same move in several different ways, from a more relaxed and "informal" mode to a more structured one.

The Point of Impact

Similarly to the *aú com uma mão,* there is no point of impact for the regular *aú sem mãos*. However, there is a variation of the move called *meia-lua pulada* (jumping wheel kick), which functions as a kick resembling an *aerial meia-lua*. Actually, the difference between these two moves is that if you use the movement evasively, you could call it an *aú sem mãos,* and if you use it to attack with a kick, you will be executing a *meia-lua pulada*. In this case, the point of impact will be primarily your opponent's head, followed by any other mid-level to preferably high parts of the body, including an attacking arm.

The Technique

The *aú sem mãos* is an aerial that starts from a standing position, from *ginga* or from zero stance. As with the *aú com uma mão* (with only one hand), you should know how to easily execute a quick and perfect classic *aú* before you attempt this aerial. When you are ready, assuming that your left leg is your supporting leg, throw your body downward and swing your right leg back and immediately upward as hard as possible to start the move, and then launch off your left leg. If you execute it with enough power, your right leg will lift you up and the left leg will follow from under you to complete the movement.

Your arms should move as if they were going to touch the ground like in the classic *aú*, but, quickly synchronized with the first leg and your torso, you should do a hip-over-head rotation in which no hand support is necessary to help you spin easily in the air. Keep your arms above your head throughout the entire movement, so that if you need them, they will be there to catch you. Figure 11.1 shows the main part of the sequence.

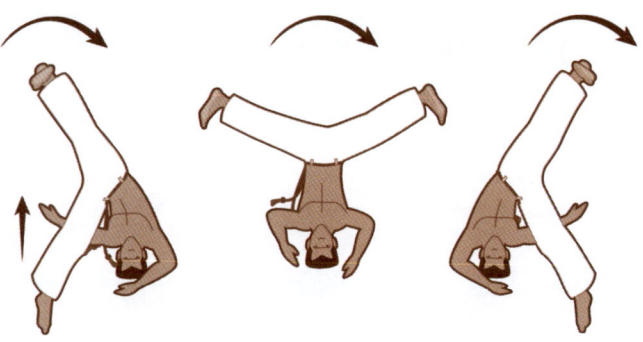

Figure 11.1: Main sequence of the *aú sem mãos* in action.

Note that before you start the sequence you have to decide whether to go vertically or horizontally, i.e., cartwheel only or kicking mode (see *meia-lua pulada*).

Practicing Alone

Since there is no tumbling belt to help you out, and spotting is not really an easy task, you must practice quick classic cartwheels to perfection before giving more power to your supporting leg, and then to your first swinging leg to finally do the aerial. Once you can perform the *aú sem mãos*, do it in front of a reference point, such as your training chair and your training bag. You should try both long ones (when you move away from your reference point) and short ones (when you stay closer to it). This will give you the confidence you need to perform a perfect *aú sem mãos*.

Defenses and Counterattacks

Obviously, there is no point in trying to use a *rasteira* against an *aú sem mãos*. If your opponent is doing an aerial cartwheel and you weren't able to stop him, it is because he had already "read" your intentions or your guard. He knows your position in relation to his potential next move, which can be a treacherous one.

Try to be decisive enough and fast enough so as to do your own *aú sem mãos* in the opposite direction, always keeping an eye on your adversary. Actually, for every capoeirista this procedure demonstrates the importance of mastering both right and left skills. If your opponent's *aú sem mãos* comes on his first (left) supporting leg, you will do the same, whereas if he starts with his right leg, you will also have to start with your right leg in order to execute your aerial in the opposite direction. Afterward, get yourself together and start your combat all over again. **Note**: do not use kicks against an *aú sem mãos* unless you are completely sure of your timing and your success.

However, if you can be fast enough to execute an *aú sem mãos* in the opposite direction, you will probably be able to knock down your opponent with one or two kicks, instead. Of course, I don't expect you to try a *cabeçada*. Follow the opponent's movement by twirling and executing a *chapa giratória* or a *chapa de costas*, to get him before he finishes his move. You must seize the moment he starts his aerial and start twirling, just like a twister along his move, in order to deliver your *chapa* right on his thigh or torso.

Bananeira

The handstand. See also *aú giratório*. This is a great technical contribution to capoeira, which most of the time is neglected by capoeiristas. It is a valuable asset to Olympic gymnasts, as it gives you considerable control over your body, which is of tremendous help in learning complex ground movements executed with the support of your hands. It is one of the best ways to gain the confidence you need in order to develop advanced capoeira skills.

The name *bananeira* was inspired by the banana trees, which first grew in the coastal regions of Brazil after the sixteenth century, introduced by the Portuguese. The name came from West Africa, where the fruit was called banema and later banana, probably from the original banan spoken by Arab traders long before the Portuguese arrived in Africa. The move itself, though, resembles the fruit. I'm inclined to believe that the move was known as a "banema" sort of move back in precolonial Africa, perhaps as a humorous analogy.

I will comment and compare both styles: the capoeira and the Olympic gymnastics handstand, for this will help you to understand why their mechanics are slightly different and to take advantage of both versions.

Objectives

The main objective of the *bananeira* is to practice body control. You can use the handstand to stroll along your capoeira gym, to be still for balance control and mind concentration, or to deliver kicks, such as a *chibata,* with the ball or top of your foot from the classic upright handstand or from a more flexible and relaxed position. In combat, though, the objectives of the *bananeira* are similar to those of the classic *aú* and the *aú fechado,* except that you don't want to move, but rather wait for your adversary's moves. Unless you fell like a spider or a crab (and why not?), in actual fighting it's not as cunning or efficient as an *aú* in motion.

The Point of Impact

Doing the *bananeira,* you will have the same points of impact as with the classic *aú* and the *aú fechado.* Normally, a capoeirista executing a capoeira handstand during a *jogo* or in real combat does one or two *chibatas,* using the last one as a springboard for a *ponte,* and eventually launching another set of *chibatas* on his way back.

The Technique

Begin by keeping your fingers spread out and facing forward. This will allow for better control and stability in your handstand. Like in Olympic gymnastics, the fingers are an important part of controlling the balance of your *bananeira*. Keep your arms far apart.

Right after you position your hands, thrust your first and second legs up. Here you have two distinct choices: if you want to do the traditional handstand, keep both legs straight and together, arms always straight at shoulder width, head between your arms to form a straight line. If you are doing an original capoeira handstand, though, you can keep your legs straight and relaxed, together or apart.

For the capoeira style, place your arms apart but limit the distance between them to a comfort zone, in which you can keep them fairly straight. In Olympic gymnastics, the athlete has to keep both arms straight and at shoulder width. Shoulders must be locked, with straight and stiff arms aligned with the head, torso and legs. In capoeira we put a little more strength on the arms, so as to prepare

BANANEIRA

ourselves for ground navigation or other complex moves. I prefer the relaxed, "strolling" type of *bananeira*, with legs relaxed and bent and head extended, looking at the ground ahead, as in the left-hand illustration on the next page.

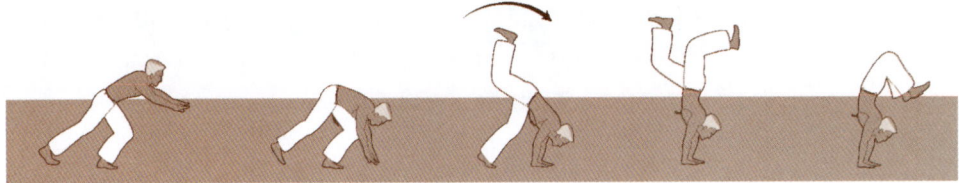

Starting with two supporting hands.

Again, if you want to do a straight Olympic gymnastics-style handstand, tense your abs and try to feel the connection of your whole body straight up from your fingers to the tips of your toes. If you want the best freestyle capoeira, relax your abdominal muscles and compensate your balance with your legs turned toward your backside, and let your feet compensate for your weight. Your torso should be slightly bent toward your backside. You can use this *bananeira* to stroll on your arms, to freeze the movement or to engage in other strategic moves. This is capoeira's best style for body control in motion, which basically differs from the stiffer style of Olympic gymnastics. With practice, you should feel lighter when executing this *bananeira*.

Figure 12.1 shows the capoeirista in a typical straight *bananeira* with arms bent at the elbows and legs slightly apart. Since he has his arms bent, he is ready to engage in one of several possible ground movements, such as a *queda de rim* or a *negativa,* or he may try one or two *chibatas* and execute a *ponte* afterward.

Figure 12.1: A typical straight *bananeira.*

A traditional capoeira *bananeira*. You can walk on your hands forward or backward, whichever is more convenient for you.

Bananeira Giratória

The spinning handstand can be done with both hands or one hand. The mechanics are similar to that of the *aú* giratório except that you don't start the move sideways, but rather facing front. From standing position, pull your right leg back and put your left hand down on the ground. Kick up onto your left arm and try to achieve some rotation while balancing on the supporting arm. Execute one half-rotation on the first supporting arm.

After the first half-rotation, put your other hand down to provide thrust for another half-turn before coming down to finish the move.

You may have noticed that I have already spent three pages discussing what seems to be a very simple move, the handstand. One important conclusion here is that you just can't practice yoga, Olympic gymnastics or capoeira without mastering the foundations of your style of handstand. They are slightly different, yet their differences are huge when we consider their specific objectives. Mastering the *bananeira* technique will raise you to a new level of capoeira. Believe me.

Escorpião

The *escorpião*, a.k.a. *coice de mula* or *rabo de arraia*, is an aggressive variant of the *bananeira*. It has the same body mechanics, but the objective is slightly different, as you intend to hit your adversary on the head or the chest with the sole or the heel of your attacking foot.

Once you have executed the strike, you can continue the movement forward to finish it in a *ponte*, or you can go back to your original standing stance.

Escorpião.

Prancha

This is clearly a *floreio* – a very elegant one, by the way, although in capoeira the moves can always harbor a surprise or two! The board, in free translation, can be a result of a *bananeira* or a new move done from scratch, which is more difficult to execute.

Prancha.

Normally, what you do is freeze the move for a few seconds, to the astonishment of your partner in the *roda* (generally he or she will not really know what to do while you are demonstrating your *prancha*).

Practicing Alone

The very best way to practice the *bananeira* is by actually strolling at will along the floor of your capoeira school. If you are in good shape, you can do some vertical pushups by slightly leaning your feet against the wall. Get the proper guidance for this exercise and, if you can, include it in your routine. Practicing the handstand gives you endurance, flexibility and muscle tone.

Be sure to practice all styles, keeping your toes and feet pointed upward and your whole body aligned straight up, for both the Olympic gymnastics version and the more relaxed capoeira style.

The advantage of keeping your legs straight and together is that this will help you gain more confidence and balance control, since it is more difficult to do the Olympic gymnastics style than the capoeira one, while the capoeira style is more resourceful. So I advise you to practice **both** styles, for the sake of enrichment.

Defenses and Counterattacks

The *bananeira* functions more as a launching pad for several other measures and countermeasures rather than as an attack or defense move in itself. Most defenses and counterattacks of the classic *aú* and the *aú fechado* will be suitable for the possible variation of moves executed from the *bananeira*.

Bênção

The Blessing. A straight front heel kick, and sometimes a push kick. There is the classic high *bênção*, the low one and the *bênção pulada*. In the *roda*, sometimes we are "blessed" by our Mestres during our *batizado* (capoeira's official initiation of a capoeirista, the "baptism" game). I remember receiving a powerful merciless *bênção* from my Mestre, Adilson "Camisa Preta," at *Grupo Bantus de Capoeira*, the original one founded back in the 1960s in the slums of Morro do Pavão e Pavãozinho in Rio de Janeiro. I fell out of the *roda*, breaking through a wall of guests and fellow capoeiristas straight to the end of the room and down flat on my back! At first I could not understand why my dear master did it. I felt awful. Then, when I became a teacher myself, I realized why I deserved such a "blessing" from Adilson. I was a strong dude, full of energy, doing well in Olympic gymnastics and karate. It was the early 1970s, and few people in Rio thought about fitness, in contrast to nowadays. And I was not at all humble; usually, I challenged my academy companions because I could show off, doing impressive somersaults and back handsprings and many karate kicks, and I was also more physically fit than most of my colleagues at *Bantus*. In my mind, I knew I was not the best. Far from it. I can still remember my pals Marcos and Fernando, Nelson, Luis,

BENÇÃO

Michel, Charuto, Sandra, and an American Capoeira pioneer named Chris, just to mention a few idols and some of my colleagues at that time. A good crop, which also gave us Mestre Paulo Siqueira, who became a master in 1980 and today runs the school of Capoeira Nzinga in several cities in Germany. Not to mention Adilson – a great master and a great character.

I guess Adilson was trying to send me a message with that *benção,* which literally exploded right on my chest, sending me on a long journey through the academy. It took me more than a year to accept a "batizado" ceremony. I always believed I was not ready and I wanted to learn more. Since more was not enough, I wanted to learn even more. But at the same time, little by little I gained too much confidence, and that had to be curbed. And it was, by Adilson's unforgettable *benção*.

Axé and thank you Adilson, my dear friend and master.

Objectives

There are two main objectives in delivering a *benção* on your opponent. One is to strike him on his chest with the flat sole of your attacking foot – or with the ball of the foot – with no delay, in order to get him away from you immediately. The other is to do the same movement, but this time with the heel of your attacking leg hitting your opponent's chest, as straight and as hard as possible, in order to "send him to hell" or beyond! More or less Adilson's style.

The Point of Impact

From the upright position, you can actually deliver the *benção* on your opponent's hips, belly, or even thighs, as a maneuver to keep him distant from you. However, the most efficient *benção*, whether a mean one with the heel, or a milder one with the flat sole or the ball of your foot, is directed against your opponent's chest, as shown in Figure 13.1.

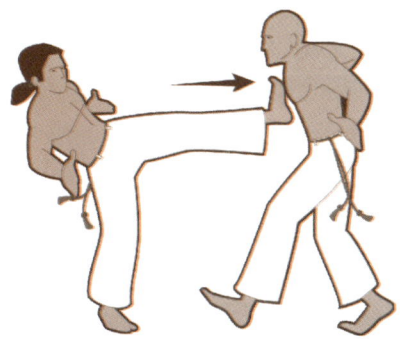

Figure 13.1: A perfect "mean" *benção.*

Figure 13.2: Sometimes a quick ground *benção* will do the trick.

A somewhat unusual but consistent point of impact is the head of your rival, especially if he is a grappler who is attempting to get hold of you or mount you. You can deliver this version of the *benção* from a *queda de quatro* or a *queda de três* when your opponent approaches you, as shown in Figure 13.2. Alternatively, you can strike his abdomen with your heel.

The Technique

For an effective *benção,* you should be in an upright position at *ginga* or zero stance. First, bend your body slightly forward to prepare for the move as you lift your knee as high as possible, keeping the foot of your supporting leg planted flat on the ground, as shown in Figure 13.3. Continue by bringing your shoulders and arms back at the same time you deliver the *benção*. Opposite the *ponteira*, you should compensate your balance by inclining your upper body backward to deliver power to your attacking foot. Use your hips to thrust your leg straight forward in the direction of your target while you pull your toes back, as you do when kicking with the ball of the foot – but this time using the bottom of your heel to hit the target. Bend your supporting leg slightly. As soon as you hit your target, retrieve your kicking leg, bringing it behind the pivot leg, resuming your original *ginga* or zero stance position.

Figure 13.3: Prepare the leverage for an efficient *benção.*

If you cannot control the surface with which you wish to hit your target, i.e., your heel or the flat sole of your foot, you can always use the ball of the foot for a regular frontward "push" kick to keep your opponent distant from you.

BENÇÃO

Also, note from Figure 13.3 that the capoeirista is in a tense guard, gathering power for his *benção*. You don't really need those tight fists to deliver a good *benção;* actually, most of the time a sly, more relaxed one (Figure 13.4) would do the trick.

Figure 13.4: Relax, but do not ever forget to transfer power to your leg.

For the *benção pulada* (flying front heel kick), your power comes from the kicking leg, as you step forward with it in order to gain force to jump as high as necessary in order to place the kick. Your thrust, however, should emphasize the forward jump more than the height, since your objective is to reach the adversary's chest. Your other leg will act as a pivot when you deliver the blow. It is the same procedure with the *ponteira pulada*. Generally, you choose this *benção* when you are far from your opponent though within a reasonable range for starting a surprise move.

Benção Pulada.

One great and beautiful move in capoeira, often seen in the 1970s *rodas* in Rio, is the combo *benção* and *ponte* (bridge). As with most capoeira moves, it can be used in real combat, as a source of *chibata,* but it is more of a *jogo* move. Execute the *benção* immediately followed by a *ponte* to the rear. The attacking *benção* leg will function as a lever for you to do a bridge in order to continue your game.

The combo *benção* and *ponte.*

Practicing Alone

Just like the *ponteira,* the *benção* can be practiced on a training bag or on a towel. Refer back to the Introduction of this book for more details and special tips on practicing the *benção* alone to improve your techniques.

Defenses and Counterattacks

The *benção* can be a very quick and objective capoeira move. As with the *ponteira,* to avoid being caught by a well-delivered *benção* you can try to step out of its range, or step back from it. However, escaping sideways and diagonally is an excellent alternative for engaging in another move and surprising your attacker. Normally, the most common quick defense would be to escape to one side and fire an *armada* to the opponent's head. The problem with this is that most of the time I see capoeiristas rotating their *armadas* out of the range of attack of their adversaries, some even completely outside the *roda* area. For an effective counterattack against a well-executed *benção* in real fighting, the best choice would be to escape diagonally to the side of your adversary, within his range of attack, and fire your crescent or spinning kick. Make sure to control your speed, though, if you are in a game of capoeira rather than in real combat.

Of course, you could escape to the side while delivering a good *rasteira* to the adversary's pivot leg, if you are able to foresee his *benção* coming before it renders you defenseless.

Other countermeasures, such as a *meia-lua reversão,* can also be effective if you are playing capoeira in the *roda*. Just remember to time your *esquiva* (the moment you dodge to the side to engage in the move) with your opponent's *benção* in order to fire your *meia-lua reversão* right over his attacking leg.

If you are really fast, you can use a *chapa lateral* on your opponent's hip and descend to a *negativa* to prepare for an *s-dobrado* with a *martelo* or a *chapéu de couro,* or, once you are on the ground, from the *negativa* you can choose a *macaco* (to hit or approach the adversary) or a *tesoura.*

Bloqueio

Blocking movements are a second art in capoeira. A simple move that can displace your opponent in the *roda* or in real fighting, the *bloqueio* can be both elegant and persuasive, or aggressive and definitive.

A gentle *bloqueio*, such as the *cruz* shown above, can simply avoid the attempt of a *benção* (or of an *aú reversão* and an *s-dobrado,* for example, as shown in Figure 14.1) and gives you time to think of a new strategy. It may also give you the opportunity to develop bitter consequences, such as sweeping your opponent's supporting arm or doing a *giro* to connect an immediate low *meia-lua de compasso,* while your partner is trying to regroup after your first *bloqueio*. The most common use of a *cruz* is the one shown above, where your arm and shoulder perform the functions of blocking and throwing your attacker's leg up and backward before he regains control of the situation. Watch for kicks on your head, though, as you dodge down to prepare the *cruz*.

Bloqueios are so important in capoeira that a good Mestre can play with them throughout a whole *jogo* without even having to execute a single attack move.

Nevertheless, *bloqueios* are seldom used to their full potential – perhaps because of the danger they may pose in a *roda*, or maybe because they were forgotten by some capoeiristas who traded the art of capoeira for a disciplined system of acrobatic moves. Make no mistake: capoeira has beautiful acrobatics, but its *bloqueios* are not dissociable technical resources. Therefore, they should be used in every confrontation.

Figure 14.1: The *cruz* can also be used to block an attempt of *s-dobrado*.

Objectives

The objective of technical blocking in capoeira is to use a *bloqueio* to intercept an attack from your opponent before he can complete his movement. You can do that by simply avoiding the conclusion of the move, or as a kind of counterattack when you force your adversary to fall down in an awkward and vulnerable position.

Figure 14.2 shows the technique that is also explored in the chapter on the *rasteira*. Here we have some additional comments. In (1), your approach can be either a direct one, seeking the left supporting leg of the attacking opponent – as you can see in the *banda* described in the *Rasteira* chapter – or you could bump his back with your upper body in order to displace him. However, if you do that, chances are that he will not be able to rotate his *armada*, and you will not complete your *bloqueio de dentro*. In (2), you can complete your *bloqueio* by avoiding his *armada* (which will lose power on your shoulder) while at the same time applying a *banda de costas* to his supporting leg.

One thing that I don't mention in the *Rasteira* chapter, though, is the fact that you can choose to do the *banda* while forcing your shoulder (and your head) against his *armada* to help displace him more quickly. It is exactly at this time that

BLOQUEIO

you will choose to simply upset his balance, or to still use your *banda de costas* in order to make him fall hard on his back and/or on the nape of his neck.

You can "bump" his back before going for the *banda de costas*.

Here you can displace his attacking leg to make him lose his balance.

Figure 14.2: The *bloqueio de dentro* offers a number of alternatives.

Figure 14.3 shows a *bloqueio* done with a *giro* (which is discussed in the *meia-lua de compasso*). Note that if you are too far from your opponent, he may get you on your back with a set of *chibatas*, so you better do the *giro* in a timely manner and at an appropriate distance, from which your adversary will not have time to reconsider his attack.

In the *meia-lua de compasso*, I discuss the *giro* from the point of view of a "fake *meia-lua*." Here I want to focus on the versatility of this simple, yet highly opportunistic and elegant move. With the *giro*, you can always fake a *meia-lua de compasso*, execute a *bloqueio*, do two *giros* in a sequence or perform the *giro* as a *bloqueio* and hop back with your two feet the moment you rotate in front of your opponent's attacking move, so as to collide with his moving body and knock him down.

For instance, in the *giro* of Figure 14.3, you could simply rotate close to his *macaco* or *aú de costas*, and your opponent would end up hitting your backside with his belly and thighs, doing you no harm. He would miss his attack, but would be able to recover himself quickly. On the other hand, if you execute the *giro* and hop-slide back vigorously, heels together, you will have the chance to slam his body and make him fall down hard.

Be careful when trying to bump on a *meia-lua*.

Figure 14.3: Slide-bump your opponent with a *giro* before he accomplishes his attack.

Figure 14.4 shows an attempted *xangô* intercepted by a *bloqueio* before the move is up in the air. This *bloqueio,* also done with a *giro,* is helped by a short hop backward, which is supposed to cause your hip to hit the attacker's upper body and terminate his *xangô*. This technique is an attempted *tombo da ladeira*.

The *tombo da ladeira* is another great classic (and old) capoeira *bloqueio*. You can do it against show-offs, especially if you are an advanced capoeirista capable to control the results of your countermeasure to your advantage, without hurting your partner or yourself.

Figure 14.4: *Bloqueios* are great defenses against aerials, especially if you are an expert capoeirista.

Figure 14.5: A classic *tombo da ladeira*.

It is done when you advance with your *giro,* for example, *under* your opponent's aerial move, before he (or she) completes the move. The idea is to intercept your attacker while he is still in the air, thus interrupting his move. It is a great asset against the *mortal,* the *compasso pulado* (as shown in Figure 14.5), and the *xangô,* just to mention the most common uses.

BLOQUEIO

The Point of Impact

I refer here not to impact in the sense of a blow, but mainly those of your hips and backside against the thighs, chest, legs and hips of your adversary.

A capoeirista generally uses his feet and hands in a game of capoeira or even in real fighting. The head may also be used both for promoting the flow of motion or in a traumatic attack, like in a *cabeçada*. From time to time, though, especially if you are in real combat, you can use your arms and hands to block a hand blow, such as the *galopante* shown in Figure 14.6, and complement your defense with a countermeasure, such as a *meia-lua de compasso,* done under the attacking arm and on your opponent's back or the nape of his neck. You block his *galopante* and use your *bloqueio de braço* as a lever to launch your *meia-lua*. Don't do this in a *roda*, where your main role is to use your *esquivas*.

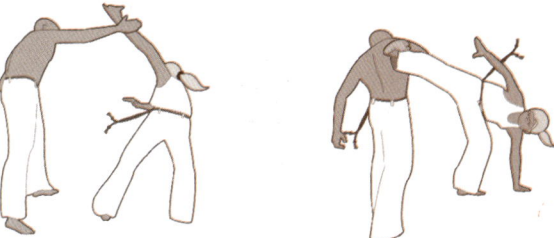

Figure 14.6: Block and move equals surprise!

The Technique

Normally, a *bloqueio* is done with one or two steps to get you where you need to be in order to block the opponent's move. You always use your hips, shifting them back, forth or sideways against a beginning move. DO NOT use your arms and hands to defend against a capoeira kick, like in karate. Avoid unnecessary body contact. Note that the *galopante* shown in Figure 14.3 was blocked when she started to turn for her *meia-lua*, thus reducing the impact of the bald-headed capoeirista's blow to her forearm.

Study Your Approach

Be extra careful with *rasteiras, bloqueios* and *esquivas,* for these techniques require that you approach your adversary when he or she is executing a move or preparing to execute one. See *esquiva* for additional and important information.

If you are not an advanced capoeirista, watch the experts doing – and teaching – the *tombo da ladeira* before trying one. The result may not be what you expect if you make a wrong move against a dangerous aerial, such as the *compasso pulado*.

The good thing about the *bloqueio* is that you can always revert your approach to another move, i.e., you can actually give up a *giro* and come up with a *meia-lua* while your smart opponent already believes you are going to really do a *giro* this time – and not a *meia-lua*; from your *bloqueio de dentro*, you are able to actually execute a quick and powerful *banda de costas* even before you get to block his *armada*. Or you could "go around" your opponent's rotating kick with a *rodeio*, if he does a lazy or careless *meia-lua*, as shown in Diagram 14.1. See *esquiva* for more information.

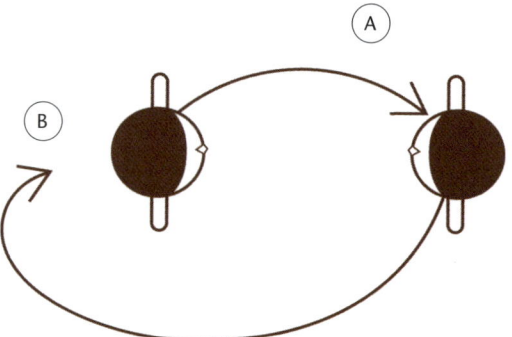

Diagram 14.1: If your moves are timed with your opponent's moves, you can go around him and avoid a rotating kick.

Note that in (a), the attacker has fired a rotating kick at his opponent; in (b), the opponent defends himself by simply (and in a timely manner) circumventing the attacker's attempt to strike him using a *rodeio*.

Be aware: Don't perform this move if you are not sure of your superiority in the *jogo* or in real fighting.

Bear in mind that you can go around your opponent's *meia-lua* if you feel you are faster than his rotating kick. He does not need to fire a "lazy" kick for you to succeed in your *rodeio* counterattacking his kick and get him, most unexpectedly, with your own kick.

BLOQUEIO

Practicing Alone

Believe me, it's impossible to obtain good results by practicing a *bloqueio* alone. Clarify it with your master, and get a good partner to practice your *bloqueios*.

Defenses and Counterattacks

As with the *esquivas,* there is not really a defense or counterattack procedure aiming specifically at the *bloqueio* techniques. If you notice that your partner or opponent is going to try a *bloqueio* against one of your moves, follow with a new move or simply try to escape with a *fuga*, which could mean dodging down or to the side – and away from his *bloqueio*. However, it is always good to remember that if you are an advanced capoeirista, it is your obligation to "offer" moves that will mislead your adversary to a point where he thinks he can use an efficient *bloqueio* against your move, so that you can then "get him on the corner," which was actually your original (and hidden) intent.

Chapa

A lateral kick that can also be used for blocking. There are three types: the low, the medium and the high *chapa*, called *chapa lateral*, a.k.a. *esporão* or *pisão*; the *chapa giratória*, which is the rotating *chapa*, similar to the *meia-lua de compasso* (but without the arch and still kicking laterally); and the *escorão*, which is a *chapa* done with your supporting hands on the ground (if you simply place your hands on the ground and kick straight back with your heel or with your flat foot, then you've got yourself an *escorão*, a.k.a *coice de mula*, the mule kick).

The *chapa lateral* is a direct lateral kick done mainly with the ridge of the foot, although you can also use your flat foot. If you are attacking your opponent, the high one should aim at his neck, his mandible or the side of his head. The medium one is supposed to strike deeply in your opponent's ribs. The low one is to be delivered to his thighs, shins, knees, hips or abdomen, and can be used to block his movements. Be aware: the *chapa* can cause severe bone damage to your partner in the *roda*, which is why you should avoid completing the move when in a *jogo*.

CHAPA

Objectives

The *chapa* is one handy technique when you need capoeira as a martial art, and it is a great move if you want to show your partner how good you are with your legs (as long as you do not complete the movement when in the *roda* – unless you are using your *chapa* as a blocking technique). The main objective in real fighting is to knock down your opponent without having to worry too much about the flow of motion, which is the main characteristic of capoeira. You can surprise your opponent by executing a straight and unexpected *chapa lateral* or a *chapa giratória,* which is especially efficient if you do not have enough space to spin a round *meia-lua de compasso,* or if you want your opponent to believe you are going to spin one – and you come up with a *chapa*.

Figure 15.1 shows a *chapa* used as a *bloqueio* technique. You can block a beginning kick by hitting your opponent's supporting leg or attacking leg, or you can block an attack by striking at his hip before he completes his move.

Figure 15.1: A timely *chapa lateral* blocking the leg of the opponent.

The same *chapa, as* shown in Figure 15.1, can be used to strike the opponent's ribs during his rotation of an *armada,* for instance, or as an attack initiative of your own.

The *chapa giratória,* shown in Figure 15.2, is a powerful timesaver. You don't really need to use a *meia-lua de compasso* if you just want to get your opponent quickly.

Figure 15.2: The handy *chapa giratória*.

The *escorão,* shown in Figure 15.3, is the version of a *chapa presa,* i.e., a *chapa* with two supporting hands on the ground, also known as *coice de mula* (mule kick).

Figure 15.3: The *escorão,* a.k.a. *coice de mula.*

The Point of Impact

There are innumerable points of impact in a *chapa,* although the classic targeted ones are the ribs, the abdomen, the jaws and the head of the adversary. The blocking preferences are the hips, the thighs and the lower legs.

The Technique

You can also use the palm of your foot, or even your heel, to strike these kicks. A strong and effective *chapa lateral* should be done at a 90° angle with a stiff foot and calf and a straight leg, with the thigh muscles contracted for maximum leg power.

The *chapa giratória* can be regarded as a "reduced" *meia-lua de compasso.* You have the *presa* and the *solta* styles, and you rotate your body to fire them in the *giratória* version. However, the *chapa lateral* is unique in capoeira (though present in most martial arts with their characteristic names). It is a straightforward and highly versatile kick that can be delivered with the edge of the attacking foot, with the heel, with the ball or the sole of the foot, all depending on the amount of aggressiveness you need to apply to your target. By the way, never complete the move in a *roda* unless you are perfectly sure that your partner will know how to defend against it properly.

You can also use an attacking leg with stiff thigh and calf, for a more powerful *chapa*, or a more relaxed posture, depending whether you are in a *ginga* motion

CHAPA

or are coming from a zero stance. *Also, as* with the *meia-lua de compasso,* you can use the *diagonal factor,* especially with the *chapa lateral* (see *meia-lua de compasso* for more details on this technique).

Chapa Pulada

As with most capoeira high kicks, the *chapa* also has its jumping version, which should be delivered when you are at a certain distance from your opponent. For an optimal performance, see the techniques described for the *benção pulada* and the *ponteira pulada*. If you want an extra-powerful kick, make sure to firmly thrust your torso forward to the attacking leg. For the *chapa giratória pulada,* see the *meia-lua pulada* and make sure not to rotate your leg in a 360° turn, but rather rotate your body first and only then deliver a straight *chapa* to your intended target.

Practicing Alone

All styles of *chapa* are good to practice with the training bag. Make sure to use all the available hitting points of the feet, such as the heels, the edges, the balls and the soles of your feet.

Defenses and Counterattacks

The *chapa* is one of the easiest and most powerful capoeira kicks designed for real fighting conditions – and of course for the *roda* as well, if you do not intend to hurt your partner by completing the move.

To avoid a well-delivered *chapa lateral*, the best choice – if you are quick enough – is to fire one diagonal *armada* to the inside of your opponent's open guard. That is, if he fires his *chapa lateral* with his right leg, step diagonally forward with your right leg to his left open guard and rotate your *armada* with your attacking left leg onto his face.

If you are up against a *chapa giratória,* do the opposite and step forward with your right leg outside his range of attack, moving to his right, and choose a good *meia-lua diagonal,* against which your opponent would be defenseless. If you are fast enough and your moves are well timed with your opponent's, you might succeed in doing a *rasteira em pé* when your adversary turns his back on you while rotating his body.

I do not advise a ground defense, such as a *negativa*, against a *chapa lateral*, which could leave you defenseless on your way up to complete the kick. In addition, most of the time the inbound *chapa giratórias* are low enough to reach a *negativa* (and I recommend that you practice high ones in order to have your *chapas* well mastered).

Now, if you have to defend yourself against a jumping *chapa*, you might escape your opponent's attack by descending into a *negativa* and coming back up in a providential *s-dobrado* with a *martelo*, or a *chapéu de couro*, to take him by surprise after he lands back on the ground. If you escape on an *aú fechado*, for example, you could come back to his landing position on a *queda de rim* and execute a low *meia-lua* or a *rasteira giratória* on both of his legs, followed by a cunning and protective *relógio*. You can see this *relógio* at www.unknowncapoeira.com.

You could also fire a *meia-lua de compasso* (the *solta* or the standard type with one supporting hand on the ground) right over his attempt to deliver his *chapa lateral*, or even his *chapa giratória*. In this case, go for a high *meia-lua* on your opponent's head.

If you really time your movements with those of your opponent, you might be able to deliver a *meia-lua* on his open, less protected guard and still be behind his back before he has a chance to recover.

Of course, there are a number of other possible defenses and counterattacks against all types of *chapa*. Those described above are my own choices of what I believe are good and not-too-complex ones that may achieve quite perfect results.

Compasso

The compass. A low or high, rolling, aerial *meia-lua,** also known in some capoeira schools as *armada solta* and *rabo de arraia*. This is a great asset to capoeira. It is an original move very much appreciated by some capoeira old-timers. It is beautiful and at the same time highly efficient, both in the *roda* and in real fighting.

Essentially, there are two types of *compasso:* the first which is done with one supporting hand on the ground, and the purely aerial version, executed without the supporting hand. Both can be identified as "aerials" because the attacking leg actually flies over to the target. In both modes, you can control the lateral angle of your attack according to your strategy.

Objectives

The main objective of the *compasso* is to attack or counterattack your adversary by surprise – especially if he is not a capoeirista. Actually, a few capoeiristas will escape if the technique is used at perfection level. This move is so versatile that you can plan a ground, low, medium or high attack, whether your opponent is

---

* See *meia-lua de compasso* for additional information.

standing or navigating on the ground. In addition, you can strike your opponent with your attacking heel or your leg – in a less harmful kick.

The Point of Impact

Mainly the head of your adversary, but there are several other points. Normally, one uses the *compasso* with the supporting hand on the ground in a quick, short surprise move against an opponent who has just engaged in a *negativa* or other ground navigation technique. In this case, you will try to get him on his chest or his head with your attacking heel. This will be both an attacking and a blocking measure.

The aerial *compasso* is normally used as an attack with the heel to the head of your astonished opponent. Under "milder" circumstances, you may prefer not to hurt your adversary and fire a *compasso* using your whole leg as a weapon, striking him on his chest.

Controlling the height of your *compasso*.

The flying *compasso pulado*.

The Technique

For the regular *compasso* with one supporting hand on the ground, you can part from your *ginga* or from zero stance. You should try to use your whole body, synchronized as a lever to help power your move.

COMPASSO

Make a "swimming arch" with your supporting hand as you reach for the ground with the palm of your hand, bending your upper body forward. At the same time, bend the leg of the same side as the supporting hand while using the other leg to thrust you up and forward. Your supporting leg, which was also your pivot leg, will give you the final power to twist your body in a forward aerial lateral attack with your heel. You should land as in a *chibata,* ending the move as in a *negativa.*

For the aerial, simply explode your attacking leg synchronized with your whole body up and forward, as you throw that "swimming" hand in an arch – this time without touching the ground, and aided by the more powerful body and arm lever. The body's rotation is accomplished in the same way a diver executes a somersault twist.

In all versions, though, make sure you apply the concept of your hands used as a goal for your attacking heels. As you start to throw your supporting hand downward, like in the crawl swimming style, your target will be locked the moment you pass with your hand in front of it. If a *compasso* over your opponent's head is required, you need to pass your hand between your eyes and your opponent's head (Figure 16.1). If you want to throw your *compasso* on the opponent's chest, your aiming hand should pass between your eyes and the adversary's chest. It's pure technique!

It is very easy to choose the height and the power of this move once you get the grip. Make sure you include the *compasso* in your repertoire of capoeira moves.

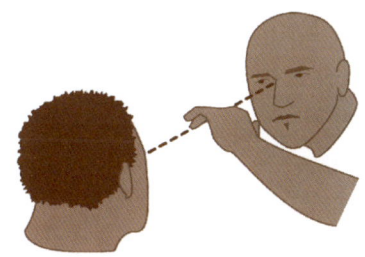

Figure 16.1: Your hand can be your secret aim.

In Figure 16.2 the bald-headed capoeirista executed a *compasso pulado* immediately after his opponent jumped on a *xangô.* This is only possible if you do a diagonal *compasso pulado,* or a straight one in case your opponent jumps for his *xangô* from a stance in front of yours to escape from your range of attack. Within this framework, you should throw your *compasso* when your adversary is still in the air and almost touching the ground on the other side.

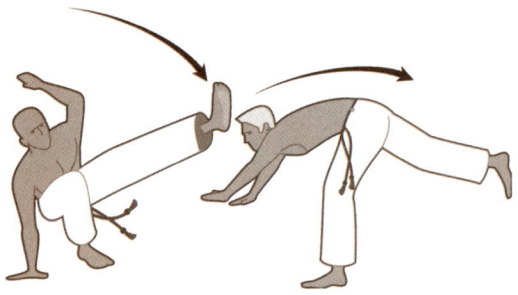

Figure 16.2: Launching a timely *compasso pulado* over an opponent's ending *xangô*.

Practicing Alone

Once you have learned, the different styles of the *compasso* can be practiced on the training bag, which can be done over a safety mat and into a foam pit, or on the beach, for instance, as long as you have the proper professional guidance and start the *compasso* with one supporting hand on the ground. This is an easy one to start with, at low speed and low height. Then, little by little, you can increase speed and height (as you improve the quality and the safety of your jump).

Defenses and Counterattacks

It is extremely difficult to escape from a good and timely *compasso*. The move is a true winner, whether in the *roda* or in real fighting. One thing you can do is to try a *bloqueio*, like the *tombo da ladeira*, which I do not guarantee will be successful. Another would be to try an *esquiva* or, if you are in the midst of a move, try an *aú fechado* and stop with your defensive feet grouped together against your opponent's *compasso*.

Esquiva

The *esquiva* (dodging) is as important as kicking in capoeira. The moment you learn how to kick, you must learn how to get out of a kick. Capoeira schools all over the world practice the *armada* and *cocorinha* combo (Figure 17.1) as an exercise of attack and *esquiva*.

You can execute a simple and efficient *esquiva* or more complex ones, which are really a combination of two or more techniques that are triggered from an *esquiva,* such as the figure above that shows an *esquiva lateral* with a loose *queda de quatro* ending in a recomposing or escaping *rolê*. You can see this move and more than 100 moves in GIF animation files that are available at www.unknowncapoeira.com.

In addition, the *negativa* is also a type of *esquiva,* which deserved a chapter of its own in this book, mainly because it plays an important role of a ground stance, allowing for capoeira's unique "ground navigation."

There are many possibilities for a move to be called an *esquiva*. The simple fact that you dodge to your right to escape a kick can be called an *esquiva*. If you simply make an inclination or hop to the side with your standing body, there you go: you've got yourself an *esquiva de tronco* (*esquiva* of the upper body).

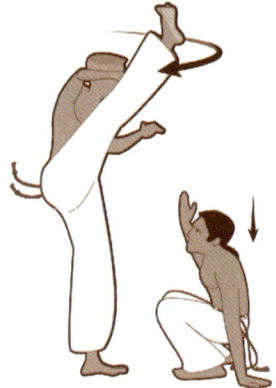

Here I have gathered the classic dodges, which are classified as *esquiva* although some may have different nicknames, such as the *queda de três* and the *queda de quatro,* for example.

Figure 17.1: The *cocorinha* done with an *armada.*

Note that the dodging capoeirista is doing a *cocorinha* with one supporting and one defending hand, which must be the one on the same side as the incoming kick. The *cocorinha* can be executed with both hands protecting the head, as an exercise, although for an experienced capoeirista it does not make much sense to do it this way, if you are dealing with a rotating kick that can only come from either side.

Cocorinha.

Compare the two types of *cocorinha*. Practice both versions, and always look at your partner when executing them.

A classic training *cocorinha.*

ESQUIVA 83

A classic *esquiva lateral*.

The illustration of the *esquiva lateral* in Figure 17.2 is a tricky one. The attacking capoeirista may be firing a *ponteira* or a *benção*. If this is the case, there is too much head exposed, and if you are not absolutely sure that your opponent will come up with a high kick *before* you duck, chances are that you will be caught by his attacking kick.

The same illustration may represent a *meia-lua de frente,* which is a crescent kick, in which case you would continue with the flow motion in order to complete your *esquiva lateral.*

Note that from the *esquiva lateral* you can execute a *rasteira*, and sweep your opponent before he has time to finish his *meia-lua de frente.*

Now, if the attacker is coming at you with a *queixada,* this means you are completely off base because his *queixada* must have started from his right and is traveling to his left, i.e., directly against the flow of your *esquiva lateral.*

Figure 17.2: Warning! The *esquiva lateral* must always follow the flow of motion.

Figure 17.3: From *ginga* to *esquiva lateral.*

You can chose to do an *esquiva lateral* as in Figure 17.4, which is very similar to a side *cocorinha*; and if you lean to the same side as your supporting hand, you can call it *resistência* (resistance). The main difference between this and the one in Figure 17.3 is that in the latter, she could easily engage in a *rasteira* and in an *s-dobrado*, whereas in the one below the capoeirista would not be so readily prepared for a *rasteira*, but would certainly be prepared for a *macaco*, a *negativa* and a *rolê*, and would also be close enough to her opponent to use a *rasteira de mão*. However, bear in mind that we are discussing a difference of fractions of a second, i.e., she would normally be able to execute practically any of those techniques from both *esquivas*.

Figure 17.4: This is also an *esquiva lateral.*

The capoeirista in Figure 17.5 is doing an *esquiva lateral* followed by a *negativa* as in a *troca* – but not as in a *troca de negativa*. Instead, she is doing a *troca* (quick switching of sides) from a dodge to the left to a *negativa* to the right, ending on a *rolê*. Compare this move to the *troca de negativa*.

Figure 17.5: She is executing a combo *esquiva lateral* and *negativa* with a *rolê*.

Objectives

The objective of an *esquiva* is to dodge away from an attack. You can do so by dodging down or to the sides, or dodging back, or dodging under your adversary's attack. You may be standing, in a *ginga* stance or at zero stance. A crucial point, though, is that the *esquiva* be performed well. It has to be elegant and nimble. This means that if you master a reasonable repertoire of capoeira moves, you should execute your *esquiva* close enough to your opponent, so as to try to continue the flow of motion to your advantage. If you are not able to do this, you might as well not try an *esquiva* at all, and instead, flee the scene...

ESQUIVA

The Point of Impact

Except for that smart leg left from the *queda de três*, no direct impact is generated by an *esquiva*. However, remember that from an *esquiva* you can engage in a variety of helpful techniques.

The Technique

There are really several personalized ways one can execute an *esquiva*. Most important is to never get hit by a capoeira kick, which could be hazardous. On the other hand, some techniques will help you not only escape from an attacking leg, but also perform more elegantly – and more safely – in the *roda*. Therefore, when you do an *esquiva*, such as the *cocorinha* for example, you can crouch with both feet flat on the ground, or you may use the sole of one foot and the ball of the other for your support. Do not invent a new *cocorinha on the heels*, though. It simply will not work.

As for the *esquiva lateral*, use your *ginga* and your defending arm as a lever to help you swing with your torso to the side. You can also execute a pendulum-like move to the opposite side before you actually do the *esquiva lateral* to the other side. Protect your head, and look at your opponent at all times.

If you do the *esquiva de frente*, you may or may not incline your head in the same direction as a rotating or crescent kick, but your *esquiva* will be executed mainly by a retracting leg that can be a large or a medium step back. In any case, you will still look at your opponent.

Esquiva de frente.

The dodging moves called *queda de três* and *queda de quatro* are commonly practiced in some capoeira schools as a defense against a *benção*. You will not use these techniques in real fighting; however, they are excellent capoeira exercises.

When you start to fall on the *queda de três* or the *queda de quatro,* use both hands to support your fall. Do not fall straight down like a log. Start by falling into a sitting position and then, when you are halfway to the ground, assume a straighter position and fall with your hands flat on the ground.

Queda de três.

Notice that the *queda de três* (fall on threes) is almost exactly the same as the *queda de quatro,* except that you leave one "teasing" leg straight up as an extra defense maneuver.

Queda de quatro.

Study Your Approach

As I have already noted in the *bloqueio* chapter, be extra careful with *rasteiras, bloqueios* and *esquivas*. These techniques demand that you get close to your opponent when he or she is executing or preparing to execute a move. Before I graduated a "Mestre" from the original *Grupo Bantus* in Rio de Janeiro, I went to visit a high-school friend, Oscar, who had been a capoeira student at the *Senzala* school of Mestre Baiano Anzol. A nice guy, Baiano, as he was often called, soon allowed me a *jogo* with him, which was a reason for rejoicing.

I was that type of young, fast capoeirista, physically fit, Olympic gymnast and full of pride due to my recent achievements as a capoeira player. You see, I am 5.57 feet tall and I was a student playing capoeira at the same level with a *Senzala* master who was 6.2 feet tall. Well, not quite! There is a problem here with my interpretation of the words "the same level." I remember throwing at him a set of very quick *meia-luas* and engaging in a high and perfect *xangô* that caught Mestre Baiano Anzol by surprise, though I didn't really reach him, as he dodged away from my *meia-luas* only to wait for my show-offy *xangô* to finish in order to fire his only move – a *meia-lua* right on my head! A few minutes later, when I came to my senses, I had the biggest headache of my life and understood the following equation: the weight of his attacking leg plus the weight of his modesty minus the weight of my arrogance equals my ignorance...

> **MESTRES, TEACH YOUR STUDENTS THE WEIGHT OF MODESTY!**

To Mestre Baiano Anzol, my deepest respects!

One interesting technique is called *volta por cima* (turn around and over). This move could well be a part of the *rasteira* chapter because you actually pretend to do – or refrain from doing – a *rasteira*, but what you are really doing is a *volta por cima*, which is almost a *relógio* – used more as a *floreio*. You can also execute the *volta por cima* as a *floreio*, although the *esquiva* is one of its best applications. It is challengingly beautiful to see a capoeira expert doing an *esquiva* by going down for a counterattacking *rasteira* make an abrupt switch to a *volta por cima*. This happens more often when the attacker fires a *meia-lua* or an *armada* and you go down for a *rasteira*, but then he surprises you with a second attempt, which is promptly answered with a timely *volta por cima*.

Volta por cima.

Practicing Alone

Esquivas are great moves to practice alone as stretching and flexibility exercises, once your Mestre or qualified coach teaches you how and when to do it. Don't forget to select a point of reference, so that you keep yourself in the smallest possible area of action when doing the moves.

Defenses and Counterattacks

Since the *esquiva* is not an attack move, there is no direct defense or counterattack against it. However, I must remind you once again that from any type of *esquiva* there may (and most probably will) come a new move, which could turn out to be a dangerous one.

Folha Seca

Literally, the dry leaf. A back flip done with one leg at a time, "kicking the moon." The *folha seca* is a spectacular acrobatic capoeira move extensively used in the *roda*, especially for public exhibitions. If you do it right, you can actually kick a chandelier – but please, don't do that!

This beautiful and impressive technique should be executed in a single movement (or several single movements). It really comes in handy for the flow of motion in the *roda* and also in real combat. *Motion,* by the way, is a key word in capoeira. *Connection* is another one. You need to control the flow of motion to be successful in a capoeira game or fight, and the more you control it, the better will be your connections to other moves. That is why it is so important to master the complete repertoire of capoeira techniques.

Objectives

The *folha seca* is a fancy move, normally used in the *roda* and explicitly for demonstrating acrobatic skills. Make no mistake, though. In real fighting, it is one of the most dangerous kicks in the capoeira repertoire. I am not talking about reaching an enemy in a balcony above your head. Think of a *ponteira*. Fortunately, this is a very rare example, but during your rotation you can actually kick your adversary on the chin (Figure 18.1). Keep in mind that as with most capoeira kicks, in a real-life situation this one can be lethal, and you don't want to harm anybody unless you need to fight to protect your own life or the lives of others.

The Point of Impact

The chin of a very dangerous and mean assailant. Use the ball of the foot.

Figure 18.1: Be aware of this dangerous and lethal kick.

The Technique

The *folha seca* is an overhead kick done while moving slightly forward. In the beginning, it looks like the "bicycle kick" in soccer. The main difference is that in soccer you fall down after kicking the ball over your head. In capoeira you do the complete rotation and land on your feet, one at a time, on the other side.

Begin with the professional assistance of a coach who can work with the help of a tumbling belt wrapped around your waist, with two straps on each side and a safety mat under you. Two partners can hold the straps and pull up when you practice your jump, so that you won't fall. As with most "mortal" types of jump, this practice builds the confidence you need to do it by yourself.

At first you may need to take a short run in order to gather momentum. With practice, though, this won't be necessary. The secret here is to start the kicking motion from ground level up to the imaginary target over your head. Think of a chandelier, or look at the clouds above your head. You have to use all the power you can muster on the first kicking leg, so that it travels up and pulls your second leg behind it for the complete rotation.

Your arms play an important role, as you throw them behind your back and up together, and then forward and up to assist the liftoff, while you turn your head up and back, looking for the ceiling and the ground behind you. At the same time, thrust your head and neck back for extra drive. The whole movement must be coordinated and synchronized with your legs. Everything must be properly timed.

Like with the *xangô*, you should look up all the time and never to the sides. Once you have passed the peak of your jump, you should land on your leading leg, i.e., if you start kicking with the right leg this will be your first one on which to land.

If you ever have to actually kick a target (believe me, strange things happen in real combat) with a *folha seca*, make sure you use the ball of the foot. If you try to kick or to simply rotate with the instep of your leading foot, chances are that your *folha seca* will not come out perfect.

The Folha Seca with a Parafuso

Let's take a moment to talk about improvements in capoeira.

In September 2007 I had the pleasure to be invited by Mestre Camisa, founder and president of ABADÁ Capoeira, for a most pleasant day on his farm on the outskirts of Rio de Janeiro. We met to talk about capoeira, Mestre Camisa's wonderful environmental and social projects, and this book. At one point, I asked his opinion about the number of new moves, notably the acrobatic ones that are from time to time introduced to and associated with capoeira. His answer was, as usual, very interesting: "Many people know how to do the 'cartwheel' he said. Some people execute perfect cartwheels, yet they can't do a simple *aú*. A real capoeirista cannot lose the essence of capoeira. There is no tradeoff. If a new acrobatic move fits in with the essence of capoeira, fine. If not, one will be practicing totally different arts!" he added to my satisfaction, since I had always done Olympic gymnastics while primarily aiming at capoeira.

I share his thoughts. In fact, I believe this is what most capoeira lovers think. So if you want to learn the *folha seca* done with a *parafuso*, be my guest, but be sure to integrate the high complexity of such moves into your level of expertise in capoeira. Nowadays it is awkward – but common – to see a novice capoeirista flying all over the place though incapable of doing a good *meia-lua* in the *roda*.

In addition, before you introduce a new move to your capoeira repertoire, make sure that space, timing and accuracy are also present.

Folha seca and *parafuso*.

You can find an animated file of this *folha seca* and *parafuso* plus over 100 other animations at www.unknowncapoeira.com.

Practicing Alone

Once you have mastered your *folha seca*, you can practice it on the beach or on an appropriate resi-pit and into a foam pit for extra safety. When you feel you have really mastered the move, try to find a good space with a ceiling on which you can hang a professional high-quality speed boxing bag with which to practice. Make sure you install a good heavy-duty speed bag swivel, so that you can kick your speed bag at will.

Do not use trampolines or springboards to practice the *folha seca*. The only way you will learn how to gather momentum is by understanding the full mechanics of the movement and of the muscles involved in the task. Just PRACTICE!

Defenses and Counterattacks

The *folha seca* can be tricky. It can also be dangerous if executed by an inexperienced capoeirista, who can ultimately end up hitting your chin (or himself) in an attempt to show off. It is quite common nowadays to find practitioners who are able to do all sorts of acrobatic moves before they even reach intermediate level in capoeira. If the capoeirista is responsible and dedicated – no problem; but if you meet an arrogant show-off, you'd better be careful. Be aware: these guys tend to show up in real combat too!

There is a story going around in capoeira circles: Once, in a *batizado* in Brazil, at this famous old Mestre's studio, a young capoeirista about to be baptized by the old master started to jump all over the place, showing his "qualities" to his master. After a number of acrobatic moves executed alone in the *roda*, the old master simply stood up and applauded! Then he added: "You are ready, son. You don't even need a partner to play with. You have just baptized yourself. You don't need me!"

If you cannot avoid having to counterattack, do as with the *mortal de frente* discussed in the *aú* chapter, and revert into a quick diagonal *aú* executed from the side of your opponent's second leg on the way across his *folha seca*. The idea is to be ready for your next move before your opponent lands and regains control.

One tip: be calm and concentrated if you have to face one or more clowns jumping all over the place. Don't do unnecessary acrobatic moves if your opponent is already doing them. Look for his open guard as you time your motion with his. Be sure to find the gap in which you can use decisive and accurate, powerful kicks at the right time and on the right targets.

Gancho

Literally, the hook kick. It is not a great aesthetic move for the *roda* and not a very complex one either, though very much appreciated, but it's a highly efficient and opportune kick to use in real fighting. Easy to grasp, you can execute it from the *ginga* or from zero stance. Make no mistake: the *gancho* is a good asset for any martial artist.

Objectives

The main objective of the *gancho* is to counterattack your adversary during a gap after he has tried to reach you with a spinning or a crescent kick. It is an objective and time-saving kick, since you should wait for your opponent's round kick to pass, i.e., to fail, in order to quickly get inside his guard with the *gancho*. Ultimately, you can use it against (after) other kicks, such as the *chapa*, the *benção* or even the *ponteira*.

The Point of Impact

Generally, the points of impact for the *gancho* are the parietal and temporal regions of the head, or the nape of your adversary's neck. It all depends on the circumstances of your fight. Bear in mind that the *gancho* is not a great resource for kicking other parts of the body (as efficiently as the *chapa*, the *ponteira* or the

GANCHO

martelo, to mention three classic examples of kicks that can be used on the ribs or neck of your adversary).

The Technique

With a little creative effort, one can interpret the *gancho* as the opposite of the *martelo.* Instead of snapping your knee, you do the opposite move and bend it before you stretch your attacking leg in the direction of your target, so as to strike with your heel behind the nape of your opponent's neck or on the side of his head, retrieving your leg while you hit the target.

The secret for performing a good *gancho* lies in taking the shortest possible path to the target at the moment you deliver a powerful kick. When you finish the move, bring your leg back to your original stance.

Note that you can execute the *gancho* from your *ginga* or from zero stance, and you can start with a rear or forward attacking leg – the most powerful move being the one coming from your rear leg, which gives you more leverage.

Practicing Alone

Best way to practice alone? The training bag is an absolute essential!

Defenses and Counterattacks

Though the *gancho* is not such a complex move, protecting yourself against a well-executed one is not a simple task. You need to be fast to try a *calcanheira,* a *rasteira giratória,* or even a *banda de costas* (if you are really fast).

Now, if you are a more advanced capoeirista, in real fighting you could try a *tesoura* or even a *rasteira de chão* to either side of your adversary's supporting leg, i.e., you could get him from inside or outside his supporting leg.

I have seen a capoeirista do an *esquiva,* followed by a *volta por cima* to a *ponte,* to come back on a successful *chibata* against a well-executed *gancho* (in this case, you have to foresee that your opponent is starting a *gancho*). The same capoeirista repeated the move, this time executing a *xangô* back from the *ponte.* As I said, it is not an easy task, but these defenses and many others are perfectly possible if you are an attentive and dedicated capoeirista.

Helicóptero

The helicopter. Though it resembles the *aú reversão* or *meia-lua reversão*, it is a more surprising move, started as a classic *aú and* then switched to a sudden rotating twist to generate an inverted kick, the purpose of which is to mislead an opponent whose counterattack strategy is based on the belief that you were actually planning to execute a classic *aú*. It is also an excellent *floreio* in the *roda*.

Objectives

The main objective of the *helicóptero* is to deceive your opponent, pretending you are going to execute a classic *aú* and then getting close enough to actually hit him with the kicking leg back in the direction you came from.

The Point of Impact

If you are a good capoeirista, you can aim for your adversary's chin, hitting with your heel, or get him anywhere on his head with your attacking foot, depending on how close you get to him from your starting *aú*. It is not an easy task if you don't practice hard to perfection. That is why the *helicóptero* is often used by the

HELICÓPTERO

most advanced capoeiristas in the *roda* as an exhibition technique, rather than as an attack move in real fighting.

The Technique

Start what would be a classic *aú*. Watch your opponent from between your supporting arms. The first leg to go up will be the last to touch the ground. Keep both legs straight, so that they function as a lever for a quick and strong twist. You can choose to start your *helicóptero* in a "star-like" traditional cartwheel, with legs straight up and parallel to your arms, or you can execute the *aú* with both legs straight and bent at the waist, so as to start an immediate thrust for the twist. As soon as you start twisting your torso, keep your eyes on the first leading leg. The moment you start rotating, you should follow the leading leg and watch your attacking foot all the way to the intended target. Try not to bend your legs until you finish the movement, after having rotated both legs. To finish the move, let your second leg bend first, followed by the first leg (the attacking one). Be streamlined, and bend those legs as little as possible.

Practicing Alone

The *helicóptero* is best practiced as an attacking kick on a training bag. However, you should practice it frequently in the *roda* as well, as these two types of practice offer different results. While you can't use your partner as a real target in the *roda*, you can beat the heck out of your training bag! Use the *roda* to position your *helicóptero* in different situations, timing it to your partner's moves, and use the training bag to practice your aim, different speeds, power and balance. That is the best way to acquire accuracy for complex moves such as the *helicóptero*.

Defenses and Counterattacks

If you believe your opponent is just executing a classic *aú*, the *helicóptero* can easily mislead you and make you choose the wrong strategy as a counterattack move. Therefore, you must be very careful not to spin a *giro*, do an *aú giratório*, a classic *aú* or even another *helicóptero* "against" an attacking *helicóptero*. If you feel you need to execute an *aú*, choose the *aú fechado agrupado* (with your legs and feet grouped for extra protection during the move). At least you will have a chance to be evasive and protect yourself against your adversary's kick, and eventually use one foot to try to push him down.

Normally, though, you don't want to stop a *helicóptero*. If your actions are really timed with your opponent's, go down to the *negativa*, always following the direction of his attacking leg. Then you can "navigate" on the ground and choose between a classic *rasteira* or even a *rasteira giratória*, to sweep your opponent's supporting hands off the ground, or you may choose an *s-dobrado* in order to come up on him while he is finishing his *helicóptero*. For additional information, see the chapter on the *aú fechado*.

Macaco

A back-walkover. Historically, the *macaco,* a.k.a. *pulo do macaco* (the jump of the monkey), is the most fascinating move of the whole capoeira repertoire. It was at the same time taboo, for being so difficult for beginners, and a goal to be achieved, as the first really acrobatic move in capoeira. This move was a success among newcomers and intermediate-level practitioners in Brazil, back in the 1960s, when the first capoeira schools started to crop up in Rio de Janeiro.

One of the first questions we used to pose to a fellow capoeirista was: "Do you know how to execute the *macaco*?" Everybody just wanted to learn the *macaco.*

An elegant move, the *macaco* is one of the trademarks of capoeira, and if you don't know how to do it well, you are not a full-fledged capoeirista – if such an appellation really exists.

A lower version, called *macaquinho,* is a resourceful variation that should be used in all *rodas*.

Objectives

There are really several objectives in doing the *macaco*. In the *roda*, it is a great aesthetic, as well as strategic, tool for a good game of capoeira. In real fighting, it is the perfect starting point for most low and ground movements, from which you can do a variation of evasive and attacking maneuvers using slightly different types of *macaco*.

In an attack, the *macaco* is a reliable choice for *chibatas* and kicks that can be executed with one or both feet, hitting with the ball of the foot, the top of the foot, and also with the heel.

When doing the *macaco lateral,* your objective will be a quick evasion, preferably keeping your eyes on your adversary at all times, or a quick *s-dobrado*-like attack.

The Point of Impact

There are several. If you are not doing an evasive *macaco,* you can use it in real combat to quickly revert to your original position, get closer to your adversary, kick-push him away from you by hitting his chest with a *macaco agrupado* (with legs grouped together), or come down on him slapping his back with the top of your feet or kicking his head with the ball of your feet.

Macaco agrupado.

The Technique

There are three types of *macaco:* the classic *macaco,* the *macaco lateral* and the *macaco s-dobrado.* The best way to learn a *macaco* is by working on your *s-dobrado* first. After mastering the perfect *s-dobrado,* start executing it with an outstretched "attacking" leg, rather than in kicking mode, until you feel you are able to do a *macaco*-like *s-dobrado,* which is a natural help.

MACACO

Place the palm of your supporting hand behind you while assuming almost a sitting position. Your palms should be fairly closed, fingers pointing out, and your arms not far from your upper body. Use your other arm as a lever, throwing it back and vertically over your head, with palm closed and fingers pointing in the direction of the move, as though you wanted to "catch the floor" behind you. The movement of arms and torso must be synchronized with your two bent legs, so as to thrust your *macaco* back. Note that for the classic *macaco*, you must look directly above you, at the ceiling, throughout the entire movement and as soon as you thrust your head, your torso and legs must follow almost simultaneoulsy. Use the balls of your feet as a launching pad. The movement must be completely synchronized in one combined effort.

To do what for me is the classic *macaco*, you must have both legs together, or put into position one at a time as in a *chibata*, and your head must always face directly up (never to the side). This is what we could call an "Olympic *macaco*." The *macaco lateral* is what some of us who were involved in Olympic gymnastics when we were young students of capoeira, back in the sixties, thought was a "wrong" style of *macaco*. Wrong idea! Though I believe that every capoeirista must know how to do a perfect vertical "classic" *macaco*, the "sideways" *macaco* is as useful as a good *s-dobrado* except for the fact that the *macaco lateral* can be a faster solution and a more evasive one, depending on the circumstances.

To execute a *macaco lateral,* simply look slightly to the side of your target when starting the move. Your body will then follow the lateral pathway.

The *macaquinho* (small *macaco*), a.k.a. *macaco de chão* (ground *macaco*) or *macaco baixo* (low *macaco*), is another great resource for ground maneuvers. It has the same techniques of the regular *macaco,* but it is done over the supporting elbow, like in a *queda de rim.*

Macaquinho.

Practicing Alone

The three styles of *macaco* are best practiced in the *roda,* at different levels of difficulty, before you practice alone. However, practicing alone is always an excellent – and complementary – way to achieve perfection and at the same time find your "comfort zone" with your own *macaco*. Practice in front of a mirror, using different angles of view, and with your training bag. Make sure to use the *macaco agrupado* to kick-push the sandbag away, and to use your *chibatas* in an attacking mode.

Defenses and Counterattacks

Be timed with the *macaco* done over the same spot by your rival. However, this will most likely never happen to you in a real fight. If you feel your opponent is preparing a *macaco* of any type, a quick and invasive *meia-lua presa* can do the trick and block his move. A second one, executed immediately after the first, can be quite devastating.

A *bloqueio,* too, is often an excellent approach against an attempted *macaco.*

Nevertheless, if you feel you are too far from your target to deliver the *meia-lua presa* or to prepare a *bloqueio,* take evasive action with a timely *aú* and go around him in order to catch him with a *compasso,* a *meia-lua de compasso,* or a *meia-lua solta,* when he finishes his *macaco.*

Mariposa

Also known as the "butterfly twist." There are three types of *mariposa:* the 360°, the 720°, which is the double one, and an intermediate one, the 540°. This beautiful acrobatic move is also practiced in Chinese wushu (a.k.a. kung fu), which has been around for centuries. Actually, I can't say for sure when this move was created in wushu or integrated into (contemporary) capoeira, but I believe up to 1983, when Tong Fei introduced it at the 1983 World Artistic Gymnastics Championships held in Hungary, it was not part of the repertoire of any Brazilian Mestre I had ever seen.

Nevertheless, we really have to accept that martial arts are constantly evolving. It is a blend we just cannot avoid. Like language, it is alive and ever-changing. So the best thing a capoeira purist can do is to carefully select – or accept – only those exterior techniques that fit in with the philosophy of capoeira and its beauty, grace and constant flow of moves – like the *mariposa*.

Objectives

The *mariposa* is one of the flashy moves generally used in the *roda* explicitly for demonstration of acrobatic skills. In a real combat, though, it is not a particularly dangerous kick, but it's always fun to see an astonished neophyte opponent encounter a good *mariposa*. Besides, to the adversary's mind, the fact that you can do a perfect, high, quick *mariposa* may mean that you are ready to open your "treasure chest" full of other capoeira surprises, and psychologically discourage him from getting into a real fight.

Do not confuse the *mariposa* with the *meia-lua pulada*. They are different techniques with slightly different objectives. The *meia-lua pulada* should be used as an attack move, whereas the *mariposa* can be used both for an attack and an evasive move, or simply as an aesthetic movement, a *floreio,* to help the flow of motion in the *roda,* or even to mislead your adversary in a real combat.

The Point of Impact

Generally, if you want to use this technique as a kick, what you really want is what we call the *meia-lua pulada* – a.k.a. the butterfly kick. The *mariposa* is best suited for evasive or tricky maneuvers, adding new action to your flow of motion. On the other hand, if you really master the move, you can use it as a kick to your opponent's head. There are three main foot points you can use to hit your target. The most powerful kick is done with the top or the ball of the foot of your second leg when completing the *mariposa*. The quickest one uses the outer edge of the first foot to touch the ground. It is not as strong as hitting with the second leg, but it will work as a surprising aerial *queixada* before you touch down.

The Technique

The *mariposa,* like some other acrobatic moves, is not as hard as it looks at first. You need to follow technical instructions to learn how to do them safely and perfectly. You must be physically fit and have good coordination.

Note that rotation control comes from your arms and torso, and not from your legs. Also, as with most acrobatic moves, you need an extra launching technique, the most common one being running, in order to gather momentum for the thrust before you can actually perform the complete move from zero stance.

Suppose you are going to execute a *mariposa* from right to left. To start preparing for the jump, take a small step forward with your right leg, bring your right arm

MARIPOSA

up straight, parallel to the ground, while stretching the other arm in front of you, also parallel to the ground. Make sure you bring both arms to each position in a swinging pendular move. At this time you should lift your left foot slightly off the ground to prepare for your thrust.

Continue the pendular movement of your arms by swinging them down to your left while stepping with your left foot back on the ground, turning your arms and torso back and around in preparation for the jump, and bending both legs for the spring effect you will need in order to lift off for the horizontal rotation of your body.

As you come around, continue to swing your arms and now your body down in a circular motion to your left. Your arms and head should go down close to the ground for the best leverage, right before you throw both arms up while taking off, powered by your left leg and swinging your right leg upward. Use your arms to lead the jump and take off. Visualize yourself helping a friend to count up to three, and then throw a heavy buddy far into a swimming pool by his arms and legs.

As you start swinging your right leg up, kick it high. This first leg to fly off the ground must be completely straight, so make sure you do not bend your knees. Keep your arms open wide as you start to fly, taking your torso upward.

Now let your right leg take control. You must have kicked it up high enough, so that you can now bring your left leg up and straight. At this point, you must be horizontally above and aligned with the ground surface, ready to start your rotation and complete your *mariposa*. Both legs must be straight and still slightly apart.

Now it's time to create the axis of rotation. Imagine yourself as a driveshaft. Turn your torso quickly by bringing your arms together close to your body, between your chest and your abdomen, your right hand touching your left hand right above it, both hands slightly closed. Your straight legs should meet in the air while your whole body forms a rotating axis.

To finish the movement, open your arms again and separate your feet, so as to touch the ground with your left foot first.

The 720°

Your prerequisite is to master the 360° completely before attempting the 720° version. All you have to do then is to move a little faster and higher, and continue to rotate before opening your arms and legs to land. In wushu, landing is sometimes done in front-splits position. This could be sometimes interesting for the 720 because gravity pulls you down after the 360, and since you'll be closer to the ground on the second turn, the front-splits may come in handy. However, if you want to land in front-splits position, make sure you learn how to do it first!

Whether doing the 360, the 540 or the 720, these steps must be coordinated as in one whole, fluid, smooth though very vigorous movement. You must know how to control grace and power for great acrobatic capoeira movements. Think of the noise that gold medal gymnasts make when they land on the floor. Watch Kyle Shewfelt or Catalina Ponor win their gold medals at the 2004 Olympic Games, or look for more recent examples at the 2008 Olympics in Beijing. However, a capoeirista cannot afford to do that. You must control your power from the start and seek for a smooth landing, like a cat landing softly on the ground. That's why a good teacher will always tell you that doing all sorts of acrobatic jumps does not make you a capoeirista. It takes much more than that!

By the way, Kyle Shewfelt and Catalina Ponor did perfect beautiful jumps, the way they must be done in Olympic gymnastics, where they deal with pre-established routines and where the objectives are different from those of capoeira.

One last bit of advice: you should know how to execute a good *aú sem mãos* before proceeding to the *mariposa*.

Not good. Be more demanding with your *mariposa!*

Practicing Alone

It is always best to practice complex acrobatic moves over an appropriate mat, a resi-pit, or a foam pit for extra safety. Once you have mastered the three types of *mariposa,* then you can feel free to perform them on the ground and in the *roda.*

Don't use trampolines or springboards for practicing the *mariposa.* The only way you will learn how to gather momentum and lose your natural fear is by understanding the full mechanics of the movement and of the muscles involved in the task. Therefore, PRACTICE, and when you're done practicing, PRACTICE MORE AND MORE!

Defenses and Counterattacks

The *mariposa* can be exceptionally tricky. If done well, it can also be a very quick and surprising technique – especially the 720, which has to be fast enough to bear two horizontal body rotations in the air before landing. This is where the problem lies if you are a fighter in combat. A good capoeirista with perfect acrobatic skills can easily trick you into making the wrong move; and the *mariposa* is a great technique for throwing you off balance.

In addition, watch out for the kicks. If your opponent has mastered all styles of the *mariposa,* he might perfectly well be able to kick your head during his rotation, using his first or second leg. In this case, you should be ready to jump away from his attack with a *mortal de frente diagonal* outside his path.

Eventually, you can use a *mortal de costas* or even an evasive *aú,* but using this *mortal de frente* technique will allow you to be ready for a quick comeback with your own *mortal de costas,* a *xangô,* an *aú de costas* or a *macaco* to win the fight.

Martelo

The roundhouse kick. The *martelo* honors its meaning of "hammer" in Portuguese. It is one of the most efficient, most accurate, and fastest kicks in capoeira. It is present in practically all martial arts in the world – like karate, where it is called *mawashi geri*; tae-kwon do, called *dollyu chagi*; wushu, named *bian tui*; muay thai, known as *dteh! wiang*; savate, called *fouetté; and* krav maga, as *be'itat magal*, to mention a few. It has been a real solution for a clean, quick, real fight for those martial artists who can master it.

The capoeira *martelo* can be super-efficient if one really understands its potential. It can be used for an attack at any level, from the leg to the head of your opponent, with the ball or the top of the foot and even with the shin! When executed correctly, the *martelo* can be surprising and devastating. If one is an attentive fighter, the *martelo* can easily knock out an adversary when delivered to his head, or break several of his ribs.

Personally, if I had to choose, I would say that thanks to its versatility the roundhouse kick is the most efficient of all martial arts kicks. Like in the Brazilian jiu-jitsu doctrine, a shorter or weaker fighter who has mastered all versions of the *martelo* can win the fiercest combat in no time.

MARTELO

The perfect *martelo* brings the confidence necessary for any capoeirista to feel he belongs to the world of martial arts. Mastering the entire repertoire of capoeira movements means the capoeirista is one of the best and most complete martial artists in the world.

Objectives

Surprise, knock out, knock down and devastate. These words would be enough to define a good *martelo* if it weren't for its different versions. Whether the main objective is to score a fast, accurate blow to your opponent's head in order to fell him with no mercy, other objectives, such as using a *low martelo* to put your opponent's leg out of commission by striking behind his knee, or hitting directly on his thigh, or using a *medium martelo* to get him in the ribs, cannot be overlooked.

The Point of Impact

These are the most efficient: on the parietal and temporal regions of the head, with the top of the foot for knocking your opponent down, or the ball of the foot for knocking him out, or on your opponent's jaws, i.e., the lower and the upper jaw plus the cheekbone, with either the top or the ball of the foot; the ribs, also with the top or the ball of the foot and with the shin; the thigh, with the top of the foot; and the back or the side of the knee.

One very specific lethal point of impact is the nape of the neck. Normally executed with the ball of the foot, hitting the nape of your adversary's neck with a perfect *martelo* can cause him severe damage and could be fatal.

Another very dangerous point of impact is your adversary's neck, if you decide to "trespass" it by striking it with a very quick and solid (thus deadly) *martelo*. A combination nape and neck, struck with the top of the foot as in Figure 23.1, is a sure hit on the target. See *The Towel Factor* in the Introduction.

There are, of course, many other possible points of impact, but they are not as efficient or as lethal as the ones discussed in this section.

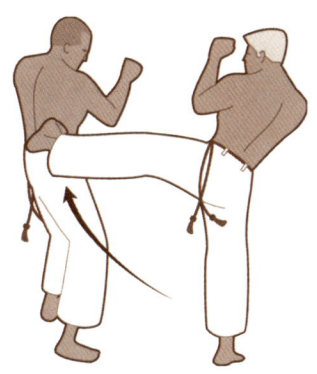

Figure 23.1: The classic *martelo*.

The Technique

For the high kick, begin by standing in a front stance. You can do it from your *ginga* or from zero stance. In my opinion, the best "real-life" *martelo* comes from the zero stance. This is where we gain our utmost propelling power. A strong, stable stance is particularly important for a powerful and accurate kick. Your hands must be positioned in a defensive manner, in front of your head and a little lower, arms level with your ribs, almost as in a boxing stance.

The attacking leg will be the rear one. Thrust the knee up and forward, using your foot like a spring. Use your knee to aim at your target at the same time you quickly snap the attacking leg out from your maximum knee height, close to your ribs. The higher your target, the higher your knee should be. Right before striking, the inner sides of your attacking knee and shin should both be as parallel to the ground as possible. At this time, still in a single movement, transfer all the power you can to your attacking leg and foot, and extend your leg at the knee to finally launch the kick at the target, while rotating your hip and your supporting leg until you have hit the target with the top or the ball of your foot.

Some fighters prefer to strike with the tarsal bones of the foot (the upper top bones), while others prefer to use the metatarsal bones (the bones of the instep). The subtle difference between these two modes is that if you hit a hard surface with the tarsal bones, chances are you will also hurt your foot, though perhaps not so badly. On the other hand, hitting with the instep may be a little less harmful to your adversary (but just a little, believe me). You can feel these differences when practicing on your sandbag.

During the strike, concentrate on transferring all power to your attacking thigh, then to your calf and down to your attacking foot. This happens very quickly, as your foot acts in a split second when reaching the target, preferably "as fast as a lightning bolt."

You may slide your supporting foot to follow your rotating movement, and slide it back if you retrieve your attacking leg to the original stance after striking your opponent. Note that you can tilt your upper body slightly to either side of your

MARTELO

kick in order to counterbalance your *martelo*. If you move away from the kicking leg, you will have a more open and "elastic" *martelo*. If you tilt your upper body toward the kick, putting a lot of pressure into bending your waist sideways, you will have a straighter, more closed *martelo* and your supporting foot will not slide on a long rotation. You may need to use this latter style, which is also a powerful one, if you don't have enough space for the former one, whether in real combat or if you simply prefer it this way. For the *roda*, though, stick to the more open style. Diagram 23.1 shows the path for the two styles of *martelo*.

For the medium *martelo*, as well as the low one, use the same technique as in the high kick though you will not need all the effort of the rotating hip and supporting foot of the high kick, rather using the straight-line technique described above. This is because the targets are nearer, and the rotating efforts will, therefore, be smaller.

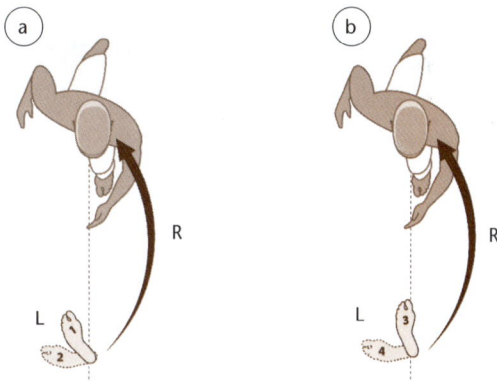

Diagram 23.1: In movement **a** (left foot, from 1 to 2), a more open and "relaxed" *martelo*. In movement **b** (same left foot, from 3 to 4), a more straight-lined, closer and "tenser" (and objective) *martelo*.

In karate and krav maga, for instance, the correct way is to retract your leg soon after the strike. In capoeira, you can engage in other moves to continue delivering a great variety of kicks. If you parted from zero stance, though, bend your knee tightly and retract your attacking leg as quickly as possible after your successful strike. You must transfer as much power as you can from your attacking foot to your target (see the section in the Introduction on practicing with a training bag and a towel) in the least possible contact time, so that the generated energy stays there and is not dissipated between your foot and your target.

During the kick, you can keep your hands closed, with fists closed and lifted like those of a boxer, or palms open, fingers tight, as in the *ginga*.

Martelo Médio

A medium roundhouse kick. The *martelo médio* is not a new move, but rather another choice of performance of the traditional *martelo*. It is an efficient option for a target that is too close, and it might also be selected for tactical reasons, if you want to dominate your opponent without doing him lethal harm, for instance.

In real fighting, the *martelo médio* is normally delivered to the ribs of your adversary in one of three possible ways: with the ball of the foot (Figure 23.2), the top of the foot, or the shin.

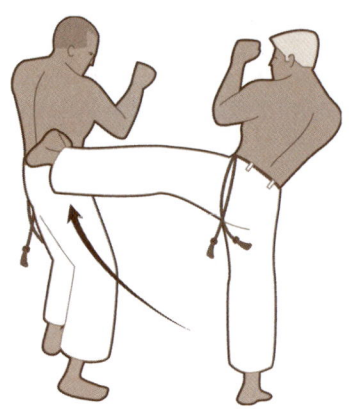

Figure 23.2: A *martelo médio* onto the ribs.

Figure 23.3: A closer shin *martelo médio* on the ribs.

The Shin Option

The best time to use your shin is when your adversary is too close for a classic *martelo* and has his arms open or above his ribs, like when someone is approaching and trying to choke you or even punch you, or to hit you with something. You can deliver the shin *martelo* to his ribs in two ways – by simply launching the move with your attacking leg, or by first holding his arm (Figure 23.4) on the opposite side which you want to strike his ribs with your shin, as in Figure 23.3. Hold his arm with your two hands, and use it as a lever to launch a powerful shin kick to his unguarded ribs.

If you execute a powerful and perfect strike, it will severely break his ribs, which is potentially lethal due to the risk of perforating his lungs.

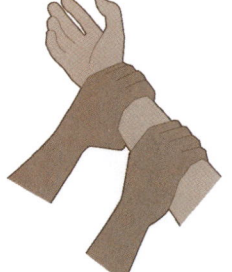

Figure 23.4: You can maximize the power of your shin *martelo* by grabbing his opposite arm.

Martelo Baixo

A low roundhouse kick. The *martelo baixo* is an efficient option for the *rasteira* or the *banda* if you need to put your opponent – and his knee – immediately out of commission. However, this is for serious combat. If this is the case, you should vigorously deliver a powerful *martelo baixo* with the top of your counterattacking foot onto your adversary's inner side of the knee , as shown in Figure 23.5, as if you were trying to pass through his leg (see the Introduction for details on practicing capoeira kicks alone). As an alternative, you can use either the shin or the top of the foot to deliver a sound kick to your opponent's thigh.

Figure 23.5: A *martelo baixo* on the back of the knee can block and cause a severe damage to your adversary.

Figure 23.6: A shin *martelo baixo* onto the thigh can bring the fight to an end.

For the *martelo pulado,* take one or two firm steps forward and vigorously hop up high for the kick. Go forward. Your first supporting leg will act as a springboard and will be the attacking leg. The first leg to go up will be your "guiding leg," and the same foot will also be the first to touch the ground after you have delivered your swift kick to the target. Synchronize your movement. You should not touch the ground before the kick.

I prefer tight fists for this movement when practiced on a sandbag or in real fighting, as it helps to maintain accuracy and power.

Martelo pulado.

This *martelo pulado* technique can be successfully used against an opponent who is too far away for your regular kicks. However, if you are quick enough to use a good *esquiva,* you could try one against an *armada,* or even against a *meia-lua de compasso*.

Then again, a good alternative option would be to use a *martelo rodado voador*.

Which to Choose?

Choosing between a *martelo pulado* and a *martelo rodado voador* will depend on some assumptions. If you are really too close to your opponent, you will not be able to hop so as to perform a *rodado*-style move. You definitely need more space for the *rodado*. On the other hand, the *rodado* carries a good part of your weight together with the movement, and this can be very handy in actual combat. For instance, you could choose to hit your adversary's neck using the "Towel Factor" discussed in the Introduction to this book. Your weight and speed would be concentrated in your attacking foot. That could be devastatingly lethal. Your life must be in real danger before you choose to use this kick! Perhaps you would better give your opponent a second chance with the *pulado* version delivered to his face or his head, not without some damage, though.

In both cases, use good sense and take your distance into account in order to choose the most suitable type of jumping *martelo* – and always use the top of the foot.

Practicing Alone

Besides practicing on the hands of a friend with open palms, tight fingers and outstretched arms (only to practice aim and leg stretching and never for power), the *martelo* should also be practiced extensively on a training bag until fully mastered. When using the training bag, be sure to hit the bag with both feet. Be especially careful when practicing with your shins. To avoid hurting your shins, you need to seek efficiency in *positioning* your shin strike rather than looking primarily for power.

See *queda de rim* for information on the *martelo de chão*.

Defenses and Counterattacks

The best way to defend yourself against a high *martelo* and a *martelo médio* is by using the classic *rasteira em pé* or a *rasteira de chão*, a *rasteira de costas* a.k.a. *rasteira giratória*, a classic *banda*, or a *banda de costas* and a *rasteira* or *banda cruzada*. You could also quickly dive into a low combination of *negativa* and *rasteira de chão*, or *negativa* and *s-dobrado*, or launch a counterattacking *meia-lua diagonal* over your opponent's attempt to execute his *martelo*. For the low *martelo*, a pre-emptive counterattacking *meia-lua* would be equally great, but since this *martelo* is a more straightforward and therefore a shorter kick, maybe your best reaction would be to simply move diagonally away from his kick and deliver a diagonal *meia-lua*. In this case, using your *meia-lua* supporting hand would eventually help you to retain control and prepare for the next action.

If you intend to get close to your opponent's apparently open guard, make sure to be prepared for a possible *cabeçada* and a couple of punches. Otherwise you will be the victim of your own attempt to counterattack.

If you are attacked with a shin *martelo*, it is probably because you are too close to your adversary. Avoid that unless you are a good Brazilian jiu-jitsu fighter. As a capoeirista, your best choice would be to use a *rasteira em pé* or a *banda* against a medium shin *martelo*, or a *cabeçada* against a low one, blocking your opponent's arm on the same side of his attacking leg in order to use it as a lever and for purposes of balance.

If you are close enough, you may try to deliver a *godeme* to the attacker's eyebrow, a *galopante* to his unguarded ear, or an *asfixiante* to his throat. These should all be precise, powerful blows in order to be efficient and take your opponent out of action.

If you are attacked with a *martelo pulado,* you will most probably be out of your opponent's normal range of attack. Being a capoeirista helps you understand that; being an advanced capoeirista gives you an important edge over your adversary. You should have time to see which leg the adversary is using as his attacking leg, and execute a diagonal *aú fechado* in the opposite direction of his attack and on the side of his other leg.

Don't ever try to hold his attacking foot up in the air. If your opponent is a good capoeirista, he will certainly surprise you with part of his repertoire of capoeira moves.

> **REMEMBER: CAPOEIRA IS ESSENTIALLY A MARTIAL ART. DO NOT TRY THESE OR ANY OTHER MOVES ON A PARTNER OR A FRIEND, AND DO NOT PRACTICE WITHOUT PROPER PROFESSIONAL GUIDANCE.**

Martelo Preso

The spinning roundhouse kick or spinning roundhouse on hands, a.k.a. *chibata presa*, or *martelo rodado preso* (or simply *martelo rodado* when done without the support of the hands). Some schools call it *chapéu de couro*, although I prefer the *s-dobrado* version for this last one. It looks like an "opposite *meia-lua presa*." Some capoeiristas believe this is not as a strong and efficient a weapon as the classic *martelo* or even as the *martelo rodado voador*. The reality is that the *martelo preso* can be both a quick and violent kick, as well as a very cunning and surprising one. If you are acting kind of slow, you can easily deceive your opponent by pretending you are going to execute an *aú* or simply a malicious swinging of your upper body, toward an *esquiva*, in order to delude him – and then, suddenly, come up with a quick *martelo preso*, against which there is usually no defense.

In real fighting – and sometimes even in the *roda* – the *martelo preso* is most unexpected by your opponents and partners because if done well, it is not much of a "telegraphic" move. It is solely up to you to make it as evasive and misleading to them as the moment and your skills allow.

Objectives

The *martelo preso* is a tactical as well as an objective move. Although it can be harmful if delivered to your opponent's head, "surprise" is really the key word for this move. Done as a tool for trickery, for a quick defense by which you can show your opponent that you are resourceful in capoeira moves, and as a preparation for a counterattack, the *martelo preso* can be highly efficient and a perfect smokescreen if used to connect to other moves, especially the spinning ones, which can take advantage of its centrifugal force, such as the *meia-lua de compasso*, the *armada*, the *martelo rodado voador* and the *meia-lua reversão*, to name some of the most efficient.

The Point of Impact

The head and neck of your opponent.

The Technique

The move is executed just like a reverse *meia-lua presa*. As you start to lift your attacking leg for the spin, place both hands on the ground for support and leverage for the final spin, while looking through your arms and rotating your hips to thrust the 180° kick, hitting with the top or the instep of the foot.* As with the *martelo rodado voador*, if you try to spin with the ball of the foot, your upturned toes will interfere with the aerodynamics of your roundhouse movement and you will not have the same power.

If you are flexible and, therefore, bent over with your head close to the ground while keeping your supporting leg fairly straight, push with your hands while spinning the attacking leg. You can straighten your supporting leg according to the desired angle of attack. This means that if you want to execute the *martelo preso* at a lower level, use the combination of a gradually bent supporting leg and your supporting hands, for leverage and thrust.

For the *martelo rodado* (the version without use of supporting hands), you do it almost exactly as a reverse *meia-lua solta*, normally returning to your original position after executing the move.

---

* If you prefer, you can also execute the **martelo preso** with only one supporting hand, for a freer distribution of your weight while executing the move.

MARTELO PRESO

Practicing Alone

As with the *aú* and the *bananeira*, feel the surface of the ground under your hands. Practice the different tactile characteristics of each type of surface you touch, the aim being to familiarize yourself with ground surfaces, from cobblestone roads to sidewalks, from flat wooden courts to synthetic flooring, on sandy terrain or in rural areas. As with Parkour practitioners, don't let these all-terrain surfaces be an obstacle to your capoeira. Get professional guidance and, above all, PRACTICE SERIOUSLY!

Your best choice is, as usual, to practice your *martelo preso* or *martelo rodado* on the training bag, using different speeds and degrees of power in order to gain full command of both techniques.

Defenses and Counterattacks

You can defend yourself against a *martelo preso* and a *martelo rodado* with a classic ground *rasteira*, so as to sweep the supporting leg of your attacker off the ground. As you see his *martelo* coming, dodge down in the same direction as your opponent's kick while you execute the *rasteira* to complete the sweep. If you are too hungry for action, you can close in under his attacking leg and sweep his supporting leg and his supporting hands off the ground all at once, using your *rasteira* shin and foot. See the chapter on *rasteira* for additional information.

You can also continue the move and turn it into an *s-dobrado* back in his direction for extra precaution. A set of *meia-luas de compasso* is also a good choice for getting your opponent in open guard when he is about to finish his *martelo preso*. If you time your movements with his, you won't miss your target.

Martelo Rodado Voador

The flying spinning roundhouse kick. This version takes longer to perform than the classic *martelo*, but is an excellent strategy for real combat against more than one adversary, especially if they are at various distances from you, which can ultimately help you to use the move as a catalyst for executing other techniques.

Do not confuse this move with the *martelo pulado*, the "jumping" roundhouse kick, which is a way of thrusting the classic *martelo* into the air without having to spin your attacking leg.

Objectives

It is excellent as a counterattack move, started when you are surrounded by at least two assailants, or as a surprise attack against an open *armada* or *meia-lua*, as long as you time your movement with your opponent's, looking for an open guard right after his spinning kick, as shown in Figure 25.1 for example, or simply when you want to reach your target when it is beyond your range of attack.

Note that in real fighting, you should fly your *martelo rodado* (and most jumping kicks) first in the direction of the farthest opponent and not toward the closest one, as you might initially think. In the demonstration shown in Diagram 25.1, you are the one in the middle, being attacked by two assailants. The bad guy behind you is your nearest opponent. The one coming in front of you is the farthest assailant – the one to be counterattacked first. Your best choice would be to try to reach his head and then land on the ground, ready to fire another move toward the (now former) closest opponent who, as you jump away from him, will probably try his best to approach you again.

Figure 25.1: You can surprise his ending *armada* with a *martelo rodado voador*.

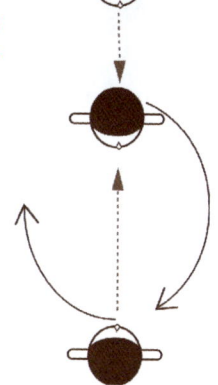

Diagram 25.1: Take care of the farthest opponent first.

The Point of Impact

Preference should be given to the neck and to the parietal and temporal regions of the head. Always hit with the top of your foot, so as to make best use of the aerodynamics. There is a big difference between using the top and the ball of the foot in a whirling front kick.

Although you may fly and spin quickly and accurately, if you don't take your weight with you during the movement, the absence of a supporting foot that should act as a perfect lever for thrusting the classic *martelo* will make you lose some power and cause less damage to your target. However, this will not hinder you from knocking your opponent flat on the ground from either of the two styles.

The Technique

At first, it looks like an *armada* followed by a *martelo* in the air. The fact is that the *martelo rodado voador* has its own personality. It's not too difficult if you practice it thoroughly – as you certainly should with all capoeira movements.

Launch your first leg in the desired direction, as if you were going to start an *armada*. At the same time, bend your supporting leg (which will later be your kicking leg) while lifting your first leg as high as it will go. The higher you fly with your first leg, the greater should be the thrust for your jumping *martelo*. As you spin around off the ground, the second leg gets dragged behind.

You should bend the kicking leg at the start of your *martelo rodado voador,* so that it acts as a springboard for the move. While twisting your upper body, which is already off the ground, stretch it and strike your target like a strong bullwhip. Hit with the top of the foot. If you try to spin with the ball of the foot, your upward-pointing toes will interfere with the aerodynamics of your performance. Aerodynamics, flexibility, agility and strength are all important assets for a good capoeirista. Believe me, these important details do matter.

You can control the power and the course of your spin, so as to land on your first leg and face your second opponent behind you or coming from the side, or to face the first opponent. With practice, you will be able to choose whether to execute the *martelo rodado voador* from your fixed stance position, or to first travel the desired distance between you and your immediate target.

There is a variation of the *martelo rodado voador,* done with the kicking leg only, called *martelo cruzado*. You jump as high as you can and delay your rotation in the air as long as possible – like a flying basketball player does – before you start your descent, completing the rotation with a powerful spin of your kicking leg and seeking to land on the ground with the same leg.

Practicing Alone

It's fun to practice the *martelo rodado voador* on the sandbag and over the hands of a stationary partner with arms outstretched. Your partner can vary the height of his hands to make you execute different jumps. You can also practice different attacking speeds on the sandbag, from the very high and most gentle flight to the most violent and quick aerial *martelo rodado*. Always practice different landing angles, pretending you were surrounded by opponents on all sides. Remember to practice with both legs.

MARTELO RODADO VOADOR

Defenses and Counterattacks

You definitely cannot use a *rasteira* to defend yourself against a *martelo rodado voador*. You shouldn't use your hands either. Your best choice would be to go down on a smooth – and at the same time quick – *negativa,* and immediately engage in an *s-dobrado* in order to catch the opponent finishing his *martelo*. One good secret between friends: never try a spinning kick while your opponent is still in the air. Besides its being an awkward move, you may hit an unwanted target and jeopardize your defense. Remember, he will have his weight to his advantage, which means that his weight could exceed the power of your move. It's better to be cautious and tactical, and think of the various angles that you can reach depending on how quick his movement is, or how hard and accurate he may be, i.e., LOOK FOR GAPS!

Nevertheless, you can use your repertoire of *meia-luas* to get your opponent by the time he lands, before he recovers his stance. And if you really know exactly how and where he will land, you can risk a flying *compasso* on his head and catch him defenseless.

Mata-borrão

Literally, the ink blotter. A great *floreio,* the *mata-borrão,* a.k.a. simply *borrão,* is also a good way to trick your opponent in the *roda* or in real fighting, as you can fall down smoothly and make a quick comeback to your original stance in no time. The good thing about it is that you can use it to dodge down to avoid a strike and make a quick return to action.

Objectives

To dodge a strike; to recover from an unsuccessful ground maneuver and quickly get back into action in the *roda;* to recover from a fall and make a quick comeback.

The Point of Impact

You should not use this move as an attack.

The Technique

Start to sit down on the ground smoothly, and let your body roll over to around one-third of a somersault. Since you are looking for a spring effect, you must feel that your back has the shape of an ink blotter. Then, with the inverted palms of your hands on the ground placed next to your ears, and your legs extended over your chest with toes almost touching the surface behind your head, spring up and back to a standing position, with the aid of your hands coordinated with your legs, which are close together, to make a perfect lever for the jump.

The process does not involve much strength, but rather the union of body shape and technique.

Practicing Alone

The best way to practice the *mata-borrão* is on a gymnastics mat, until you get the hang of the movement and feel that you can execute it over rougher surfaces without getting bruised.

Defenses and Counterattacks

Although the *mata-borrão* is not an attack move *per se,* you can easily block one by doing a half *giro* right next to your opponent when he is getting ready to come back, while his legs are still behind his head. You can also go around him, doing an *aú* by his side the moment he starts springing into the air, and get him with a spinning or crescent kick as soon as he lands.

Meia-lua de Chão

The ground half-moon. This ground wheel kick is a variation of the *meia-lua de compasso* done at a low stance, close to the ground. It is a very resourceful kick as a technical alternative to the *s-dobrado*, when you need to go down and suddenly come back up to kick high, taking your opponent by surprise. To deliver a *meia-lua de chão*, you should already be heading for the ground where your target is, at low or medium height, perhaps after a *meia-lua presa*. In contrast, on an *s-dobrado* you can start from either an upright or a ground stance, and your objective is normally to kick a high or medium-height target – not to mention the fact that the *s-dobrado* is done from a forward position, with a *martelo,* and the *meia-lua de chão* is a back wheel kick.

Objectives

The main objective in using a *meia-lua de chão* is to surprise your opponent with a seldom-executed, unexpected and highly technical strategic type of *meia-lua*. Generally, a martial artist will not perceive your intention until it is too late to react. Of course, as with most capoeira spinning kicks, you must look for the final result, which is to knock your opponent down while preparing yourself for a new strategy.

The *meia-lua de chão* can also be successfully used as a high *rasteira de costas*, through which you can sweep your opponent by hitting his supporting leg above the sinew at calf level. In its initial stage, you can decide whether to use a kicking or a sweeping type of *meia-lua de chão*.

You can also choose a reasonable height for a target with your *meia-lua de chão*, i.e., you don't need to stick to very low targets, such as an opponent on a *negativa* motion. It is entirely possible to get targets as high as the ones you can get with the *meia-lua presa*. The advantage of this resource is that you will have both legs off the ground (but will have both supporting hands on the ground, which can also represent a threat if you are careless). Figure 27.1 shows an average height of the *meia-lua de chão*.

Figure 27.1: You can control the height of your *meia-lua de chão*.

The Point of Impact

One of the targets of your *meia-lua de chão* is your opponent's head, in the parietal and temporal bone regions, as suggested for most spinning and circular kicks in capoeira. However, since the *meia-lua de chão* can be done against both a classic and a high *meia-lua de compasso*, as well as against another *meia-lua de chão*, you must also be ready to deliver it on your opponent's chest or abdomen.

Ultimately, your target could be your adversary's supporting leg – or even his two legs planted on the ground, which would cause a dramatic sweeping effect.

The Technique

The *meia-lua de chão* is an opportunistic capoeira move. Generally, most capoeiristas do not expect it in the *roda*. For all other martial artists, though, it is practically unknown and therefore *never* expected, which is exactly why you have a good reason to practice it to perfection, until you feel you can deliver one at any time and from any stance.

You can start your *meia-lua de chão* from an upright stance, preferably against an opponent who is beginning his descent to the ground or one who is already "navigating" on the ground. Try not to step away from your base – this is one big difference between this *meia-lua* and the others: you simply reach for the ground with your supporting hands as quickly and suddenly as possible, to achieve the surprise effect.

Figure 27.2: Get your opponent on his ground movements with your *meia-lua de chão*.

Your best combination will be to fire a *meia-lua de chão* immediately after a classic *meia-lua de compasso*. This is an excellent strategy for reaching your target, since the first attempt with your *meia-lua* will most likely make your opponent go down on a *negativa* – whereupon you will get him with your strategic *meia-lua de chão,* as shown in Figure 27.2.

As with all spinning kicks, follow your target during the movement. Your initial supporting leg gets off the ground and turns with your attacking leg, as soon as you start to spin the *meia-lua de chão*. Keep your attacking leg straight throughout its full rotation. Strike with your heel and return the attacking leg to the desired stance, upright or on the ground. Your proficiency in the ground techniques, especially in the use of your hands, will make the difference when you decide which type of movement to execute next.

Be sure to keep your spinning leg straight and your attacking foot rigid, at a 90° angle to your attacking leg, so that your calf and heel are hard enough to hit your target without injuring your foot, your sinew or even your leg – which could result in injury to the groin. Never relax your *meia-lua* foot, or your strike will be weak and ineffective. You can, at your own risk and discretion, bend your attacking leg while spinning the *meia-lua* if you feel the need to control the distance to your target, although this procedure is recommended more as an extra resource in the *roda*.

Figure 27.3 demonstrates a common encounter of two *meia-luas de chão*. The black capoeirista has escaped from his opponent's attack and is ready to counterattack with his own *meia-lua de chão*, delivered on the chest or belly as he turns to finish his original attack. Endless possibilities with capoeira …

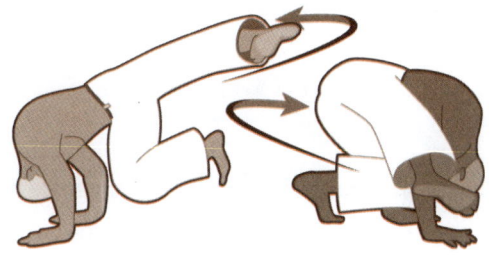

Figure 27.3: You can always engage in a *meia-lua de chão* yourself and surprise your attacker.

Practicing Alone

Besides the *roda* or with a friend, the *meia-lua de chão* can be practiced on a training bag and over a short-backed chair. Use the chair for independent movements with the *meia-lua de compasso*, the *meia-lua de chão*, and with the combination of *meia-lua solta* & *meia-lua de chão*. Refer to the Introduction for more details and special tips on practicing your *meia-lua de chão* alone to improve your techniques.

Defenses and Counterattacks

To avoid a well-delivered *meia-lua de chão*, you have the choice of withdrawing from your attacker's range of attack or descending to a lower *negativa*, the so-called *negativa derrubando* (takedown *negativa*),* or *negativa de chão* (ground *negativa*) as

---

* A *negativa*, although possible, is not the best recommendation against a **meia-lua de chão**. However, if you decide to engage in a **negativa** to defend yourself against a **meia-lua de chão**, be sure to do so only if you have no room for a different means of escape. In this case, you will first apply its defensive aspect, which is dodging down to escape your opponent's wheel kick. You will then be able to engage in another ground move and so on, but remember that your opponent will leave no supporting leg left on the ground to be swept away by your takedown **negativa**.

it is also called by some capoeiristas. However, there is a slight difference between the takedown type and the ground one: in the former, your head is lower than in the classic *negativa,* but not as close as possible to the ground as in the latter. If you step in with your *negativa* when going down under your opponent's *meia-lua* leg, watch for his other leg, which will be spinning right after his attacking leg.

However, one of your best strategies against a *meia-lua de chão* is to immediately execute a low *meia-lua* or even a *meia-lua de chão*, after your successful *negativa.* With proper timing, speed and accuracy, chances are good that you will reach your target and repel his attack.

You could also try a perfect *compasso* right over your opponent, as soon as he starts to spin with both his legs off the ground. In this case, choose the one with the supporting hand on the ground, and jump in the same direction as his *meia-lua de chão*, since the fight seems to have gone to ground level at this time. This technique will allow you to stay on the ground for further "navigation."

Meia-lua de Compasso

The half-moon. The classic wheel kick. There are several options for the capoeirista. In this chapter we will discuss three: the *meia-lua de compasso*,* a.k.a. *rabo de arraia*, or simply as the *meia-lua*, which is done with one supporting hand on the ground; the *meia-lua solta*, which is performed without any supporting hands, and is also known as the *chibata*; and the *meia-lua presa*, which is done with two supporting hands on the ground. See each specific *meia-lua*, where we also explore the *meia-lua de chão*, which is a low type of *meia-lua* done close to the ground; the *compasso*, also known as the *aú chibata*, which has a ground and an aerial variation; the *meia-lua de frente*, a forward inside crescent kick; the *meia-lua pulada*, which is a

---

* Personally, I prefer the terminology we used at the original **Grupo Bantus de Capoeira**, at Morro do Pavão e Pavãozinho, in Copacabana, Rio de Janeiro, which was a "center of excellence" for capoeira, *maculelê* and *samba*. For this reason, it was often visited back in the '60s and '70s by other important capoeira groups who would "come up the *morro*" to get together and celebrate.

At **Grupo Bantus**, the *meia-lua* with one supporting hand was known as the plain *meia-lua*. The version with two supporting hands on the ground was called *meia-lua presa*, and the *meia-lua* with no supporting hands at all was known as the *meia-lua solta*. Our *meia-lua de compasso* was what many schools now simply call *compasso* or *aú chibata*. In my opinion, **Bantus** made a major contribution to this terminology by trying to classify the mechanics of these moves according to their "roots." Note that the so-called *aú chibata* is really a deliberate wheel kick delivered with the heel in a "half-moon-like" movement, in which the jump is just the lever for powering the move, while the *chibatas* usually derive from other specific classic moves, such as the *aú* or the *bananeira*.

jumping variation of the *meia-lua solta,* often called the butterfly kick; and the *meia-lua reversão* – where you actually benefit from the use of both feet, so as to kick alternately in a typical half-moon spinning movement.

Objectives

The *meia-lua* is one of the most effective and popular movements of the entire capoeira repertoire, and that is precisely why it is also so widely used. With the richness of capoeira and its resourceful choice of movements, if you are a serious capoeirista and love the martial art that resides within it you must be careful when choosing your next move. Be sure you have mastered the move with both legs, at slow, medium and fast pace, before proceeding to the next one.

The main objective in using a *meia-lua* is to knock down your opponent while protecting yourself against kicks or even against hand and armed attacks. The *meia-lua de compasso* is a wonderful move and can be used in different situations, both during real combat and in a *roda*. For instance, you can use it to reach – or just to scare – one or more adversaries, since its mechanics allow for several strikes from a fixed spot, as shown in Diagram 28.1, or from alternating bases, as in Diagram 28.2 – all uninterrupted.

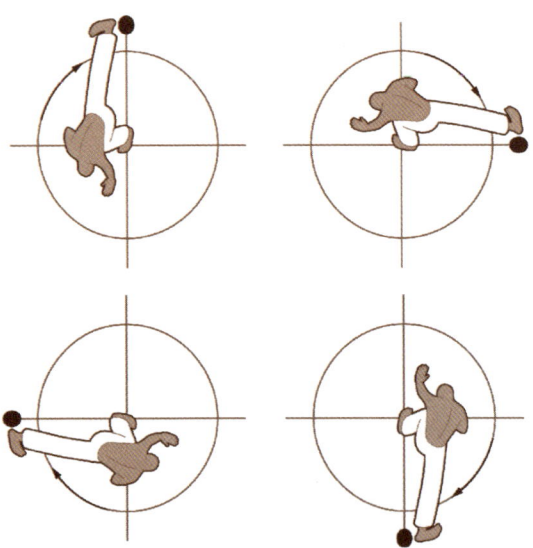

Diagram 28.1: A set of *meia-luas* from a fixed base.

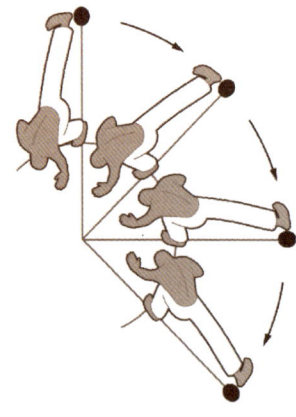

Diagram 28.2: A set of *meia-luas* from alternating bases.

Use the Centrifugal Force

In Diagram 28.1 the capoeirista can rotate on his base right before spinning his *meia-lua* and still keep his range of attack. His supporting, pivot foot does the trick by placing him in front of his target after each move. The four moves are done within the same area.

In Diagram 28.2 the capoeirista does not rotate on the same base. He chooses to step aside, forming an arch with his supporting leg right before spinning his next *meia-lua de compasso* in a new attack range. As in Diagram 28.1, his supporting, pivot foot also places him in front of his target after each move, but the four moves are done *outside* the original area. Note that the capoeirista does not need to follow a circular path as shown in the diagram. He can change his targets at will, but by doing so he will lose momentum. His natural and best choice would be to deliver additional circular strikes, considering the centrifugal force achieved in spinning and crescent kicks, which suggests a continuous pathway.

In practical terms, this means that in a *roda* you can change the direction of your movements at will, like doing a *meia-lua* to the right followed by an *armada* or a *martelo* to the left, according to the strategy of the game, but in actual fighting, time and accuracy are of the essence and you must not make any concessions.

Therefore, you can also use the *meia-lua de compasso* to reach your opponent and quickly proceed to a ground movement, such as a *negativa* and an *s-dobrado,* or use it as a lever for other high kicks, such as a *martelo,* an opportunistic *armada,* or a *chapa giratória* – but be aware of your directions!

Always keep in mind that the *meia-lua* can be a lethal form of attack. Play with it in the *roda* in order to improve your motion, time it with the several possible moves from your peers, and practice it to perfection – but do not deliver one on a colleague. Save it for a real combat, if you ever need it.

The Point of Impact

The three classic types of *meia-lua* discussed in this chapter must all aim at the parietal and the temporal regions of the head, just as with the *armada*. A defensive, counterattacking *meia-lua de compasso*, or the highly technical *meia-lua diagonal*, which is even more effective than the diagonal *armada*, can also aim at your adversary's face, catching him by surprise. The *diagonal* technique is explored in detail later in this chapter.

Figure 28.1: An opportunistic *meia-lua de compasso* against an *armada*.

A good way to control your balance and time your movements with those of your attacker is to apply a *meia-lua de compasso* right on your opponent's *armada* and over his passing attacking foot (actually a split second after he starts to turn with his attacking leg up). This way, when you finish your *meia-lua* you will be in a *ginga* stance and ready for your next movement.

Always look at your adversary during a capoeira move, so that you can gauge his intentions. Figure 28.1 shows a classic *meia-lua de compasso* done against a passing *armada*.* Note the fighter's close attention to his adversary while he is making his thrust.

Other points of impact, such as the chest, the abdomen and the ribs, are possible targets for any of the three types of *meia-lua* presented in this chapter. In actual fighting, however, I recommend these moves only if they are performed strictly and specifically according to the approach explained under *Practicing the Attacking Moves Alone*, in the Introduction to this book, with special attention to the section entitled *The Towel Factor*.

What I am trying to say is that if you lose some of your power or disregard some of the "rules of perfection" but plant a good *meia-lua* on your adversary's head,

---

* Watch for speed if you want to use a ***meia-lua presa*** to counterattack an efficient ***armada***, because it is normally slower than in the ***meia-lua de compasso*** or the ***meia-lua solta***.

MEIA-LUA DE COMPASSO

chances are you will be successful in your venture anyway, whereas a reckless *meia-lua*, say on the guy's ribs, may not cause any damage at all and leave you in a precarious situation.

So, always remember to select your targets carefully and decide which movement is suitable for each context. Look for gaps in your opponent's range of attack. There is always a movement most appropriate for any given situation. Refer to the Introduction to find out about how to deal with "target contextualization" and more.

FOCUS ON TARGET!

The Technique

For an effective *meia-lua de compasso* you should be in an upright position at *ginga* or zero stance. You must look at your target first, immediately before bending over, and then look again during the movement. Your supporting hand must touch the ground firmly and completely, and it must go in front of your supporting foot during the spin. If you deliver a *meia-lua presa,* place both hands on the ground and be sure to keep watch on your target from between your supporting arms, as in Figure 28.2.

Figure 28.2: A *meia-lua presa* against an *armada*.

Positioning Your Meia-lua Presa

Figure 28.3: Positioning an efficient *meia-lua presa*.

Generally, capoeiristas prepare for a good *meia-lua presa* in two ways. One is to simply spin the kick while looking for your hand base on the ground, where you will place your two hands when your leg has already begun to turn. The other, highly classic, way is to bend down, placing your two hands on the ground and slightly twisting your torso *before* starting to spin your attacking leg, as in Figure 28.3. Your first supporting hand will be placed between your legs, followed immediately by your second supporting hand, which will be placed in front of your first hand, making a diagonal angle almost parallel to your two legs right before the kick. This gives you very good control of your move, as well as the necessary body flexibility to further engage in ground "navigation."

You can slightly bend your supporting leg as needed, but keep your attacking leg straight throughout its complete rotation. Keep the sole of your supporting foot on the ground while you turn your attacking leg, but slide-turn this foot to follow your *meia-lua* leg spin. Strike with your heel and return the attacking leg to your *ginga* or zero stance, if you do not want to execute a ground movement. In fact, this is one of the advantages of using the *meia-lua presa*. It gives you the technique and the confidence to quickly change from upright to ground maneuvers – and back again.

For the *meia-lua solta* (Figure 28.4), the rule is practically the same, but this technique has the advantage of leaving you slightly freer to launch upright kicks. Both your arms are free, and the movement is faster than in the *"presa"* style. In addition, you can always decide what to do with your arms right after you finish the move. The classic *meia-lua de compasso* is faster than the *"presa"* version and slightly slower than the *meia-lua solta*, but offers more control than the *"solta"* style. In addition, it forces your torso slightly further down than the *"solta,"* thus offering you extra protection against front crescent and spinning

MEIA-LUA DE COMPASSO

kicks from your opponent. You can still decide whether to remain standing or go down to the ground for some more action.

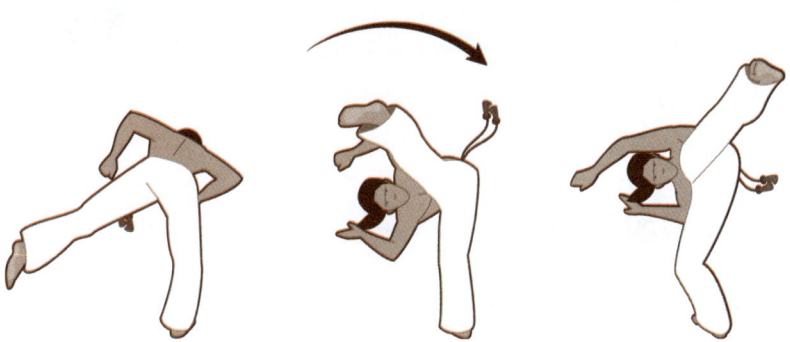

Figure 28.4: The *meia-lua solta*.

Be sure to keep your spinning leg straight and your attacking foot rigid and locked at a 90° angle to your attacking leg, so that your calf and heel are hard enough to hit your target without injuring your foot, your tendons or even your leg, which could result in injury to the groin. Never relax your *meia-lua* foot, or your strike will be weak and ineffective. You can, at your own risk and discretion, bend your attacking leg while spinning your *meia-lua* if you feel the need to control the distance to your target, although this procedure is recommended more as an extra resource at the *roda*. In all three techniques, you can also control the height of your *meia-lua*.

The "Fake" Meia-lua

Much of the fun of capoeira lies in misleading and deluding your opponent, whether he is your partner in a *roda* or your worst enemy challenging you in a back street. You may have noticed that in this book I keep pointing out moves that are "good for the flow of motion." In my view, these moves, if executed at exactly the right moment, represent the very soul of capoeira. Trickery is a major factor in capoeira, and I am dead serious about it. It's when you turn the ludic aspects of the game into a fierce fight, as easily as you flip a switch on and off. Capoeira Angola has it, and so does Capoeira Regional, the contemporary capoeira and capoeira as a martial art, which is our main focus in this book.

One of the most interesting and efficient tricky capoeira moves is the *giro* (Figure 28.5), where you spin on your heels as though you were going to deliver a perfect *meia-lua* – but you don't! What you really do, besides misleading your opponent, is carefully follow his spinning attack kick and use your hips or your buttocks to block his move, or to push him away and upset his balance. After that, you will still have time to engage in a new technique and continue "the flow of motion."

Figure 28.5: Do the *giro* inside your opponent's open guard...

Meia-lua Pulada

There is a jumping version of the *meia-lua de compasso,* called *meia-lua pulada,* also known as the butterfly kick. A beautiful version can be seen in figure skating, although with a slightly different technique and, of course, purpose. Though it is widely used in other martial arts, capoeira is where we mostly find grace as an ally of efficiency, and a great possibility for connecting to other techniques without having to interrupt one's flow of motion.

The *meia-lua pulada* is best done as the flying version of the *meia-lua solta,* such that it tends to allow for a little more action and flow of motion than the former technique. In real combat, we generally use flying kicks when we encounter more than one opponent at the same time and need to shorten distances while retaining control of the flow of moves. That's one big advantage of capoeira. See Diagram 25.1 on the *martelo rodado voador* for more detailed information.

Meia-lua pulada.

MEIA-LUA DE COMPASSO

For an effective *meia-lua pulada* you should be in an upright position at *ginga* or zero stance. You must look at your target first. Suppose you are going to do a *meia-lua pulada* to your left. Stand on your right foot while starting to rotate as in the *mariposa*. Your arms and palms should be pointing straight up, in a small v-shaped angle, almost parallel.

Sink your arms down in an arch over to your left while using your left foot as a support for the jump and the rotation with your right leading leg.

In this example, your left leg will be your attacking leg and the leg that will first touch the ground when you complete the move.

Meia-lua Queda de Rim

Very much used as a *floreio*, the *meia-lua queda de rim* is an excellent resource for ground navigation. Best done with a *meia-lua presa*, you start the movement as if you were going to fire a *meia-lua presa*, but before you spin your attacking leg you keep low and turn your torso together with your leg, engaging in a *queda de rim* (that will end in a *negativa* before you go on to the next move).

Meia-lua queda de rim.

You can use either your attacking heel or the sole of your foot to strike your opponent; your attacking leg can be a more relaxed or a stiff one, which will give you more power. Most capoeira kicks have this characteristic: you can stiffen either your calf or your thighs – or both, all depending on your objective or on the type of kick you intend to execute. For instance, for a front kick like the *ponteira*, a stiffer calf will produce a more powerful kick, whereas for a *benção*, your stiffer attacking thigh (and still your calf) with your heel will produce a very powerful kick.

The Diagonal Factor

A diagonal wheel kick, the *meia-lua diagonal* is pure lethal martial art. It is difficult to practice in a *roda* due to its element of surprise, its accuracy, and its power. Done without warning, no *Vale Tudo* fighter could withstand its force. If you do it perfectly, even if you are practicing or fighting against a more advanced capoeirista, there is a chance that you will hit your target with dramatic consequences. Against crescent or spinning kicks from any martial art, the *meia-lua diagonal* is the ideal counterattack. It is so efficient that it can be done against a boxer or a grappling specialist, with a very good chance of success.

You should start your *meia-lua diagonal* right after your opponent starts preparing his attack. Suppose he is attacking you with a *martelo* or an *armada*. Take a quick, long step forward at a 45° to 50° angle to the side of your *armada* attacker, and immediately deliver your *meia-lua* to his head. Diagram 28.3 shows how this should be done. Always be very careful. Don't try this in a *roda*, as it may be a blow against which there is no defense and cause your opponent severe harm.

Meia-lua Diagonal

In number (1), the black arrow indicates your *meia-lua de compasso* from your normal face-to-face *ginga* or zero stance position relative to your adversary. In number (2), the colored arrow indicates the sudden shift from your original position (a) to the new position, from which you will deliver your *meia-lua*

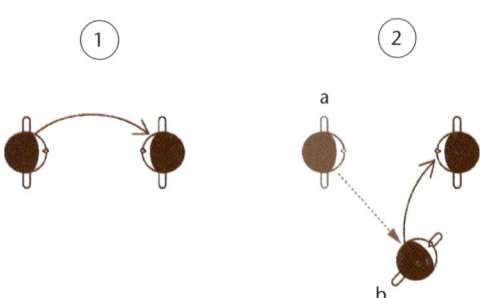

Diagram 28.3: Paths to a lethal and precise *meia-lua diagonal*.

diagonal to your opponent's head before he turns his *armada* (or his *martelo*) in your direction (b). Note the angle of your shoulders in relation to position (a). You are looking at your opponent, but your body is still in the position to which

MEIA-LUA DE COMPASSO

you had stepped up. The shorter black arrow in number (2) also shows that your *meia-lua* will actually have the same span as the regular one, except that it should strike your opponent in the center of his face at full speed and maximum strength, before losing momentum.

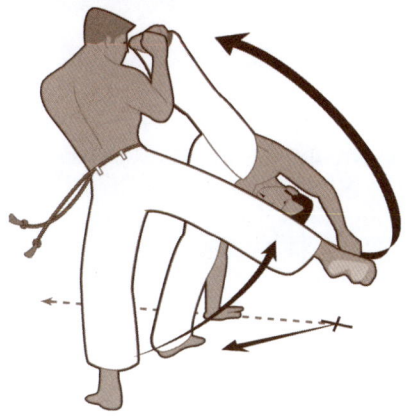

Figure 28.6: Making space for a quick *meia-lua diagonal* on the same flow and over a beginning *martelo baixo*.

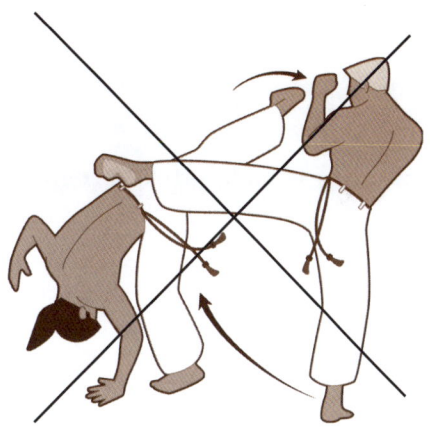

Don't row against the flow: never cross kicks in capoeira!

You can use the "diagonal factor" on many occasions, and with other capoeira moves as well. In Figure 28.7 an opportunistic *meia-lua* is delivered against an opponent who has just finished his *xangô*. This can be done with either a diagonal *martelo* or a diagonal *armada*.

Figure 28.7: Catch your opponent when he is still finishing his move, with a surprising *meia-lua diagonal*.

Practicing Alone

The three types of *meia-lua de compasso* discussed in this chapter can all be practiced on a training bag and over a chair with a short or a tall back – but not on a towel. Refer to the Introduction for more details and special tips on practicing your *meia-lua* alone to improve your techniques.

For the *meia-lua pulada*, be extra careful and make sure you have enough space before attacking the sandbag. Start elegantly at a slow pace, and increase power and speed only when you feel safe and have become used to the sandbag.

For the *meia-lua queda de rim*, simply select a point of reference, or a short obstacle, in order to practice the move to perfection.

Defenses and Counterattacks

The *meia-lua de compasso* is one of the fastest capoeira moves. It deals with several variables, including the height of the attacker's strike. As with all other capoeira techniques, always try to choose a faster counterattacking strategy according to each new combat situation.

To avoid a well-delivered *meia-lua*, the best choices are a perfect downward *esquiva lateral*, a classic *rasteira*, a *rasteira giratória*, a *rasteira de mão*, a *giro*, an inside *negativa* followed by a *tesoura,* or an outside *negativa* followed by an *s-dobrado* or a *meia-lua de chão*. A common counterattack, though, is to fire an immediate *meia-lua* over that of the attacker, if you feel you will really get him on his *meia-lua*. However, watch for the "telegraphing" aspect of most spinning kicks, as your opponent will be able to prepare a countermeasure. That is one of the reasons I always prefer the classic *meia-lua de compasso* with one hand on the ground, which gives you more flexibility, as well as an option to engage in a variety of other moves suitable for emergency situations.

Two advanced styles of *meia-lua* are excellent counterattacks if you master them to perfection – as I insist for all movements in this book. I am referring to the *meia-lua pulada* and the *meia-lua diagonal*. The *pulada* (flying) version can be delivered as soon as your adversary spins his *meia-lua,* as you would do with the classic move, but with the advantage that you can jump forward while you get off the ground to spin the kick, allowing for greater accuracy and affording a better chance of reaching your opponent's head before he tries another move. The diagonal version is probably the most efficient upright kick in capoeira. It is best done with the *meia-lua de compasso* (with one supporting hand) or with the *meia-lua solta*. These kicks are the same traditional ones, except that the *diagonal effect* is the strategic *angle* in relation to your opponent, from where you start your *meia-lua*.

Be careful with *negativas*, and do not try a *bloqueio de dentro* against a *meia-lua*. You may get caught before achieving your goal. If you want to go to the ground, be sure to master the diagonal *negativa* and the other styles of this defense technique.

Meia-lua de Frente

The front half-moon. This inside front crescent kick is a handy capoeira move. It is not a complex kick, technically speaking, but it is a valuable source of surprise attacks and an efficient typical defense weapon in capoeira. You can use it at high or medium height as an attacking kick, or as a defense and counterattack against an armed assailant, and you can also use the *gafanhoto* style, which allows you to quickly engage in a ground move after firing your *meia-lua de frente*.

Capoeiristas who do not take capoeira as a serious martial art generally overlook the *meia-lua de frente* and use it only in a *roda,* as part of their capoeira game. Make no mistake: the *meia-lua de frente* can be a dangerous and efficient weapon!

Objectives

There are distinct objectives in choosing a *meia-lua de frente* in real combat. One is to quickly attack an opponent who is moving toward you. Normally, if you are in front of him you would use a *benção*. However, if you intend to prepare for other spinning kicks, if you are diagonally in front of your opponent, or if there is more than one opponent advancing in your direction or around you, the *meia-lua de frente* could be your best bet.

The Point of Impact

As usual with high capoeira kicks, the main target of your *meia-lua de frente* is your adversary's head. However, if you are perfectly attuned with your kick, your primary target would be the region comprising the jaws, that is, the mandible and the maxilla plus the cheekbone, as shown in Figure 29.1. Your secondary target would remain the combination of the parietal and temporal bone regions of the head, as in the *armada* and most wheel kicks.

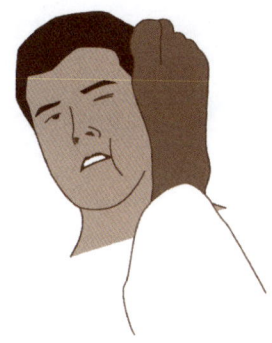

Figure 29.1: The primary point of impact of the *meia-lua de frente*.

Another important point of impact is reached by a medium or low *meia-lua de frente* quickly delivered on the leading arm of your attacker, especially if he is holding a weapon, or just to upset his balance or distract him from your next kick.

The Technique

The *meia-lua de frente* can start from your parallel legs, or from the rear leg in your *ginga* or zero stance. The best technique, though, is to step forward with your supporting foot, followed by a long, high and archlike progressive movement, where the peak power will always be at the target. You must strike with the entire inside edge of your foot, paying attention not to hit with the side of your big toe or with the side of your heel. Be sure to flex your toes up for the movement, as you do when delivering a *ponteira,* since this way you will have a stronger leg, and hence a stronger blow.

Gain extra thrust by pushing your hips forward as you fire the kick, but do not relax your arms or spread them out, as this would cause you to lose precious power and balance. The *meia-lua de frente* is a strong and strategic kick; don't underestimate it by its apparent simplicity. The right moment for it, together with the correct technique, will make the difference for you when the time comes. Figure 29.2 shows the ideal angles of a powerful *meia-lua de frente* done at medium height.

Figure 29.2: You should create a wide-open angle for firing a powerful *meia-lua de frente*.

If you choose to hit your opponent with the inside of your lower leg, make sure not to strike on hard parts, such as the head, or you could fracture your tibia. In this case, your best choice would be to hit your opponent's neck, chest or abdomen with the inside leg, anywhere from the ankle to the calf. This is a great technique overlooked by many capoeiristas, and it is best used when the adversary is in a position diagonal or perpendicular to your own, and never when he is in front of you, face to face.

In karate it is common to displace the opponent or upset his balance by hitting with the front hand on his outside front arm or wrist. In capoeira we can do that with the *meia-lua de frente* by using a technique that I like to call *shell,* in which your foot turns inward in order to provide a grip "around" the assailant's arm during the strike, as shown in Figure 29.3 and Figure 29.4.

Figure 29.3: Using the "shell" and speed to displace your opponent.

This *meia-lua de frente* done with the sole of the foot can also be a great warning "foot slap" to your adversary's face, as shown in Figure 29.4.

Figure 29.4: The sole of your foot is a handy tool in capoeira.

Figure 29.5 shows the detail of the "shell" technique of your foot position to fit the assailant's arm, almost embracing it in order to deliver the most effective *meia-lua de frente* and displace your opponent with an excellent grip. This is an efficient technique, as you don't need to get too close to your opponent and expose most of your body by using your hands to displace him.

Figure 29.5: Find the best grip by using the "shell" and speed to displace your rival.

Another point worth noting is that the faster and harder you hit his arm, the greater your leverage for retrieving your attacking leg back to the original stance. That is, your opponent's arm will function as a springboard.

After displacing the adversary with your *meia-lua de frente*, you will be able to engage in another high, medium or low kick, or in a *passa-pé* (front-foot sweep) on his forward supporting ankle by using the same "gripping" technique.

Note that you can always continue your movement forward, instead of retrieving your *meia-lua* leg back to the original stance, and choose to fire an *armada* with the other leg or a *queixada* with the same *meia-lua* leg.

The Gafanhoto Style

This is an old combination of moves, which contemporary capoeiristas call *gafanhoto* (the grasshopper). You fire your *meia-lua de frente* and finish the movement on the ground, in a *negativa de frente* (which could be a *chibata* before the landing). All is done in one complete move, as shown in Figure 29.6. You can also find an animated GIF file for this move, plus over 100 others, at www.unknowncapoeira.com.

Figure 29.6: The *gafanhoto* alternative for a strategic *meia-lua de frente*.

The Jumping Meia-lua de Frente

The *meia-lua de frente pulada*, a.k.a. *parafuso*, is a jumping version of the *meia-lua de frente*. The best way to do it is to start with a wide-open angle, thrusting your torso to the side opposite the direction of your attacking leg for a powerful *meia-lua de frente*, and going down quickly but smoothly with your attacking heel in a vertical descent, which will give you a bonus *chibata* in the end. This move is seldom used as a *chibata* or much more, just as a jumping *meia-lua de frente*, but in some *rodas* I have seen it work as a perfect *chibata*.

Meia-lua de frente pulada, a.k.a. parafuso.

Practicing Alone

Besides in the *roda* or hitting on the hands of a friend with outstretched arms, the *meia-lua de frente* can also be practiced on a training bag and over a chair with a short or a tall back. When using the training bag, be sure to hit the bag

alternating your left and right feet, as well as your left and right legs. Gauge your efforts per your teacher's or your physician's discretion, to make sure you do not hit so hard as to fracture a foot or ankle bone or damage your joints, ligaments and tendons – or so weakly as to get no results at all from your kick. Always practice safety and efficiency!

Defenses and Counterattacks

There are several ways to defend yourself against a *meia-lua de frente*. Among a number of possibilities, the *meia-lua solta,* or the *meia-lua de compasso* with one hand on the ground are great counterattacks. So is a *martelo baixo* delivered on the medial collateral ligament of your opponent's knee or exactly behind the knee. The diagonal *meia-lua* or the diagonal *armada* are also excellent choices of defense, but always remember that these dangerous kicks are not to be executed against your partner.

You can also descend on a *negativa* in order to escape the attack and continue with a *tesoura* on your opponent's supporting leg, or you can choose to work with a set of *rasteiras,* such as the *rasteira giratória,* the *rasteira de costas* or the classic *rasteira em pé,* especially if done diagonally or high, at knee level. Alternately, you can use a low *meia-lua de chão* on the opponent's supporting leg. These are your best moves, if you keep track of your adversary's action and time your counterattack with his *meia-lua de frente.*

Meia-lua Reversão

Like in a *roda,* in real fighting you may need to get your attacker on a second try if you don't get him on the first. You may want to surprise your opponent, or you may have more than one opponent during a confrontation. The *meia-lua reversão* (a.k.a. *meia-lua de coluna),* the reverse wheel kick, is an excellent strategy for getting your attacker with an open guard or even to distract him, and get back to ready stance prepared for the next adversary, especially if he is coming from behind you. If you are looking for a second strike, starting with the *meia-lua reversão* could be a great idea because this technique offers excellent flow of motion for high, continued kicks.

This said, the real benefit that this strike brings to your repertoire of capoeira movements is that it keeps you on the move through a complex and scary set of agile, flexible and rapid movements, which may even disperse your enemies before you need to engage them in a real fight.

Figure 30.1 shows a typical *meia-lua reversão* done against an *armada* – the greatest victim of spinning and aerial fast kicks, due to its distinctive open guard. Figure 30.2 shows a common practice (1) of the *meia-lua reversão* against a *meia-lua de*

MEIA-LUA REVERSÃO

compasso, where the attacking leg follows after and above the opponent's *meia-lua*. Great maneuver for a *roda*. In number (2) the timing was much more efficient, and the capoeirista waited a split second more to deliver the right *meia-lua reversão* to the opponent's head. A good maneuver for real combat.

Figure 30.1: An opportunistic *meia-lua reversão* thrust against an *armada*.

Objectives

The *meia-lua reversão* is gaining popularity in the *rodas,* as capoeira becomes more international day by day. Although new combinations of acrobatic and flexible movements do not always mean effective ones for real combat, the *meia-lua reversão* is a great technique and an excellent means for taking one or more opponents by surprise, as well as adding extra gracefulness to the *game* in the *roda*.

Because in order to perform a perfect *meia-lua reversão* you actually have to divide your concentration and power between both attacking legs – whereas in a regular *meia-lua de compasso* you have more concentrated lethal power on one attacking leg, the objective in using a *meia-lua reversão* is to reach your opponent while at the same time keeping him away long enough to allow you to prepare for another attack. The first good thing about it is that you can always do another *meia-lua reversão* after the first one. The second is that if you get your opponent at full power, you can knock him flat on the ground.

The Point of Impact

As with other styles of *meia-lua* and most high capoeira kicks, the *meia-lua reversão* must aim at the parietal and temporal regions of your opponent's head. Other points of impact, such as the neck, chest, abdomen and ribs, are also possible targets, but since the power of your kick will be split between your two legs, I do not suggest these secondary targets unless you are using this technique to scare or mislead your adversary, or just push him away.

Figure 30.2: Learn to time your moves and you will be able to choose the best effect of your strike.

The Technique

The *meia-lua reversão* is a style of *meia-lua* where a second kicking leg swings over your body after the attacking leg of the first *meia-lua*. You benefit from the use of both feet to kick alternately in a typical *meia-lua presa* spinning movement, one right after the other. Start from a standing position, from *ginga* or zero stance. After spinning the first *meia-lua*, flex your torso for the second leg to take off and kick, following practically the same trajectory, and then return to the original stance. Finish the movement with only one supporting hand leaving the ground. Be sure to stick to your attacking range area. Do not travel away with your movement. I have seen some capoeiristas begin the move in one position and finish it six to nine feet (two or three meters) away.

During the spin, keep your spinning legs as straight as possible before touching the ground. At the peak of the kick, at target level, try to keep your attacking feet stiff and locked at a 90° angle to your attacking legs, just as you do with a regular *meia-lua de compasso*.

Practicing Alone

The *meia-lua reversão* is not as compact as the classical *meia-lua de compasso*. Your attacking legs and feet tend to relax during the movement. For this reason, you have to master the movement to perfection until you feel that you can practice on a training bag. At first, focus on the bag just as a target reference, in order to practice your aim and your range area of action, and only after you are proficient in the technique should you start hitting the bag with both feet. Take your time. Practice several hundred times with both sides before actually hitting the bag graciously hard (meaning you can hit hard and still relax).

Once you feel you can hit the bag but still retain balance and total control of your movement and your strength, practice different speeds and power on the bag. Do this numerous times until you are able to keep your legs straight while hitting the bag with alternating power.

Practicing in the *roda* is always a pleasure, and, of course, I strongly recommend doing it as many times as you can. However, establishing your best balance and total control over your movement and power is only possible if you can actually "feel" the result of your work. That is what you get with the training bag, and the *meia-lua reversão* is a great example of this interdependence.

Defenses and Counterattacks

Getting rid of a good *meia-lua reversão* in real combat is not an easy task once you are within the range of your attacker. Actually, there is little you can do here, unless you have sufficient space and time to simply evade the attack. Assuming you don't, your best shot would be to dodge his attack, engaging in an inside diagonal *negativa escala* while trying to come back quickly in a classic *rasteira* to sweep his last supporting arm off the ground. However, if you do not succeed in this first attempt, try to sweep his first supporting leg as soon as he lands it firmly on the ground and before he lands his second foot. You can also try a classic *rasteira* right from the beginning, if you are fast enough not to get caught by his first attacking foot.

These are difficult techniques, and you have to be a very good athlete in order to perform them properly. The *roda* is a great place to practice them, especially because in capoeira we don't focus on hurting the person against whom we play, rather on demonstrating our skills. At the *roda,* we always prefer to demonstrate the movement without completing it, reinforcing our technical superiority or just showing our skills in a competitive though friendly environment. (Besides, in the *roda* most capoeiristas don't play the complex and most dangerous moves for real, as they tend to execute them at a distance from their partners). If your opponent cannot dodge your slowest attack, there is no reason to use your fastest one. As you notice that he follows your rhythm, you may increase speed and complexity in your next movements. Remember, each incoming attack will give you a chance to practice an evasive technique or a counterattack, and this is a great asset in your capoeira repertoire.

For more detailed information on the diagonal approach, refer to the chapter on the *meia-lua de compasso.*

Mortal de Costas

The backflip, also known as the back tuck by Olympic gymnasts. The *mortal de costas,* or simply *mortal* or *salto mortal*, is an impressive acrobatic demonstration, even more impressive than the *xangô* for most capoeiristas. Different from the *xangô*, though, the *mortal* should be executed in a single movement and is seldom used for attack, though it can be.

You know you are doing a perfect backflip when you can execute it without warning at any time and over almost any terrain, and of course, without hurting yourself!

Objectives

Great in the capoeira *jogo,* the *mortal* is a spectacular move, which can be performed at a *roda* both for decorative and for tactical purposes. In real combat, it serves as an opportunity for a quick escape or to scare your adversary, as it is also great as a warning tool. Many assailants will give up defying a capoeirista who quickly shows how skillful – and how prepared – he or she is.

The Technique

If you don't know how to do the *mortal*, don't attempt it at home or even in your backyard (actually, this is a valid advice for all capoeira moves). Find a specific place, such as a gym, with a suitable open space unencumbered by obstacles that could cause unnecessary injury. Make sure you have a proper soft mat, such as the one used in floor exercises – as well as a qualified coach. As with the *xangô*, you can also use the aid of a tumbling belt wrapped around your waist, with two straps on each side. Two partners would hold the straps and pull up when you jump back, so that you won't fall, strictly following the available technical and professional guidance. The same thing exactly is recommended for learning the *xangô* and the *mortal de frente*. This practice will build the confidence you need in order to execute spectacular acrobatic moves by yourself in the future.

However, there is one good basic training action you can do on your own, shown in Figure 31.1. For the full *mortal*, make sure you have a proper mat.

Practice the preparation jump first. From an upright standing position, bend your knees and move your arms back, and then forward and up, as a lever to help you jump as high as possible, as if you were going to reach for a fruit hanging on a branch high above and slightly behind you. You must start the move at one point and end it some three feet behind. This means you need a slight inclination when jumping backward.

Figure 31.1: Feel your jump before you tumble.

MORTAL DE COSTAS

Practicing the correct technique will help you conquer your fear, which is a natural feeling that can interfere with any successful athletic accomplishment and is nearly always present when learning acrobatic moves. If you are afraid of doing the *mortal,* don't do it! Talk to your instructor first. Discuss the problem with your peers. Study the technique and build up your internal strength first.

BUILD CONFIDENCE!

For a good *mortal de costas,* start with your arms down and your feet shoulder-width apart. You will soon move your arms back, and then forward again for momentum.

Don't ever look down. Find a spot higher than your head level. You will soon be looking for the sky during the move.

Thrust your arms back and behind you, so as to gain momentum to launch your body up into a full back flip, as you squat at an 80° angle to your knees preparing to push yourself off the ground at maximum power, with both feet.

Look up while slinging your arms back and up. At this time, your arms take control leading you up into the jump. This is a very important step. You need your arms as a synchronized lever in order to gain height for a safe jump.

When launching into your jump, make sure you burst off the ground, swinging your arms back over your head. Your arms must pull you upward. This is the time you would prefer to do the *mortal* over a resi-pit or a foam pit for extra safety.

Jump up, vertically. Do not jump or look back. You need a high vertical push before you complete the rotation. Keep looking forward, slightly up if you want to gain height.

At this point, start bringing your legs up to tuck your arms and legs in, close to your chest. This combination is exactly what you need in order to roll over perfectly. It is what we do in capoeira, in floor exercises, and in diving as well.

You can do the tucking by grabbing the front of your knees, by hugging the legs or by grabbing the hamstrings, behind the legs. I prefer to grab my knees. It's faster.

To finish the move, once you have rotated completely, extend your knees back and stretch out your legs to land fully on the soles of your feet, bending your legs again just enough to soften the impact of your weight on the ground.

Practicing Alone

Once you have mastered the technique, you can practice the *mortal* on the beach or on the floor, as long as you understand that you need to warm up adequately before doing the flip. If you want to practice on rough or irregular surfaces, you can do so if you have really mastered executing a perfect *mortal* in a buoyant and elegant manner, so as not to hurt your feet.

Make sure to practice first on a resi-pit or a foam pit for extra safety and more fun.

Defenses and Counterattacks

It's all a matter of behavior. If a capoeirista does a good *mortal* before you in a real combat, you should start to worry about what will come next! Time to recall Mestre Touro, from the suburbs of Rio. His *mortal* was (and still is) a traditional mark of his always much-welcoming *rodas*. On the other hand, if you are timed to your opponent's moves, no one can escape a good *tombo da ladeira*.

Mortal de Frente

The front flip, also known as front tuck by Olympic gymnasts. The *mortal de frente* is an easier acrobatic move than the *mortal de costas,* to be done in a single or double movement in a capoeira environment. However, make no mistake: it is still difficult to perform at perfection level, and it offers more outcomes than the *mortal de costas.*

Just as with the *mortal de costas* and most acrobatic moves, you know you are doing a perfect one when you can execute it at any time and over almost any terrain without much of an effort.

Objectives

Good for a *roda,* the *mortal de frente* is a flashy move, which can be used for both aesthetic and tactical purposes. In real combat, it is slightly more aggressive than its counterpart, the *mortal de costas,* as you can use it to jump over your adversary, delivering a powerful *chibata* with your heels on his head or upper body.

One great application of the *mortal de frente* is to execute it in the flow of motion of the *jogo* or in actual fighting, as escaping and evasive techniques. In Figure 32.1 the capoeirista is executing a *mariposa* toward his opponent, from point (1) to point (2), as either an attacking or an evasive mode.

The attentive defending capoeirista will perceive the attacker's intention. However much he tries not to, the attacker will end up "telegraphing" his *mariposa*, which needs a minimum space to be performed. By the time the *mariposa* reaches the midpoint where the defending fighter is standing, he will have escaped on a *mortal de frente* diagonally away from his attacker, from point (3) to point (4).

Note that he will be at a good distance for using a combination of *xangô* (a.k.a. *pulo do gato*) and *mortal de costas,* and still get back into action against his frustrated *mariposa* attacker.

This whole scenario also produces a beautiful flow of motion, which I have been explaining in the previous chapters.

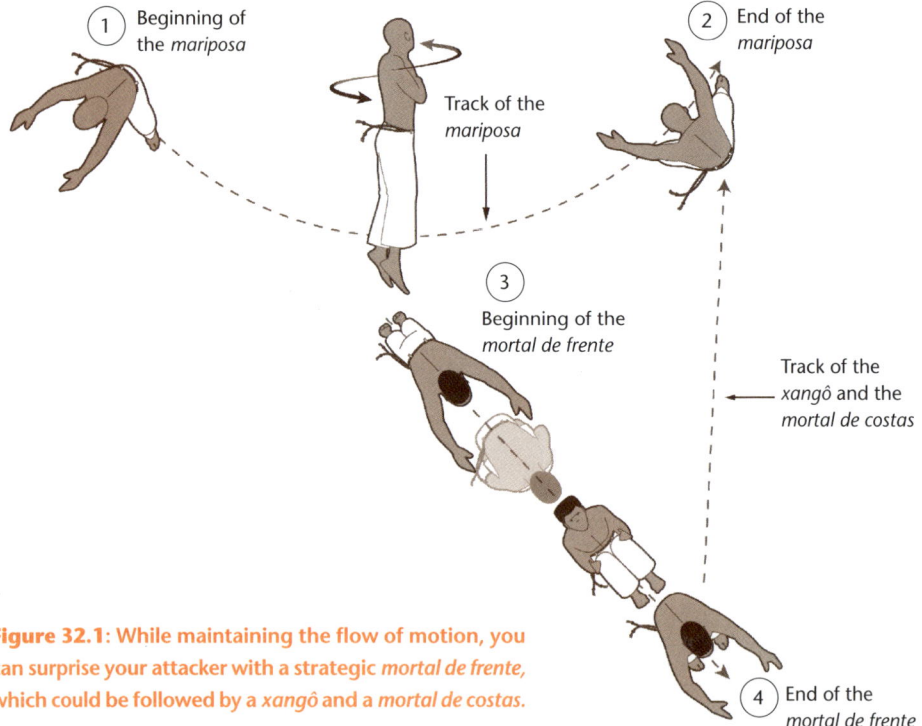

Figure 32.1: While maintaining the flow of motion, you can surprise your attacker with a strategic *mortal de frente*, which could be followed by a *xangô* and a *mortal de costas*.

The Point of Impact

When not using the *mortal de frente* for aesthetic or evasive purposes, you can come down on your adversary's head with a sort of *chibata* with the second foot of your *mortal de frente*, which landed on the first foot. With your attacking heel you will be able to get his frontal bone, his nasal bone and his lower and upper jaws. Ultimately, you will be able to reach his clavicle or his chest with your heel or with the sole of your attacking foot.

The Technique

As I recommended in the chapter on *mortal de costas,* if you don't know how to do the *mortal de frente* don't do it at home or in your backyard! Find a gym with a suitable open space, unencumbered by obstacles that could cause unnecessary injury. Make sure you have a proper soft mat, such as the one used in floor exercises, as well as a qualified coach. Use the aid of a tumbling belt wrapped around your waist, with two straps on each side. Have two partners hold the straps and pull up when you jump back, so you won't fall. Follow the technical and professional guidance. Seek safety, perfection and confidence right from the beginning.

As with the *xangô* and the *mortal de costas,* do the preparation jump as a warm-up exercise. Note that the same prep jump is used for the *xangô* and the *mortal de costas,* but the one used for the *mortal de frente* is slightly different (Figure 32.2).

Figure 32.2: Feel your jump before you take off for the *mortal.*

Starting from an upright standing position, bend your knees and move your arms back and up, and then forward and up, as a lever to help you jump as high as possible, as if you were going to take off like a rocket. Bring both knees close to your chest and quickly hug them while you are up in the air, loosening your hands to land in the original standing position. You should start at one point and end the move over exactly the same spot.

There are two types of *mortal de frente* used in capoeira. One is to take a short run to gather momentum for your jump. This is highly recommended if you are practicing alone, over a safety mat and into a foam pit. The other is to execute it from a standing position. In both cases, though, you can land on both feet simultaneously or on one foot first, using the other for a *chibata* kick, just like in a *compasso* (a.k.a. *aú chibata*).

For the running version, your first step would be to start your short run toward your *mortal*, I would say some four to six running steps before you hop.

Your last running step would be used as a trigger for landing on the ground with your feet together, seeking thrust as in a spring effect.

Bring your arms up and slightly extended behind your head, and at the same time hop with your two feet together, further than the vertical position of your head.

At this time you are still going forward, preparing to gain momentum for the vertical phase of your move.

Now jump, as if you were going to fly up and over an obstacle. Think of building an imaginary arch with your body. You want to get to the other side and land on your feet, and you don't want to land on your back!

Look ahead, slightly above your head. Don't look down, or you will abort your flight.

At this moment, when you are starting to fly toward your *mortal* with arms still extended, you must prepare to rotate during your forward lift-off. That is why you must have a perfect, powerful and high "flight." If you take too long to start rotating, you will end up short of time for the rotation. Therefore, you must rotate now, while you are still building momentum, on the same spot where you have gained altitude.

Time to tuck. Bring your arms in to hold your knees, pulling the knees together and tight against your chest. This will give you the needed rotation.

MORTAL DE FRENTE

At this time, I really hope you are practicing over a safety gymnastics mat!

When you feel that your body is coming down to a horizontal position while still in the air (i.e., when your back is parallel to the ground), it is time to start untucking. Be sure you are on a good rotation speed before you untuck, so that you pick the right time to stretch your legs back and touch the ground. Note that once you are proficient in your *mortal de frente,* you will be able to untuck one foot at a time. And if you get "really" proficient, you will be able to use your other foot for a strong vertical downward kick, an aerial *chibata.*

For a good standing *mortal de frente,* first make sure you have learned a perfect running one. The principles are exactly the same. The only difference is that in the running version we have to run and then bounce, so as to gain momentum as we take off. All you need to do is hop from your standing stance as hard as you can to initiate the move. Once you have mastered this technique, your next step depends on your physical fitness. If you have a good body with fairly strong legs, you will be able to simply leap for the *mortal de frente* from your thighs without even having to hop for the "springboard effect." You will just do the *mortal* from scratch.

Practicing Alone

Once you have mastered the technique, you can practice your *mortal de frente* on the beach, or on an appropriate resi-pit, or on a foam pit, for extra safety. However, an excellent way to improve your skills is to jump over an obstacle. Start with a cushioned object at knee height, and gradually increase the height of the obstacle until it is at chest height. Remember, you should use your arms as a guide to take off from the ground, as if you were going to fly like a missile, before you start bringing your knees to your chest.

Once you have mastered the move over these obstacles, i.e., when you have good thrust to take you off the ground, you can even increase the height of the obstacle up to your own height. However, the higher the obstacle, the greater the distance you will need to run for your *mortal de frente.*

I recommend a gymnastics spotting block consisting of vinyl covering with dense foam core, or trapezoid sections with polyurethane fillers, which can easily be mounted one on top of the other (Figure 32.3) for increased height and used as safe spotting blocks.

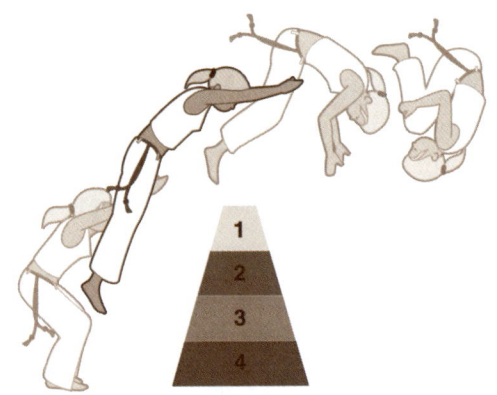

Figure 32.3: Trapezoids can be mounted one on top of the other for different heights.

I do NOT recommend using trampolines or springboards for practicing any kind of *mortal* for capoeira. These devices are much too unnatural, and the capoeirista could end up being addicted to unnecessary artificial aids. However, this is my own personal opinion, and if your Mestre or your coach believes these pieces of equipment can be beneficial, please do not hesitate to follow their instructions.

Defenses and Counterattacks

Watch for the *mortal de frente*. It can be tricky. It can be fast, and get you on the head with that second *chibata* leg. A good and elegant choice for defending yourself and counterattacking a *mortal de frente* would be to quickly step back and execute a diagonal *aú* and start all over again. If you are as quick as Mestre Preguiça used to be at the *rodas* in the *Associação dos Servidores Civis do Brasil* in Rio de Janeiro back in the 1970s, "where it all began," then you will certainly be ready for your next move before your opponent notices your intentions. On the other hand, like with the *mortal de costas* and with most aerials, if you are timed with your opponent's moves you can execute a good *tombo da ladeira*, which is not so elegant but is certainly very efficient!

Negativa

Besides being a versatile ground stance, the *negativa* falls within the concept of the moves called *desequilibrante* (to take down the opponent, to upset his balance) and *esquiva* (to dodge away from an attack). Its variability, and therefore its importance to capoeira, deserves a chapter of its own. See *esquiva* for more details on the several types of dodging moves discussed in this book.

You can drop, go, descend, duck, slide down or fade into a *negativa*. It all depends on the kind of *negativa* you need. I would risk suggesting that, strictly from the martial art's point of view, the *negativa* used at the original *Grupo Bantus* in Rio in the 60s and 70s, also known as *escala* – or what I simply like to call *descida na negativa* – is perhaps the most efficient variation in real combat situations.*

---

* Not to be confused with the hand strike called **escala**.

The *negativa* is one of the techniques that maintain the beautiful flow of motion of capoeira. It is also an important stance, from which you depart to engage in several other techniques, such as the *rolê*, the *aú*, the *s-dobrado*, the *chapéu de couro*, the *macaco*, the *meia-lua*, or even the *cabeçada*, among many others that can be connected to your current *negativa* position. An array of measures and countermeasures can arise from one *negativa*, such as changing your orientation, retreating from combat, closing in on your opponent, avoiding high kicks and misleading your adversary, using different postures and speeds.

Objectives

The main objective of the *negativa* is to protect yourself against high kicks while you "navigate" on the ground and plan a countermeasure, which could be another low or ground move, or a set of moves leading back to a standing position and then to additional combinations of moves. A timely, well-executed *negativa* can be responsible for winning a real dispute and for your success in a good *roda*.

The Point of Impact

Not an impact in a sense, but the perfect fit of the *negativa* foot on the opponent's leg is an important issue. Though this will probably happen more in a *roda*, it is nevertheless mandatory during your training sessions. Make sure to drag his leg by the ankle in a perfect fit. Even so, you will find yourself many points of impact from the combinations of moves produced by the *negativa*.

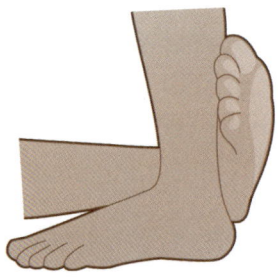
Look for a perfect fit.

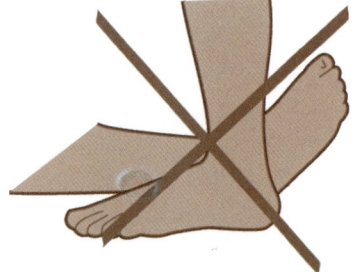
A poor posture will always result in poor capoeira.

NEGATIVA

The Technique

There are actually two groups of *negativas,* which demand rather different body mechanics. One is the *escala,* which is said to have originated in Rio de Janeiro, and the other is the *classic* group, mostly inherited from Bahia, although both groups can be seen in different capoeira schools worldwide.

You can slide down and fade into a *negativa* quickly and smoothly from your *ginga* or from zero stance, either toward your opponent (inside his guard) or away from him. One evasive and elegant *negativa* is the V-shape, a.k.a. *escala* or *descida na negativa,* where you choose to navigate practically underneath your adversary by sliding your descending, stretched leg forward (as in the illustration at the beginning of this chapter), with more pressure on your bent supporting leg, or by sitting backward, bending your supporting leg first and then leaving your stretched leg out to maneuver, supported initially by the heel. This is generally also the most efficient type of *negativa* in real combat situations, because it gives you more control over further ground navigation.

Your stretched leg would normally be lying on the ground, but it can also be slightly above it with a tenser thigh and calf and with the foot at a 90° angle, ready to connect with other moves. The toes of the outstretched leg should point outward. The supporting foot can be either on the flat sole or the ball of the foot, depending on the kind of ground navigation you choose. Keep the palm of the supporting hand on the ground. During the move, keep the other hand rather relaxed, with palm open and fingers tight and next to your head, for extra protection against surprise incoming kicks.

The backward *negativa* (*escala*).

Although many inexperienced capoeiristas don't realize it, this is a very comfortable and intimidating move. It's excellent both for the *roda* and for real combat. If you master capoeira, you can actually start any fight on the ground from this *negativa*

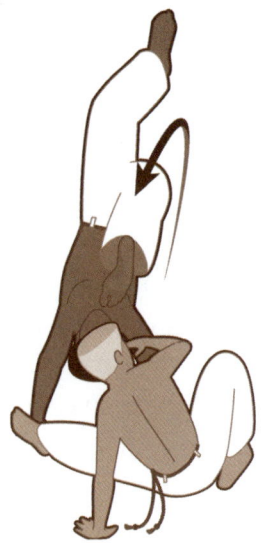

stance. When doing it, always time your descent with your opponent's move to the side, opposite the incoming kicks. However, you must always watch for kicks from up there, my friend. Do not just do reckless *negativas* all over the place, exposing yourself to your opponent's *chibatas*, as seen in Figure 33.1.

Figure 33.1: A V-shaped but careless *negativa escala*.

In the classic takedown style, the *queda na negativa,* you actually drop down or "fall" into the *negativa* when a high kick comes toward you, like a classic *martelo*, for instance, placing your outstretched leg strategically under your opponent, close to his supporting leg. Some capoeiristas call this move *negativa derrubando*. The idea is to hook your opponent's foot and pull his supporting leg toward you or a little to the outside, simply by retracting your attacking leg with the help of your supporting hands.

Unless you are otherwise instructed by your Mestre, in a real combat situation I don't particularly recommend that you actually "fall" on or "drop" down into a *negativa* because you will end up hurting your wrists. In fact, you can also execute the takedown style with grace, without the *"queda,"* and still be quite fast and timely. First of all, I expect you to be physically fit. You will need strong thighs and good knees for this maneuver. Think of a Russian polka dancer as an illustration.

What you have to do is go all the way down with your weight on your bent supporting leg, putting all the pressure on your thigh muscle while extending your takedown leg and turning to the side, where you will have both supporting hands with palms on the ground (same side as the outstretched leg). The takedown foot should be pointing outward and at a 90° angle to the shin, as in Figure 33.2.

NEGATIVA

The idea behind this technique is to be able to drop into a graceful *queda na negativa,* as quickly and silently as a cat's leap.

> **IF YOU DOUBT THAT IT IS POSSIBLE, WATCH A GOOD POLKA DANCER!**

Figure 33.2: The "takedown" *negativa.*

There are some disadvantages about this *negativa* in Figure 33.2 that are worth discussing. First, I have already said that the traditional *"queda"* into the *negativa* is not a very healthy practice; second, the bald-headed fighter is in a reckless posture, with his head too exposed, and third, he is defending himself against a *benção,* which is definitely not a good practice because he could get caught in the head by the attacker's kick during his descent.

Normally, this type of *negativa* requires that the attacker execute roundhouse, crescent or spinning kicks, such that the defending opponent can drop into the *negativa* to the opposite side, protecting his head (Figure 33.3) so as not to get hit by these incoming kicks.

Figure 33.3: Always protect your head; leg up a little and foot at 90°.

One word of advice: capoeira moves are complex and difficult to perform at perfection level, and the takedown style of *negativa* is no exception. Therefore, if you want to try it in real combat you must be pretty sure of your opponent's (lack of) ability, in order not to be frustrated with an ineffectual attempt!

Another variant of the classic *negativa*, called *negativa lateral*, originated before Mestres Pastinha and Bimba founded their Capoeira Angola and Capoeira Regional, and despite the fact that it is part of the repertoire of the good Angola schools, it is now widely used both in Capoeira Angola and Capoeira Regional. There is actually some confusion related to the takedown *"derrubando"* style, the angola style and the *negativa lateral* seen in Figures 33.4: *"Na queda de lado"* and 33.5: "Classic lateral."* The takedown *negativa* is used in all forms of capoeira – Regional, Angola or contemporary. For many masters, though, what some contemporary capoeiristas call *negativa angola* is just what they see as simply the classic *negativa*.

I have seen some nasty variations of *negativa*, such as using the fingers instead of the palm of the hands for support, a short-angle V-shaped *negativa* with an upright vertical upper body, palms of supporting hands closed or head touching the ground – none of which I would recommend within the scope of capoeira as a martial art. All the same, I do respect those Mestres who can demonstrate the usefulness of such moves in a *roda* and of course their safety as well, not to mention their beauty.

There are basically two very beautiful types of classic *negativas* besides the *escala*: you can drop on a lateral or on a front *negativa*. Both show their heritage from old capoeira. For the lateral one, you get very close to the ground with your whole body, the tips of both feet touching the ground, one leg outstretched and one leg bent, upper body and head only a few inches from the ground, supported by the hand in front of your chest and the other supporting hand behind your back, both palms wide open and touching the ground.

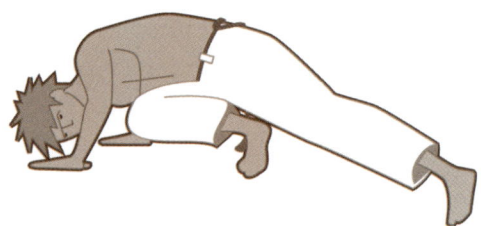

Figure 33.4: An inherited lateral *negativa* from classic capoeira.

---

* Nowadays, most capoeiristas, including this author, prefer to assume that their repertoire of movements belongs to the realm of "capoeira," regardless of the fact that one given move had its origin in the early forms of Angola or Regional.

The *negativa lateral* in Figure 33.5 shows different legwork, inverting the legs of the *negativa lateral na queda de lado* (lateral *negativa* on a side fall or side dodge) shown in Figure 33.4.

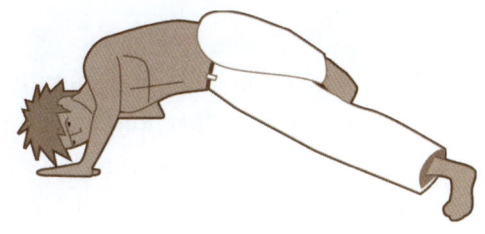

Figure 33.5: The classic lateral *negativa* with inverted legs.

There is also a subtle variation of these two types of lateral *negativa*, which is called *negativa lateral de solo*, done with the extended leg and the face actually touching the ground.

For the classic *negativa de frente*, the front *negativa* (Figure 33.6), you keep your upper body vertical, with one or both supporting hands on the ground and the toes of the outstretched leg facing up.

You have the choice of doing the front *negativa* in a more retreating manner or in a more straightforward position, ready to come back up for an attack at any moment (Figure 33.7).

From any of these forms of *negativa* you can also engage in several kinds of combinations, such as the *meia-lua presa*, *rolê*, *queda de rins*, *s-dobrado*, *macaco*, *aú*, and all their natural connections.

Figure 33.7: A tenser front *negativa*.

Figure 33.6: A more relaxed classic front *negativa*.

Troca de Negativa

The *troca de negativa* (a quick and smooth leg switch before proceeding to the next move, also changing its direction) is an indispensable strategy for capoeiristas doing a *negativa*. It is most common with the classic front *negativa*, where the capoeirista goes down into the *negativa* leaning to one side and, before engaging in another move, exchanges his *negativa* legs, inverting sides and thus the direction of his next move. This technique can be best seen in the collection of animated GIF files at www.unknowncapoeira.com.

From Other Moves into the Negativa

Almost all capoeira moves are an invitation to engage in a *negativa*. It would be redundant, and also overly presumptive, to try to include all possibilities in one book. To give you an example, I include next the sequences of the *negativa* and *chibata* and the *meia-lua* and *negativa*.* Both of these movements can be seen in the collection of animated GIF files at www.unknowncapoeira.com.

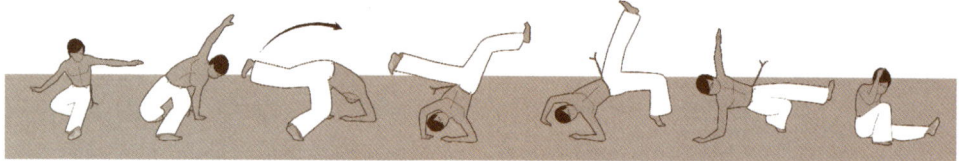

Negativa and *chibata*.

Meia-lua and *negativa*.

The *negativa* has to be seen as a capoeira stance almost as the same as a *ginga*. From the *negativa* the capoeirista can engage in a rich variety of moves, both for ground navigation and for standing maneuvers.

---

* I particularly dislike capoeira moves done over the elbow and the forearm (or the head). We see nowadays many variations of moves executed this way – and I do not recommend doing them on a hard surface.

NEGATIVA

There are really many resources you can use from a *negativa* (as well as from capoeira as a whole). I have given some examples to illustrate my own choices, so as to give you a good idea of the diversity of capoeira.

A good example of a timely *negativa* is the one used against a *martelo rodado voador*, shown in Figure 33.8. When I say "timely," I mean it! If you are always in tune with your opponent's moves, you can use the *negativa* to engage in a *martelo de chão* (you don't complete an *s-dobrado*, but just use your supporting hand to help you quickly whip your attacker the moment he lands from his aerial rotation. Your supporting leg does not leave the ground like in an *s-dobrado*).

Figure 33.8: A timely *negativa* to counterattack a *martelo rodado voador*.

From a *negativa* you can also increment your *ginga* (or you could increment your *negativa* from your *ginga*) as in the illustration below, where the capoeirista is using her *negativa* to go down and come back up, crossing her arms to protect her guard against upcoming strikes.

Sequence of *negativa* and defensive crossed arms.

Practicing Alone

All styles of *negativa* can be best practiced in the *roda* with different levels of capoeiristas. This way you will not only vary the level of expertise, but also practice different speeds and opportunities for your *negativas*. The good thing about practicing alone, though, is that you can concentrate your efforts on equalizing both sides of your move, right and left, and pay special attention to details, such as the "silent *queda na negativa*" or to the question of which combos are best from a specific style of *negativa*. Enjoy!

Defenses and Counterattacks

Actually, all styles of *negativa* are defenses and counterattack moves *per se*. Conversely, you may need to defend yourself from a tricky and sneaky opponent, such as an expert in Capoeira Angola, to mention one specific experience I had in Rio de Janeiro back in 1972.

At that time, I had the privilege of being among the large crowd of capoeiristas at the *Associação dos Servidores Civis do Brasil (ASCB)*, where every Saturday many capoeiristas from all streams gathered around a huge, free, friendly *roda*, hosted by *Grupo Senzala*, where we could see together on one evening Mestre Rafael, Mestre Gato, Mestre Preguiça, Mestre Borracha, Mestre Mosquito, Mestre Baiano, Mestre Baiano Anzol, Mestre Itamar, Mestre Gil Velho and my personal friend Mestre Peixinho – all highly respected, legendary capoeiristas.* On this particular Saturday, Mestre Camisa Roxa, a legend in himself, presented his folk group called Olodumaré, which had brought their show "Furacões da Bahia" (Bahia's Hurricanes) to Rio de Janeiro, and introduced some fine capoeiristas (including his brother, the acclaimed Mestre Camisa, whom I am proud to call my friend), into that already-rich cultural scenario.

I remember one amazing Afro-Brazilian capoeirista named Gatinho who entered the *roda* looking rather indifferent. He soon faded into a *negativa* in a slow, lazy and cunning manner. His partner followed him, trying to keep up with his agility and his special, intriguing low speed. Suddenly, as if out of nowhere, there came a myriad of spinning kicks, swirls and twists at various speeds, all low, close-to-

---

* I am sorry I can't remember the names of all the fine capoeiristas who used to play at this wonderful *roda*. To those great Mestres and athletes, my apologies and my special gratitude for the many wonderful and unforgettable evenings.

the-ground, accurate maneuvers, difficult to engineer even in the best Hollywood science-fiction computer labs today.

It was capoeira Angola at its best!

In actual fighting, in the event that you encounter such a confident fighter:

a) if you are not a very good capoeirista, RUN!

b) if you must engage in combat, be sure you fully understand which blows and kicks can be struck from low (and seemingly "slow") stances. They can be deceptively variable and catch you unaware.

> **DON'T EVER GET CLOSE TO AN EXPERT CAPOEIRISTA IN REAL ACTION UNLESS YOU ARE AN EXPERT YOURSELF!**

Ponte

Literally, the bridge. A great *floreio* while being extremely useful both in real fighting and in the *roda*, the *ponte* is an excellent way to escape some high kicks and dodge some attacks, and primarily to reorganize your combat strategy during a *jogo* or a bout.

Objectives

To make the *roda* more beautiful. To dodge a strike; to change from a ground maneuver and engage in a new action.

The Point of Impact

You may use it to deliver some *chibatas* on your opponent's head or back on your way down. It is best done with the tops of the feet.

The Technique

You can choose to go down directly from your standing position, or to squat before you turn back to reach the ground with your two hands, as if you were preparing for a *macaco*.

PONTE

To do the *ponte* you must be fit and stretched, besides warmed up – as you should be for all physical activities.

To start, stretch your arms and palms, fingers slightly together, while seeking a point vertically over your head (the roof of your school, for example). Continue the movement downward, now seeking to look at the surface behind you, until you touch the ground. Keep your arms outstretched all the way through in order to avoid hitting with your head. Keep your supporting leg as straight as possible, but bend it to your comfort zone. You may use the sole or the ball of the foot as support, though using the sole gives you greater flexibility (but it takes time and skill to reach this level).

Remember to control the power of your bridge with your thigh muscle, or else you may simply drop your weight down hard on the floor behind you, the consequences of which may not be so pleasant.

As you reach the ground, you can choose to flip right away or you can wait in the bridge position in order to engage in another ground move from the *ponte*.

Practicing Alone

The best way to practice the *ponte* is on the wall of your gym. It is a great exercise. Simply execute the movement by crawling down the wall with your hands until you reach the floor behind you. Make sure you are able to do this first. You may need the help of a friend.

When you start, look for the part of the wall that is right behind your head and then crawl down on it with your *ponte* hands. As you get used to it, you may reach for lower levels until you don't need a wall for your practice.

Defenses and Counterattacks

The *ponte* can easily turn into a *chibata* attack. For this reason, avoid being in front of one soon after your partner or opponent engages in one.

A normal technique is to use the diagonal *aú* discussed in the classic *aú* section, and elegantly get rid of his *ponte* and *chibata* threat, while you reorganize your strategy – which could include an immediate *meia-lua de compasso* or a *compasso pulado* on your opponent's head, as soon as he has finished (or while he is finishing) his aggressive *ponte*.

Ponteira

Front snap kick. There are six types: the first three are the low, the medium and the high classic *ponteira*, all of which are direct snap front kicks. In addition, there is the straight-up style, a.k.a. *ponteira esticada*, perhaps the most traditional one, used merely as a warning sign or as a threat in a *roda*; the *ponteira lateral*, which starts as a *ponteira* and finishes by striking laterally with the edge of the foot, something like a reverse *queixada* – you could even call it a fake *ponteira* or a vertical *queixada*; and the *ponteira pulada* (flying or jumping front snap kick).

As an additional countermeasure, the *ponteira* can also be used for blocking your opponent and upsetting his balance, against an *armada* or a *meia-lua*, by kicking your opponent's pivot leg or his hips when he starts to spin for his attack.

Objectives

The most important goal of the *ponteira* is to strike your opponent with precision and at the highest possible speed, without any delay characteristic of the spinning kicks, in order to take your opponent out of combat immediately.

PONTEIRA

Be aware that this kick is used extensively in real fighting. You should never complete it in the *roda*.

The Point of Impact

The perfect attacking high *ponteira* must aim at the chin of the adversary, hitting with the ball of the foot, as in Figure 35.1.* However, you must find the right moment to use the high *ponteira*, otherwise your adversary will be able to anticipate your attack and simply draw his head back, easily escaping it.

For this reason, the high *ponteira* is a very opportunistic move and should only be used if your opponent is in an inferior position in terms of reaction, proximity or balance.

Figure 35.1: Although it is a fast snap front kick, think before you choose the high *ponteira*.

Figure 35.2: A deep front kick *into* your adversary's abdomen is a harmful strike.

The medium *ponteira* must aim at your opponent's abdomen, and the kick should be delivered as deeply as possible *into* the target with the ball of the foot, as in Figure 35.2. You can also aim at your opponent's groin. Although the high *ponteira* may knock your opponent down, the medium one is the most harmful *ponteira* of its family. And that is why we seldom see in the *rodas* the full *ponteiras*, discussed in this chapter.

---

* It is easier to hit the targets with medium and low **ponteiras** because of the reduced reaction time available to the adversary and the shorter path to a closer and sometimes larger area of the body.

The low *ponteira* can be used for a powerful kick on your adversary's genitals, using the top of the foot as the striking surface, as in Figure 35.3. Alternatively, the low *ponteira* can be used for powerful kicks on your opponent's shin or knee. Refer back to the Introduction for more information on how to practice a truly powerful *ponteira*.

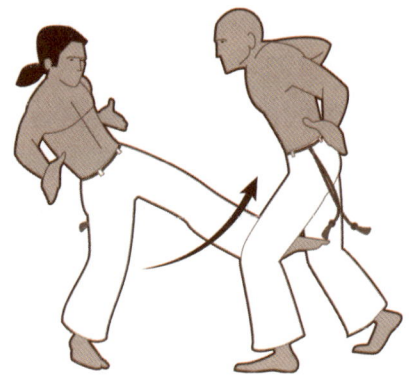

Figure 35.3: Use the top of the foot to take your adversary out of action.

The Technique

For an effective classic snapping *ponteira*, you should be in an upright position and augment your balance by inclining your upper body slightly forward to send power to your attacking foot. Keep the supporting foot of your pivot leg planted on the ground, but place more weight on the ball of the foot as you snap the knee of your attacking leg. Slightly bend the knee of your pivot leg in order to retain the ideal balance while sending power to your kicking leg. As soon as you hit your target, retract your kicking leg, bringing it behind the pivot leg to your original *ginga* or zero stance position, and get ready for the next move if necessary.

You can have both fists closed for extra leg power (you may also choose to use an *asfixiante* or two) or palms and fingers slightly open, for a more relaxed posture (and still very good leg power), if you are really in control of the situation, as in Figure 35.3.

The straight-up *ponteira esticada*.

PONTEIRA

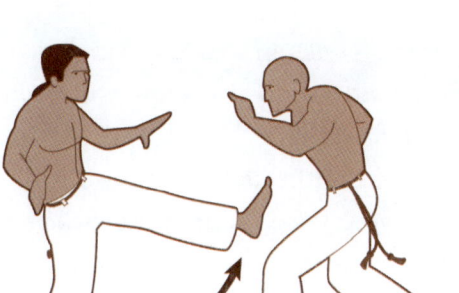

Figure 35.4: A deceptive front kick used in the *roda*.

The technique for the straight-up style (Figure 35.4) is widely used in the *roda* as a means to deceive your opponent or keep him at a distance. Yes, it can do some harm if you want, but far from the accuracy and power of the snapping *ponteiras*. You simply swing your attacking leg upward, making an arch without bending and snapping your knee, and retrieve your leg to the original *ginga* stance position.

Ponteira pulada.

For the *ponteira pulada* (Figure 35.5) or *ponteira voadora* (flying or jumping front snap kick), your power comes from the kicking leg, as you step forward with it in order to gain force to jump as high as necessary for the kick. The other leg will act as a pivot when you deliver the kick. You generally choose the flying *ponteira* when you are far from your opponent, but within a reasonable range for a surprise move. Your target may be within range of your attacking leg or slightly further away, in which case you should gather momentum to jump up *and* forward.

Figure 35.5: A timely flying *ponteira* can be very useful.

Use the *ponteira lateral* as a counterattack against a *benção*, an *armada* or a *queixada*, for example. All you have to do is fire a classic *ponteira* and just before you reach the desired height and latitude of the kick, make a short lateral arch and hit the target with the edge of your foot. At the peak of the kick, slightly shift the weight of your upper body in the direction of your target, so that the kick gets the most out of its power. This type of *ponteira* is very useful when you have little space or time to counterattack an incoming upright direct, spinning or crescent kick, or simply against an opponent who approaches you for an armed attack, a *cabeçada* or a *joelhada*, in which case you should aim immediately at his ribs (Figure 35.6).

Note that in the specific case in Figure 35.6, the (seldom-used) *ponteira lateral* is more efficient than the *benção* because it needs less space and is delivered faster.

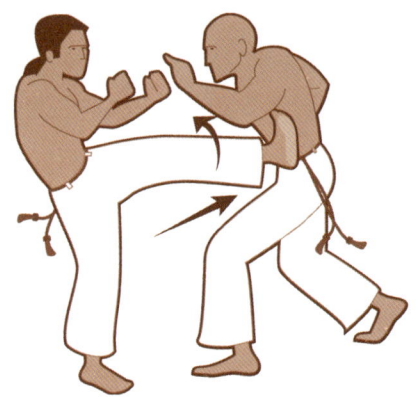

Figure 35.6: A *ponteira lateral* can be very useful if your opponent opens his guard.

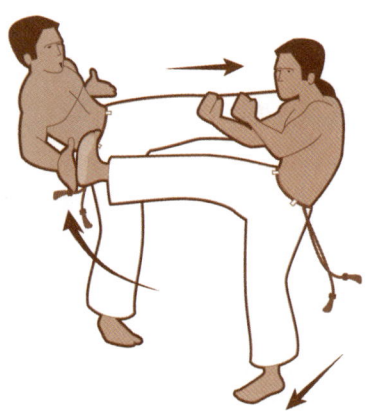

If your opponent attacks you with a *benção*, you can take a diagonal stance and use your weight in your favor to counterattack him with a *ponteira lateral* (Figure 35.7), and still use his ribs as a launching pad for retracting your attacking leg and connecting a *meia-lua* with the same *ponteira* leg, or for using the other leg to fire a *martelo* on his head.

Figure 35.7: A *ponteira lateral* against a *benção* is an invitation when your opponent has an open guard.

PONTEIRA

Practicing Alone

All styles of *ponteira* should be practiced on a training bag and on a towel. Refer to the Introduction for further details and special tips on practicing your *ponteira* alone to improve your techniques.

Ponteira lateral.

Defenses and Counterattacks

Like the *benção*, the *ponteira* is a very quick and objective capoeira move. In practical terms, little that can be done against it if it is done precisely and in a timely manner. Actually, in real combat, a *ponteira* can initiate and terminate a fight. Karate and similar oriental martial arts have their own very precise styles of *ponteira* and different ways of blocking it. In karate, for instance, *gedan-barai* and *soto-uke* are very efficient blocking motions using the arms and hands against a *mae-geri*. In capoeira, we learn escape techniques rather than expose our body to defense tactics. This may be difficult against straight attacks, such as the *ponteira* or the *mae-geri*. Nevertheless, one can always avoid a *ponteira* by stepping out of its range or stepping back from it. Escaping sideways and diagonally is also an option, and you can always engage in another move, such as a *chapa lateral*, a *queixada* followed by an *armada* or by a flying *martelo rodado*, an *armada diagonal* or an *armada pulada*. However, the magic word for a good counterattack against a well-delivered *ponteira* is **range**. If you escape from a *ponteira* but find yourself completely outside your opponent's range, you will not be able to counterattack efficiently. Therefore, you need to master the capoeira moves that leave you **outside** his *ponteira* range, but **within** an attacking range.

Luckily, capoeira offers many maneuvers that can be executed as defenses and countermeasures against a good *ponteira*, such as escaping diagonally outside your opponent's kick in order to deliver a *meia-lua,* a *chapa giratória* or an *armada* to his head. Alternatively, you can quickly step into his open guard for a straightforward *banda* or a *rasteira de costas.* If you are really fit and have mastered your capoeira moves, a strategic *meia-lua reversão* – also done diagonally – would be an excellent choice to maintain your flow of motion and the control of your body. You could then connect an *armada dupla* or a *rasteira de costas*, or go down to ground navigation.

> **AVOID MOVES THAT TAKE LONGER THAN YOUR ADVERSARY'S ATTACK.**

If you decide to go to the ground as a defense against a *ponteira,* bear in mind that once you are down on the ground, "your aim is no game," i.e., you will have to "bounce back" as quickly as possible to get your adversary; you will have to hunt him down from your ground position with the fastest combination of the fewest moves. Remember that the *ponteira* is a quick and accurate move, and if you are lucky enough to escape to the ground from one, you might as well bounce back with a good strike to immediately surprise your opponent with a sharp blow. In real combat (as opposed to the *roda* game), you cannot lose momentum and miss a strike – you may not have another opportunity.

Therefore, if you are on the ground, better be on a *negativa* and come back with an *s-dobrado* using a set of *chibatas* or a quick *martelo.* If you feel that your opponent's supporting leg is "available," make no concession and spin a quick *meia-lua de chão* or *rasteira de chão,* or a *rasteira de costas de chão,* depending on your stance.

Queda

The result of any type of efficient takedown is the opponent's *queda* (fall) to the ground. In this book I have focused separately on sweeps and takedowns. Even though there is the *negativa* takedown, meaning merely a type of *negativa*, the takedown techniques are not related to the *negativa* or the *rasteira*. They come from ancient African fighting systems, generally a mixture of wrestling, boxing and stick fighting. Also, incidentally, several techniques were mixed with other existing martial arts. Make no mistake: it is pure capoeira at its best!

Objectives

A takedown technique may have several objectives. You can simply throw your opponent to the ground, or you may need to do that and make him fall on the nape of his neck. Both are a kind of *queda*.

Many capoeiristas do not value these techniques, and some are not even aware of their existence. However, the great Mestre Bimba, founder of Capoeira Regional, created his famous sequence, which uses some of these techniques. Mestre Bimba's sequence, a historical reference, is described in a special chapter toward the end of the book.

The Point of Impact

Yes, there are some points of impact for some takedown techniques. For instance, you can use your head or your shoulder to hit your adversary on the right spot, to cause him to fall down as you planned, or you can use both your legs to strike your opponent hard on his chest to make him fall.

The Technique

The technique varies with the repertoire of moves. You will choose the most suitable one according to your distance from the opponent and based on the opponent's moves and skills. Enjoy.

Tesoura

The scissors. As with many capoeira techniques, there are two types: you can choose to catch the two legs of your adversary or only one leg, in which case you catch it from the inside. Whenever possible, choose the direction in which your opponent is leaning, in order to execute your *tesoura* and use the opponent's weight and power to your advantage. Both moves can start from the *negativa* or from a standing position.

The *tesoura* in Figure 36.1 shows a common approach, which is to grab the opponent's legs at the upper thighs, near the hips. To be successful, you should execute a good lever, using your weight in your favor. This is normally done from your *ginga,* but is perfectly possible from zero stance as well.

Figure 36.1: A high *tesoura,* catching the opponent's legs from the outside.

You can also go from your *ginga* or zero stance straight to his lower leg, from the inside. This way you get only one leg, which is called the "outside leg," i.e., the leg that indicates your opponent's direction or disposition.

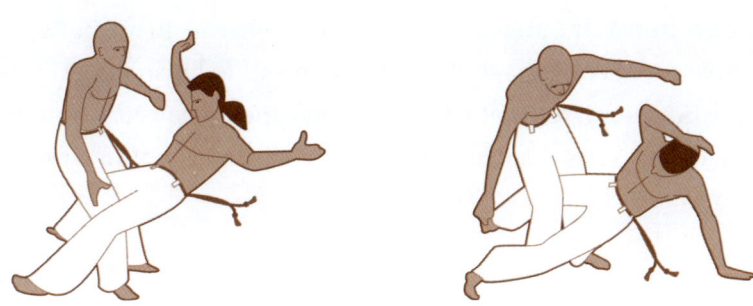

Figure 36.2: The *tesoura* catching one leg from the inside.

Figure 36.3 shows a more elaborate *tesoura*, executed from a *negativa*. This type of *tesoura* is generally executed after you defend yourself against a high turning kick, such as a *meia-lua* or an *armada*, by escaping down to the ground in a *negativa* and then coming back with your *tesoura* to catch your opponent's leg from the inside. You must be fast, though, in order to keep up with the opponent's rhythm and not lose momentum.

Take a moment to study the concept of *timing* in capoeira. Let's follow the representation in Figure 36.3 together. In (a), the black capoeirista is in a *ginga* stance – and so is the bald-headed one. In (b), the black capoeirista initiates his attacking *meia-lua de compasso*. At the same time (better to say "a split second later"), the bald-headed capoeirista goes down in a *negativa* and starts turning in

Figure 36.3: The timely *tesoura* launched from a *negativa*, catching one leg from the inside.

the same direction as the attacker's *meia-lua de compasso*. In (c), both the *meia-lua* and the *tesoura* are taking shape. The attacker needs to finish his fast *meia-lua*, but right before he does that (d), the bald-headed capoeirista gets his supporting leg with a perfect low *tesoura* and completes the technique by throwing the attacker to the ground (e).

Alavanca de Pé

The foot lever. This is a good, opportunistic takedown, seldom used nowadays. However, it is an excellent tool for a slow game in the *roda* or even in real combat, if you happen to be on the ground. The best way to execute it is when you are in a *negativa*, a *queda de três* or a *queda de quatro*. You simply use one foot as in a takedown *negativa* to grab one of your opponent's legs from behind his Achilles tendon and pull toward you, while using the sole of your other foot to push on his shin, thus creating leverage with sufficient pressure to throw him back onto the ground, as shown in Figure 36.4.

Figure 36.4: The *alavanca de pé* from a *queda de três* or *quatro* may surprise your partner in the *roda*.

Vingativa

There are some slightly different ways to do the *vingativa*. You can enter your adversary's side without much of a dodge, or simply dodge and engage in the *vingativa*. The idea is to use one fixed *rasteira* leg behind his supporting leg, while placing your elbow on your attacker's chest in order to force him down to the ground, as he launches a high crescent kick, such as an *armada* or a *queixada*. Normally, when you get to this point (of waiting for an *armada* leg to pass over your head), it is because you are sure enough of yourself to choose between a *rasteira de mão*, a *boca de calça* or a *vingativa* – whichever suits you best, once you

QUEDA

know you are in control of your timing. Figure 36.5 shows a traditional *vingativa* after a defense against an *armada*.

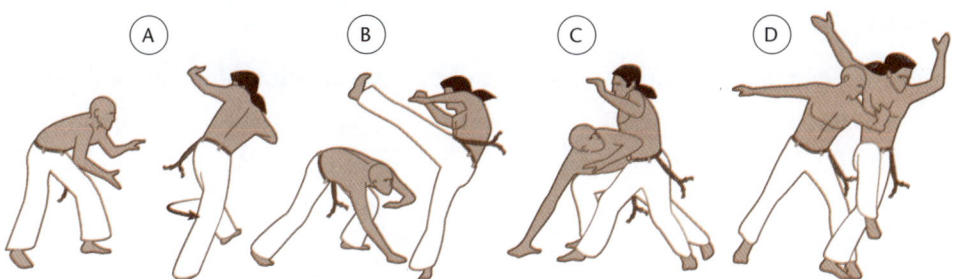

Figure 36.5: Entering a *vingativa*.

Arrastão

A takedown where you move in closely, under your opponent's guard, shoulder to his chest, grab his thighs and throw him to the ground (Figure 36.6). If you pull hard and high, the assailant will most probably hit the ground with his skull.

This technique is normally used as a defense against a punch thrown at your head. You can execute it from the *ginga* or from zero stance.

Watch for your opponent's intention, and when you notice that he is going to throw a direct punch at you, go for his legs at the back of his knees, with your head facing the other side of his attacking arm. Assume a good posture, so as to give yourself a solid base, and grab his two legs firmly, quickly pulling them toward the side of your ribs while using your shoulder to push his body vigorously down to the ground.

Figure 36.6: You may choose to execute an *arrastão* against direct punches.

If you execute the move at perfection level, the assailant will fall down heavily and you will have time to escape the "scene of the crime" elegantly in an *aú*.

Cabeçada Baixa

There are several types of *cabeçada* (headbutt) in capoeira. Some are extremely traumatizing moves, while the function of others is more to upset the opponent's equilibrium. These next two *cabeçadas* are efficient takedown moves and are very good for the *roda*.

The *cabeçada baixa* (low headbutt) in Figure 36.7, is a simple move that the capoeirista can execute on someone performing an *aú*. From *ginga* or from zero stance, all that the attentive capoeirista has to do is turn sideways, almost parallel to the *aú*, at the moment the opponent starts the cartwheel, and throw a lateral *cabeçada*, or, if you prefer, just go straight with your cabeçada at a 90° angle to his *aú*.

Figure 36.7: A *cabeçada baixa*.

Normally executed in a *roda*, this *cabeçada* is intended to upset your partner's balance (he will probably fall on an *aú dobrado*, a *queda de rim* or something similar).

Cabeçada de Chão

The ground headbutt (Figure 36.8) is used more in the *roda* as a *floreio*, or a demonstration of the capoeirista's intelligence, delicacy, timing and accuracy. It is also extensively used in Capoeira Angola. Once Mestre Adilson (Camisa Preta) and I were talking about dogs at *Grupo Bantus* in Rio, and we started discussing animals and martial arts, like kung fu (wushu), judo, and capoeira. That was an unforgettable afternoon. I had arrived at our capoeira school early, and my dear master was cleaning the premises, preparing for class – which was to begin a few hours later that evening.

We talked about how nature had inspired the earlier martial artists and founders. He told me about the tumbleweeds in the desert and the *aú*, I mentioned the subject of heavy snow on the strong and the weak branches of a tree, and we continued talking about the influence of nature in martial arts and the origin of the Brazilian names of capoeira moves (the *rabo de arraia*, the *meia-lua*, the *macaco*, the *s-dobrado* and many others that are worthy of a book of their own).

We also discussed the several types of *cabeçadas*, and Adilson suggested that very old warriors in ancient Africa could have been inspired by the crocodiles, the rhinoceros, the zebras and – surprise! – the quadruped puppy mammals that butt their mother's breasts with their heads in order to get more milk.

Figure 36.8: The *cabeçada de chão*.

Vôo do Morcego

The flying bat. Don't ask me why the heck they call it a "bat," but the fact is that a well-executed and surprising *vôo do morcego* will most certainly knock you down in no time. Believe me, I have seen it.

You don't need to run to do it. What you do is take a large step forward to quickly thrust your second leg up into the air (which will actually be your first leg in the air), with your weight concentrated on your target. You can hit with your heels, or with the flat soles of the feet (which will cause less damage to your adversary), or use the balls of the feet to hit-push your opponent instead of knocking him down mercilessly.

Figure 36.9: Watch for the *vôo do morcego* on your slow, open guard.

Practicing Alone

Apart from general and stretching exercises, and from exercises for flexibility, all professionally guided, the takedowns need to be practiced with a partner in order to be effective. For instance, you can't practice the *tesoura* by yourself. Instead, practice with your partner on an appropriate mat, taking turns until you both feel you can execute perfect low and high *tesouras*.

Defenses and Counterattacks

There are many techniques that can be used against a capoeira *queda* provoked by your adversary.*

Defending against a *tesoura* may seem simple, but it is not. Nowadays, it is easy to see good *rodas* with successful *tesouras* everywhere on the planet. The problem is that when you see a *tesoura,* it is generally too late for an efficient response. Therefore, if you are caught by one, firstly, do not swim against the current, but instead, go with the flow and try a *queda de quatro* to commence your reaction.

Now, for the *alavanca de pé,* go back to Figure 36.4 and take a look at the man's right leg. Notice that he has this leg back, as a base which he can use against (or at least, delay) her attacking *alavanca de pé*. In a continuum, if you were this man, you could simply "accept" her *alavanca de pé* and go down on a *negativa escala,* trying to draw back your left leg and start your counterattack response.

If you have to defend yourself against a *vingativa,* you will need a *saída da vingativa* (literally an "exit" from the move). You can easily accomplish that once you are a more advanced capoeirista, by simply going around and over his attacking leg (actually using his thigh for support) when he tries to complete the *vingativa*. Otherwise, you can choose to escape the *vingativa* by engaging in a *negativa* and a short *rolê*. Simply extend your back leg (in Figure 36.5 that would be your left leg) forward, while going down in a *negativa escala* the moment your opponent tries to go around you and escape outward and to your left by doing a quick *rolê*

---

* Do not confuse the concept of **queda** (a fall provoked by your opponent) with the **queda de três** or **queda de quatro,** which are **quedas** that you choose to do as a type of **esquiva.**

to get back to the *ginga* stance. You can also use the *tesoura* on either of his legs for a classic escape, going forward with your right leg under his right leg, or back on his left leg to begin your *tesoura.*

For both the *arrastão* and the *vingativa,* you can use your closest hand to force your opponent's back downward, so as to prevent him from concluding the movement. Follow it with a *joelhada* on his head as a complementary move. For the *arrastão,* you can also use both hands to force the opponent's back downward at the same time you extend one of your legs as hard and as far back as possible, so that he cannot grab both of your legs. In that case, though, you will still have the advantage of using a *joelhada* on his head.

Of course, you have to be careful with a *cabeçada* in the *roda,* but being attacked with one in real combat is no fun at all...

I have fainted twice in my life. The first was when I was still a capoeira student, teaching a friend in my backyard. Since he was inexperienced in capoeira, I was always too close to him, trying to guide him. He struck a powerful *cabeçada* on my nose, by accident. One of those incidents that is not really incidental if you are not exactly qualified to teach! I described the second time in the *esquiva* chapter.

The *vôo do morcego* is something of a telegraphing move. Use your repertoire of *esquivas,* and do not go on a *negativa* if you happen to be attacked by one. In this case, the best procedure is to do an *esquiva* to the back of your opponent's attacking leg (in Figure 36.9, to your left, behind the female capoeirista's flying legs) followed by a quick *aú* in order to maintain control of your stance and start all over again, or else get her when she lands with a surprise *compasso pulado.*

Playing capoeira in a *roda* is great fun, but sometimes we face certain challenges when we meet someone better or more experienced than us. Those challenges are greater still when your partner wants to play "for real." When this happens, and we are playing within striking range – as must be the case in a good capoeira game – things may get pretty rough, and you must be especially aware of the *rasteiras, bandas,* and other takedowns.

Queda de Rim

The kidney escape is a beautiful and traditional *floreio*, as well as a strategic move that can be executed from a variety of techniques, such as an *aú*, a *rolê* or even a *meia-lua*, to name just a few. It is also a great technical resource that can be done at different speeds and for different purposes. Primarily, it is really a *floreio* and an escape; however, it can be unexpectedly turned into a low attacking weapon, like when you use a *martelo* to surprise your rival. Here we show an initial *aú* followed by an escaping *queda de rim*.*

Objectives

Definitely a tactical move. On the other hand, if you add the low *martelo* it can be harmful if delivered on your opponent's head. Nonetheless, "surprise" is really the magic word. Used as a tool for trickery and for a quick defense – where you can show your opponent you are resourceful in capoeira moves, the *queda de rim* can be very efficient.

---

* Many capoeiristas call this move *"queda de rins,"* which is not the correct form, since we fall on only one kidney (*rim*) at a time.

QUEDA DE RIM

From the *queda de rim* you can connect to many other moves.

Queda de rim and *martelo de chão*.

The Point of Impact

You have to be a fit and attentive capoeirista to execute a perfect and quick *queda de rim*, or the point of impact will be your own head hitting the ground! As for the "extra bonus" *martelo de chão*, your natural target will be the head or anywhere on your opponent's upper body.

The Technique

Start your *aú* and support your body weight while dropping slowly down onto your elbow, which will now be supporting your upper body from under your kidney with the help of your other supporting arm. Doing the *queda de rim* with only one arm is useless as a real combat strategy. You would feel like an uncontrolled propeller. Use both hands for support and retract both legs, knees together, ready for the next move.

Don't lean or place your head on the ground. This may be decorative for street exhibitions of capoeira, but is definitely not recommended if you don't want to risk hurting your head.

Once you are steady on the *queda de rim* and watching your opponent's action, you can use your legs as a lever for a good low *martelo*, done either with the top or the ball of the foot, as in the illustration above, or for a *chapa*. These kicks can be highly efficient against a distracted opponent trying to approach you with an *aú* or other low, sneaky moves.

Here the *martelo de chão* works like the porcupine's hiding technique, i.e., at first you show a strictly defensive action, only to surprise the adversary who is approaching you and counting on your apparent inactiveness. Great Mestre

Adilson told me that this move might have been inspired by African snakes in their characteristic waiting state, when they are actually ready to attack – if you insist on getting too close.

Normally, you get out of the *queda de rim* by engaging in a *negativa* followed by an *s-dobrado* or a *macaco,* or by executing a more contemplative *ponte* in order to continue in a waiting mode while planning your next move. Don't worry, sometimes you'll look like a contortionist, but these low moves and transitions are the secret of highly efficient and shady unique capoeira moves that can win a fight.

It is time to remember that in contrast to the objectives of a *roda,* for the purpose of real fighting using your capoeira knowledge, every capoeira move must be highly technical and provide for the perfect escape and/or the perfect kick. There is no space or time for unnecessary maneuvers.

Two great *floreios* that could turn into dangerous weapons.

Practicing Alone

Simulating the *queda de rim* and its several connections in front of a mirror is a great way to improve your technique. The training bag is also an excellent companion. When I was teaching in Rio, I had one in my bedroom – which was really more of a compact martial art studio – with different levels of height for the steel chain on the ceiling hanger. This way I could lower the bag any time I wanted to practice low kicks and movements with it. I also had a wall mirror with which to practice most movements, correct posture and improvement. And I also had a great dog, Igor, who used to get in the way while I was practicing!

Practice your "dive" so you can do it at different speeds. Control of speed, extent and intensity of moves are indispensable assets to the serious capoeira athlete.

Defenses and Counterattacks

If a capoeirista ever challenges you in real combat with an apparently inoffensive *queda de rim,* you will probably already be in the midst of a move of your own, and he most likely wants to draw you near him. Unless he is a total moron, he will not do a passive *queda de rim* and find himself vulnerable just for the heck of it.

This means that if you are in the midst of an *aú,* for instance, use your *chibatas* or do an *aú fechado* to protect yourself against your opponent's connecting moves, such as the low *martelo*. You can always make a transition from your *aú* to an *aú dobrado* and evade your opponent's kick.

If he tries an *s-dobrado,* be quick enough to sweep his supporting arm or push him away with your *chibatas* or with a low *chapa* to his chest.

Queixada

A chin kick, the *queixada* is an outside front crescent kick, which can be done after a dodge to the side of the opponent or directly from a stance, such as in the *meia-lua de frente* technique. You could say that the *queixada* is a "half *armada*" or a "reverse *meia-lua de frente.*"

The *queixada,* likewise the *meia-lua de frente,* is a handy capoeira move. It is not a difficult kick, technically speaking, but it is a valuable source of lateral and diagonal attacks and counterattacks, best used high, at head level, for optimal leverage and power.

It is very common to see capoeiristas of all levels using the *queixada* in a *roda.* It gives leverage and thrust to several other kicks and techniques, and for this reason is a very aesthetic movement. However, believe me, the *queixada* can be a destructive weapon in the feet of a capoeira expert.

Objectives

There are several objectives in choosing a *queixada* in real fighting, if you are standing in an upright position. The most common is to dodge to the side of

QUEIXADA

your opponent's straight kick, such as a *benção* or *ponteira*, and come back with a *queixada* before he can evade it. As I said, this is a common approach. An uncommon though efficient *queixada* can also be delivered opportunistically on the back of your opponent's head.

As with other high spinning kicks, you can use the *queixada* in real combat against more than one opponent as a stand-alone kick, or in a combo as a great launching pad for an *armada,* or after a *meia-lua de frente*. Using it from a diagonal standpoint in a combination of techniques will allow for more strategic targets, such as the nape of the neck or the face of a distracted and dangerous adversary.

The Point of Impact

The anticipated target of a *queixada* is your opponent's head, in the region that comprises the lower and upper jaws, as in the *meia-lua de frente*. The best point of impact, though, is the back of the head of a distraught adversary. This means you were able to dodge to his side and have positioned yourself strategically – diagonally or directly behind him. You may or may not hurt your foot if you are barefooted, but hitting on the back of his head may be your best chance to overpower more than one opponent.

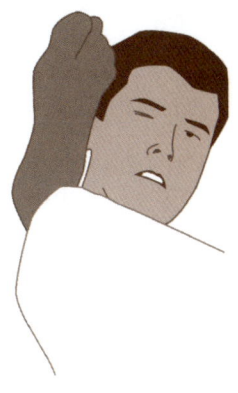

The *queixada* attacking foot.

The Technique

The *queixada* should start from your rear leg (the *queixada de trás*) or from the leg that has advanced to the side of your opponent. Either technique will be effective if you choose the one that best suits your distance or strategy. If you start from your rear leg, directly from the original stance, execute a long, high, arch-shaped progressive movement, where the peak power will always be at the target. Keep your body straight, and gain extra thrust by flexing your torso in the direction opposite that of your starting *queixada* leg, in order to offset your weight and maintain your balance. Keep your attacking leg straight all through the movement. Strike with the outer edge of your foot, which must be at a 90° angle to your attacking leg. Bring your attacking leg back to the original stance.

Queixada de trás (coming from the rear leg).

Should you choose to dodge to the side of your opponent, first start turning both arms, bent at the elbows at a 90° angle, followed immediately by your attacking leg and body until you are parallel to your opponent's shoulder. Step in with your pivot leg to create leverage for your kick, and deliver your *queixada* high and at a wide "half-moon" angle until your attacking foot is in *ginga* stance, behind your pivot leg. Do not take your eyes off your adversary during the movement. Note that your arms should always be as high as your head and ready for action if necessary.

In both styles, keep your attacking foot at a 90° angle to your leg till you complete the movement.

Practicing Alone

An excellent way to practice the two styles of *queixada* is by hitting a training bag and over a short-backed chair and a high-backed chair, just like when training with the *armada*. Alternatively, if you are not in the *roda*, you can practice on the hands of a friend, whose arms shall be outstretched.

Another effective way to improve your *queixadas* with a friend is through the combination of *benção* and *queixada*, where your *queixada* leg will be outside your partner's *benção* leg (if he executes his *benção* with his right leg, you do your *queixada* with your right leg). Practice extensively with both legs, seeking perfection, until you have the sensation that you can watch yourself in slow motion, no matter how fast your legs are moving. When you get to that point, you will be able to improve your techniques.

Defenses and Counterattacks

If the *queixada* comes as a telegraphic move, a good *rasteira em pé* will do the trick. If possible, a good counterattack would be going down on your rival's supporting leg for a *rasteira giratória*. Be sure to free your head while spinning. Although this technique can be too time-consuming, it would be the perfect defense.

An alternative and rather easy countermeasure would be a *rasteira de costas,* done from your upright standing position. The advantage is that you will lose less time to engage in the counterattacking procedure, but be aware that your head would be at stake.

Last but not least, there is always the possibility of firing an immediate *meia-lua solta* or a *meia-lua de compasso* with one hand on the ground, as efficient counterattacks against a *queixada*.

Remember to time your counterattack with your opponent's movements. On the one hand, this is not an easy task, since he will do his best to surprise you in a real fighting situation and get you on his very first try. On the other hand, capoeira is all about synchronization, timing and flow of motion. Training hard and seriously is one of your missions; studying in order to develop your capoeira is another. I believe there are a number of good books that discuss the several aspects of capoeira. "Go for it!" Read and practice. There was a time when we couldn't find good reading material on capoeira. That's long ago now.

Rasteira

Capoeira is very rich in sweeping techniques. Sweeps are a trademark of this Brazilian martial art. Having said that, one could consider the *rasteira* as its most prominent representative – the "logotype" itself. In this chapter we will deal with several kinds of sweeping techniques, called *rasteira, banda, passa-pé* and *boca de calça*.

The classic *rasteira* can be both the standing and the ground forward sweep, like the classic one that opens this chapter. To many people in Brazil, capoeira was first known by its *rasteira*. The ability to sweep the supporting leg of a moving assailant, or of another martial artist, in a great many situations was seen as an amazing feat and as an exquisite move at a time when Oriental martial arts were more of a mystery, a novelty, in the West.

For the capoeirista, the *rasteira* is almost an institution. There are several classes and many different situations in which you can use one to actually end a fight, or give your advanced though impertinent student or partner an unforgettable lesson in the *roda* (in which case, you should make your best effort not to be a presumptuous capoeirista yourself, and make sure you do not hurt your student or partner).

RASTEIRA

There are several distinct techniques: standing or ground sweeps, and forward or back sweeps, all of which can be done with a foot grip (the *rasteira* type) or with a kick (the *banda* type). There are some schools that prefer to call *rasteira* only its ground versions, and banda all the other standing ones.

Objectives

Most capoeiristas think the *rasteira* is used to sweep the supporting leg of an opponent. Very well, this is true. However, what many don't know is that it can be used to sweep the legs **and** the arms of your adversary. Nevertheless, do not execute a full *rasteira* in the *roda,* unless you are sure that your partner will defend himself and get out of your trap soon enough not to get caught.

A good *rasteira* must be capable of taking your opponent down by sweeping one or both of his legs off the ground, or one or both of his arms, and even his supporting leg and his supporting arm at the same time.

The Point of Impact

For the *rasteira,* you don't have a "point of impact" as long as you don't transform your move into a *banda* (which is a quick-kicking *rasteira*). However, you have to look for a perfect grip, as shown in Figure 39.1.

Figure 39.1: Go for your *rasteira.* Get a good grip!

On the other hand, when doing the *banda* you will actually hit your target with the top or the sole of your foot, with your heels or with the Achilles tendon.

The Technique

For a perfect *rasteira,* you need a keen sense of time and excellent agility. In addition, you need the best grip, so that you do not miss your attempt. The "takedown" *negativa* is a good example of how to fit your foot on your opponent's lower leg for a good *rasteira* grip. Here are the techniques for all *rasteiras* and *bandas*:

Rasteira

For the classic *rasteira*, a.k.a. *rasteira baixa* – or what I prefer to call *rasteira de chão*, the ground sweep – suppose a high rotating or crescent kick comes your way from the left. As with the *rasteira em pé*, you bend down to the right immediately (which is an "automatic" *esquiva* from your opponent's attack). You are now starting your *rasteira*. Keep your weight over your right (supporting) foot while reaching for the attacker's supporting leg with your left foot connecting behind it, as shown in Figure 39.2.

During this stage of the move, place your right hand on the ground, palms completely flat, for support and balance. This hand will also work to augment the leverage for the *rasteira*. Your right knee should now point away from your target and your *rasteira* leg should be outstretched, with the toes "grabbing" your opponent's leg from behind.

Figure 39.2: Fitting your *rasteira* on his *armada*.

Use your left arm for protection, as you do with the *cocorinha* or the *esquiva*. Feel the grip of your *rasteira* foot on your opponent's Achilles tendon and pull hard. Your power should come from the *rasteira* foot at a 90° angle and from your calf.

At this point, if you want the traditional *rasteira de chão*, extend your right arm as far as possible over your head to place your other hand on the ground for ultimate control. This will create leverage for your *rasteira* leg to swing around until the end of the move.

Again, be careful if you want to use a *rasteira de chão* against a good *benção*. Use the best of your *esquiva* technique to first get out of the kick, while you quickly

RASTEIRA

position your *rasteira* on his supporting, pivot leg. Your *rasteira de chão* will be like the one shown in Figure 39.3, and your opponent's fall will be a spectacular – and dangerous – one. **Do not** use this technique for real in a *roda* or with your friends!

Figure 39.3: You can escape either to the outside or the inside of his attacking leg.

Figure 39.4: Dodge and go for a *rasteira* without getting caught.

Always keep in mind that, to engage in a *rasteira* against a capoeira efficient kick, you must escape the attack with a good *esquiva* while at the same time invading the opponent's guard in order to apply an efficient *rasteira*. The *meia-lua de compasso* is one great example of this combo technique, as shown in Figure 39.4. If your opponent observes your intention to engage in a *rasteira* (i.e., if you are that slow) against his wheel kick, he will be able to change his strategy and lower his *meia-lua* leg, or adopt a new stratagem to foil your countermeasure.

Before executing a *rasteira,* be sure to time your movements with those of your opponent. You need perfect timing to find the right gap in order to use a successful *rasteira de chão*.

It's common for a capoeirista to learn to "always move in the same direction of an attacking rotating kick," which is, in fact, a good motto. However, it all depends on the timeliness of your response and on your distance from the opponent. Taking this advice into consideration, you could then use your ground *rasteira* and your skills against an opposite rotating kick.

As you have already noticed, capoeira has endless technical resources, which provide for a continuous flow of motion both in the *roda* and in real fighting.

However, the fact that you could engage in a *rasteira* against a *meia-lua de compasso* does not mean you are going to be entirely successful – and you must be aware of that!

In the example shown in Fig. 39.5, the attacking capoeirista almost accomplished his *rasteira*, but the opponent felt his *rasteira* foot at the last second, still in time to use his two *meia-lua presa* supporting hands in order to roll over to a *negativa* and avoid the imminent fall.

Figure 39.5: Your opponent may be better than you think. Always be ready to continue the flow of motion.

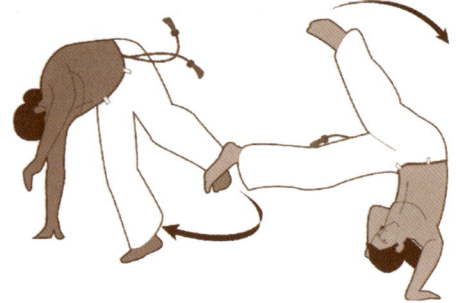

Figure 39.6: Executing a classic *rasteira* against a *martelo preso*.

For low circular kicks, such as a low *meia-lua presa* or a *martelo preso*, you can use your *rasteira de chão* to move inside his guard and sweep both his supporting hand and foot, as shown in Figure 39.6, now to the left. Always be sure that your timing is right.

Rasteira Giratória

A ground back sweep. Very efficient when done well, the *rasteira giratória* (a.k.a. *rasteira de costas de chão*) functions like the *banda*. It has more or less the same power and will do the same damage. The advantage is that you are low, close to the ground, and thus less vulnerable than when you are standing tall; this is because you have less physical mass exposed to an eventual attacker's strikes. You can choose using a *rasteira giratória* for a takedown technique, instead of a standing *rasteira de costas*, a regular *rasteira* or *banda,* if you sense the opportunity and if your timing is right.

Rasteira giratória.

The *rasteira giratória* functions like a very low *meia-lua*, as shown in Figure 39.7. You must hit your opponent's supporting leg with your Achilles tendon just above your heel, as in the standing *rasteira de costas*. If you time your movement with that of your opponent, you can go down for the *rasteira giratória* the moment he starts rotating his *armad*a (1). If both of you are quick, chances are that you will succeed in getting his supporting leg when he passes his *armada* attack over your low, counterattacking body (2). Note that the entire combination should be executed in a split second.

Keep in mind that, like the *banda*, the *rasteira giratória* is a dangerous and violent counterattack against your adversary's high spinning kicks.

One special advantage of the *rasteira giratória* is the fact that you can use your supporting hands to quickly execute another ground move, such as a *bananeira*, an *escorpião*, an *aú*, a *queda de rim* or a *ponte*, to mention a few common options.

Figure 39.7: A timely *rasteira giratória* against an *armada*.

To sweep an opponent doing a quick *benção,* position yourself under his guard, always outside his pivot leg, as shown in Figure 39.8. As capoeira is a creative art, full of resources, it is possible to use the *rasteira giratória* performed from the inside of his attacking *benção,* but if you think of real fighting, that it is not the most advisable technique.

Figure 39.8: It is rather difficult to execute a *rasteira giratória* against an efficient *benção.*

Relógio

The *relógio* (literally, the clock) is an eclectic move that can be considered as a *floreio,* an attacking low *meia-lua* or an efficient back *rasteira.* Its versatility allows you to come from a *queda de rim* and engage in the *relógio.*

Although it looks like a difficult move, its complexity derives from a rather easy leverage effect, which is a mechanical impulse to rotate over the base formed by the *queda de rim.* If you come from a rotating move, such as a low *meia-lua* or from a *rasteira giratória,* for instance, then rotating for the *relógio* is even easier, as long as you know how to do the *queda de rim.*

A timely *relógio,* if done under your opponent's guard, is an extremely efficient, as well as beautiful, sweeping move.

Relógio.

Corta-capim

From the *negativa* you can start a *corta-capim* (cutting grass), as shown in the next page, which can be both a *floreio* and an offensive sweep. In addition, the

RASTEIRA

corta-capim can also serve as an excellent, "trampoline" for transition from the ground to a standing position.

The technique for the *corta-capim* is an easy one once you are physically fit. From a *resistência*, or any other kind of *esquiva*, or from a *negativa*, you start to rotate your outstretched leg like a propeller under your supporting leg, switching your supporting hands in order to maintain balance while your rotating leg is still moving. You can see both the *relógio* and the *corta-capim* at www.unknowncapoeira.com.

Corta-capim.

Rasteira em Pé

For the *rasteira em pé*, done from a standing position without putting your hands on the ground, always be sure to come in fast toward your target (the lower leg, on the Achilles tendon, a little below the soleus muscle of the calf or slightly above the ankle). Make sure you "grab" his leg with your toes turned up, with a firm foot and leg. The moment you touch his defenseless supporting leg, reduce your attacking speed to a gentle touch, so that you have time for the right grip. Then, all in a split second, resume your *rasteira em pé* at high speed and with good power for sweeping his foot off the ground. This must be a quick though elegant move. People must not notice that you actually have time to think and fit your foot onto your opponent's leg before doing the sweep.

The *martelo* is perhaps the most classic opportunity for a *rasteira em pé* executed by an attentive capoeirista. There are two efficient ways to execute a perfect move: the *direct* and the *diagonal* one. Figure 39.9 shows the direct approach, where the attacker delivers his *martelo* to the opponent's head while the latter is leaning to the side of his supporting leg in order to grab-and-sweep it off the ground.

As soon as he comes at you, you enter his guard. See Figure 39.11 and Diagrams 39.1 & 39.2 for the diagonal approach.

Watch for the speed of his *benção*, though, as he may get you before you can execute your *rasteira em pé*.

Figure 39.9: Sweeping the supporting leg of a *martelo* attacker with a *rasteira em pé*.

Study Your Approach:
Analyzing an armada attack vs. a rasteira

The classic *rasteira em pé* must begin when the attacker starts turning to spin for his *armada*. You must time your movement with his from your *ginga* or from zero stance. Position yourself for the *rasteira*, entering with your counterattacking leg

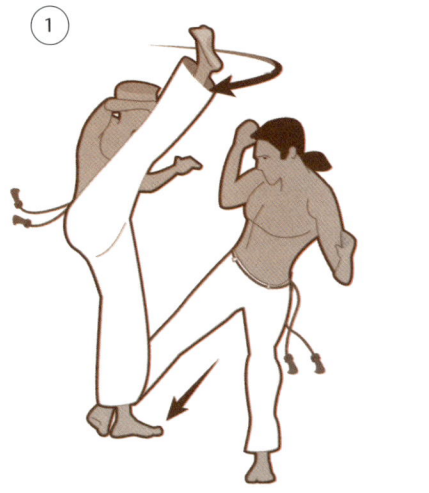 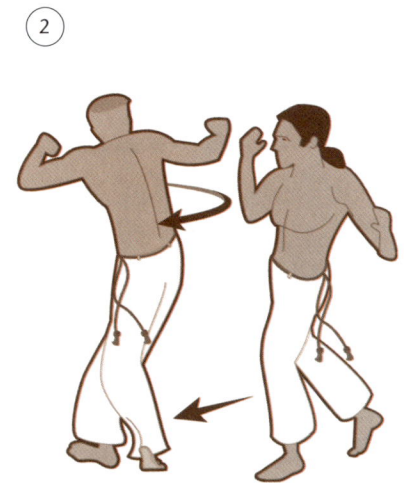

Figure 39.10: Two ways to enter his *armada* guard for a *rasteira em pé*.

inside his guard, on his outside supporting leg at the moment he passes his foot over your lowered head. Feel your foot fit perfectly behind his lower supporting leg while watching your opponent's *armada* pass by, as shown in Figure 39.10, number (1). You can also sweep your opponent off the ground, as soon as he starts to turn and before he spins his leg over your body. This is a more efficient and straightforward move, and you get your adversary's supporting leg while still in a sort of inside position, as shown in Fig. 39.10, number (2). After the *rasteira em pé* you can always go down on a *negativa*, to prepare for new moves. Don't take too long looking at your target, i.e., the opponent's supporting foot – remember to always be vigilant.

The Diagonal Approach

For a perfect approach, your primary concern is how fast you can step aside with your left foot (assuming the attacking armada comes from your opponent's right leg) in order to execute your *rasteira*. Once you have decided to enter his guard for a sweep, you can also always choose between one of the two types of *rasteira* shown in Figure 39.10 and the *banda*, which would be better done from position number (2), instead of the *rasteira*.

However, for doing a perfect *rasteira*, I personally prefer the approach of Figure 39.11, which is quick, slightly more diagonal, and safer. Compare these two different approaches. Diagram 39.1 explores the strategic details of this unique *rasteira*. See also The Diagonal Factor in the chapter on the *meia-lua de compasso*.

Figure 39.11: The best approach for a perfect *rasteira em pé*.

Diagram 39.1 shows the stages of your preparation for the best *rasteira em pé*, assuming your opponent tries an *armada*. In (1), your rival on the left starts to turn for his *armada*. Note your posture in the diagram. You are on the right. Your counterattacking *rasteira* could be started from a *ginga* stance position or at zero stance. Watch for his *armada* leg.

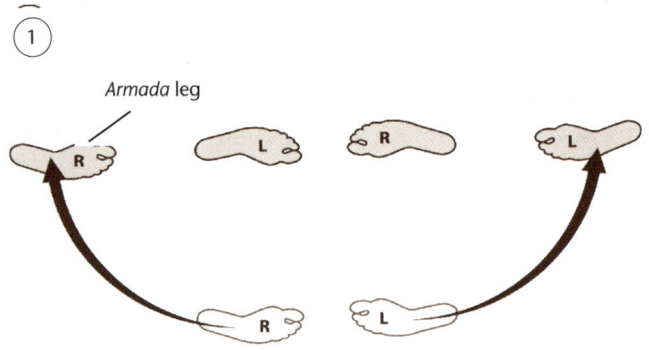

Diagram 39.1: Follow his movement and watch his *armada* leg.

Start preparing for your *rasteira* by moving quickly and diagonally to the side of your adversary while he starts to turn. In (2) (Diagram 39.2), you move away, out of range of his *armada*-to-be, in order to generate power and momentum for your *rasteira*. At this moment, your opponent is within range of your strategy.

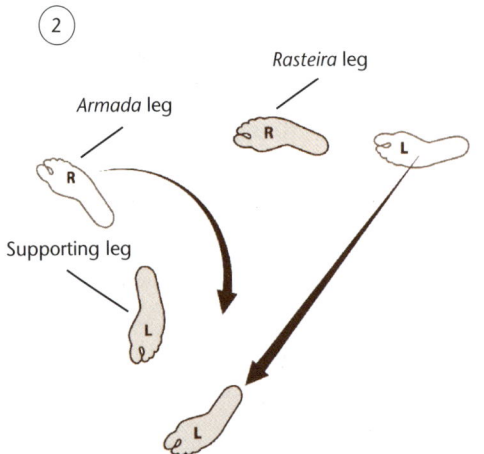

Once you execute your *rasteira em pé* with perfection, you can then follow your adversary's preparation for the *armada* while at the same time feeling the grip of your *rasteira* foot on the outside of his lower rear leg, and take time to think before sweeping his supporting leg off the ground. It is a wonderful feeling of control over the opponent that every capoeirista should have!

Diagram 39.2: Follow his spin, step out to execute your *rasteira* and move in to sweep your adversary.

Rasteira de Costas Cruzada

The *rasteira de costas cruzada* (crossed-back sweep), a.k.a. *banda de costas cruzada*, is a great asset to the capoeira repertoire of takedown moves. You can execute it on the ground, as in Figure 39.12, or from a standing position, as in Figure 39.14.

Observe the next three-frame sequence. One capoeirista is apparently in front of the other. If you look closely at the second frame, you will see that the blond capoeirista displaced herself a little to her right in order to prepare for her *rasteira*. This way she will be able to position herself inside her opponent's guard, and out of her opponent's range of attack when she delivers her *martelo*.

Figure 39.12: Sequence of a *rasteira de costas cruzada*.

Banda

A kick-like sweep. You can choose to use a *banda*, instead of a *rasteira*, if your timing is right and you feel you are in control of your opponent's open guard. Just bear in mind that this move is an even more dangerous and violent defense and counterattack against your adversary, who will most likely hit the ground violently with the nape of his neck when he falls.

There are two types of *banda* that can be executed from an upright standing position, just like the *rasteira em pé*: the classic *banda*, a.k.a. *banda de frente*, and the *banda de costas*, which is a sweep where you move in, put one leg behind your opponent's supporting leg, and push him over. The classic *banda* has two distinct moves, which are the inside *banda de dentro* and the outside *banda de fora*. The inside *banda* is easier to execute but is not the best choice against an *armada*, despite its being an excellent defense against a *martelo*. Hence, your best choice against an *armada* would be the outside *banda,* which is a little more risky to time due to the fact that you have to let the opponent's *armada* leg start rotating and only then, in a split second, execute the move, as in the *rasteira em pé,* before he regains control over a new attacking leg. See the aggressive approach and the *banda* itself in Figure 39.13.

Figure 39.13: A *banda* executed on the opponent's outside supporting leg.

Banda de Costas Cruzada

A short standing back-kicking crossed sweep, a.k.a. *rasteira de costas cruzada.* You can choose to use a *banda de costas cruzada* (Figure 39.14) for a sweeping technique, instead of a traditional *rasteira,* or a regular *banda de frente* if you sense the opportunity and time your moves with those of your opponent's.

You hit his supporting leg from outside with the muscle of your calf, just above your heel. It is a practical and fast move if you want to remain standing upright and in a diagonal position relative to your opponent.

Figure 39.14: Pay attention to your timing, and enter his *armada* guard before he rotates his attacking leg.

RASTEIRA

Since you can move into your opponent's guard diagonally, as we do with the *bloqueio de dentro,* you can decide whether to sweep your opponent off the ground by hitting his lower rear leg before he spins his *armada,* or by sweeping his ankle or lower shin right after he passes over your defensive head, as in Figure 39.13. This decision will make a major difference if you want your adversary to fall flat on his back, with the nape of his neck on the ground, or if you wish him to fall forward. Both can be fairly hard falls, but chances are that if you choose to make him fall forward he will have a better chance of using his hands to avoid hitting his head on the ground. However, if you decide to sweep your opponent the other way, remember to time your movement with his *armada* and to take the risk of waiting for his attacking leg to get close to you, which could be a little more dangerous and time-consuming. Always remember to use your soleus muscle (below the calf) to hit the opponent's supporting leg.

If you want to use your *banda de costas cruzada* against a *benção* (which I hope you will not do against your friends), be sure to move quickly to the side while executing your *banda.* See the ideal angle in which you should be at the moment your *banda* foot catches the opponent's leg, as shown in Figure 39.15. Try this and all the other sweeps with the *benção* to be proficient in this difficult move.

Figure 39.15: The *banda* is quite a difficult technique to use against a good capoeirista.

Calcanheira

The *calcanheira* is literally a heel sweep, a *banda* that can be done with a loose body than the more rigid *banda de costas.* You can use your heels or your Achilles tendon to hit your adversary's supporting leg on the ankle, soleus or lower shin.

Pay attention to an important detail of Figure 39.16. You can see there that, at the moment the female capoeirista, starts her *meia-lua* in (a), the male capoeirista prepares to counterattack; in (b), the woman has a full attacking leg while the man is still preparing his *calcanheira*. Note that this is normally the time when the counterattacking capoeirista has already struck the attacker's supporting leg – and most of the time this counterattack is done the other way, i.e., in the same direction as the attacker's kick. The idea here is to show that, if you are a fit capoeirista, capoeira offers you the chance to choose a non-orthodox approach, as the man did in (c), where he chose to wait for the woman's *meia-lua* to pass over his head in order to catch her by surprise on her inside ankle. The result here should be a painful experience, with the blond capoeirista possibly still standing, but awkwardly unbalanced – which is exactly what the counterattacking capoeirista wanted in the first place!

Figure 39.16: A sly *calcanheira* against a *meia-lua de compasso*.

Passa-pé

The *passa-pé* is a simple though highly efficient type of sweep. Due to its nature (of sweeping by hitting instead of by fitting and pulling), it can be classified as a *banda*, though I strongly recommend that you still try to "mold" the sole of your attacking foot onto the opponent's legs. Like with the *calcanheira*, there are two ways to execute it: the outside and the inside *passa-pé*, and the hoped-for results are pretty much the same. See Figures 39.17 and 39.18.

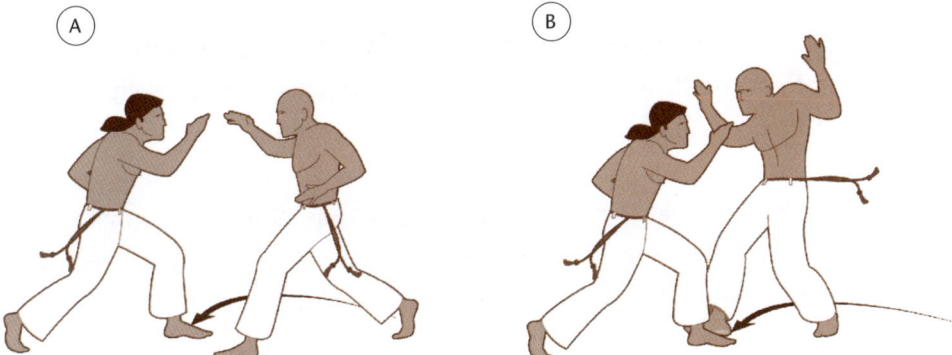

Figure 39.17: The classic *passa-pé*.

Note that the *passa-pé* in Fig. 39.17 is the traditional one, where the opportunistic capoeirista can "see" the opponent's balance (a) and simply (as well as quickly and vigorously) sweep his supporting foot from outside his ankle (b), using the sole of his foot. Depending on the adversary's stance, he will most probably fall flat on his side, twisting his ankle along the way.

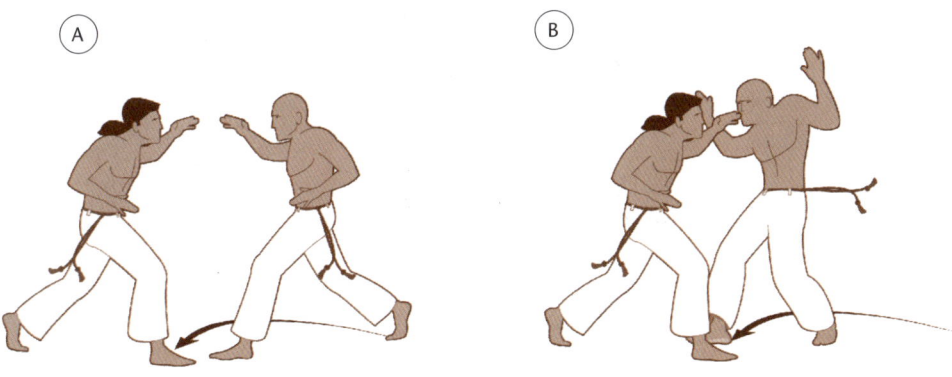

Figure 39.18: The surprising inside *passa-pé*.

In Figure 39.18 the opportunistic capoeirista unbalances the opponent by striking a painful and unexpected inside *passa-pé* on his ankle.

Bloqueio de Dentro

Move in to block before takedown. This is an advanced defense technique and a preparation for a good *banda*. It sems – but only seems – to be an easy defense. You need to be very cautious and attentive in order to pinpoint the exact time to enter the attacker's open guard, just as if you were playing jumprope with two friends. You complete the movement when your shoulder is blocking the attacker's *armada*, which will not be effective and will lose power, doing you no harm. Be aware of the attacker's arms and hands, as he can surprise you with a *cutelo rodado* (the spinning ridge of the hand) or even with a *cotovelada* (an elbow strike) while he is still rotating his body. Both are common moves when a good fighter observes your intentions and gives up his intended kick. Figure 39.19 shows the moment when you should invade your opponent's open *armada* guard.

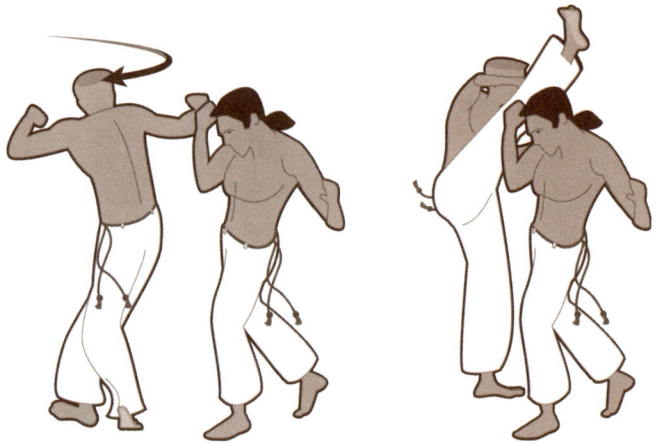

Figure 39.19: Invading his *armada* guard for an efficient *bloqueio de dentro.*

Some capoeiristas learn and practice *bloqueio de dentro* to block a *ponteira* or a *benção*. **Do not** do that! Such moves require that you lower your upper body even farther, while you move in under your opponent's attacking leg. However, both the *ponteira* and the *benção* are kicks that travel from the ground up, vertically toward the opponent. These kicks can render you defenseless, and reach your upper body and your head if you try a *bloqueio de dentro*.

Bloqueio de Dentro and Banda de Costas Combo

Takedown with heel sweep while you move in to block. This is a continuation of the previous technique. When you are side by side with the attacker, sweep away his supporting leg by hitting with your contracted sinew on the back of his lower leg, between his sinew and his calf, vigorously sweeping his leg off the ground, while his attacking leg is still up in the air on the way to completing his *armada*.* Be sure that your attacking foot is at a 90° angle or less with your leg, so that you have a powerful sweep. You can also use your hand to help thrust your opponent down, by pushing his chest. In the example of Figure 39.20, that would be your right hand. Be aware of the danger that this movement might present to your opponent. He may fall flat with the nape of his neck hitting the ground first. Don't ever try to practice this and other capoeira movements without proper and professional guidance!

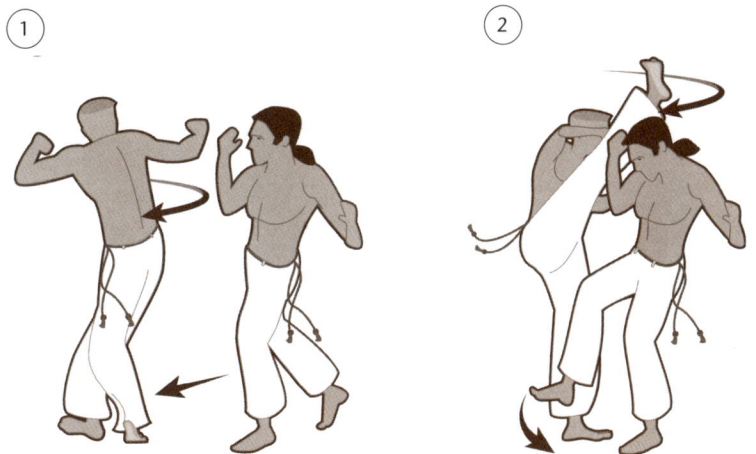

Figure 39.20: A complete *bloqueio de dentro* with *banda de costas*.

---

* You can also use the **cruz** (cross) as a **bloqueio** of a **martelo** while executing a **banda de costas** from inside his supporting leg. I don't particularly like this movement because it brings the defending capoeirista too close to his attacker, and therefore, leaving him too vulnerable. See more details in the chapter dedicated to the **bloqueio**.

The inside *banda* **can** be used against an *armada* in a more direct action. If you choose to use a *banda* instead of a *rasteira,* act quickly and opportunistically, but most of all, aggressively. In Figure 39.21 the *banda* is performed in the shortest possible path, so as to make it quick and effective. Note the almost direct line of the kicking leg. You should kick as though you were a soccer player doing a free kick over a wall of players.

Figure 39.21: Entering the opponent's *armada* guard with a *bloqueio de dentro* and a forward *banda* combo.

See more blocking techniques in the specific chapter about *bloqueio*.

Rasteira de Mão

The hand sweep. You just wait for your opponent to pass with his leg over your low, leaning defensive body while you follow the trajectory of his *armada* in a dodge from under his leg in order to sweep his standing leg off the ground with one or two hands (Figure 39.22). You can do that in different ways: by sweeping his leg in the same direction as his *armada,* or by grabbing his ankle and yanking it sharply toward you (1) or to the side; or by using the *boca-de-calça* technique (2), which can be done by grabbing and then yanking the bottom hem of his trousers on his supporting leg. You will have to decide in a split second which form suits you better when you come in below his *armada*. Be sure to always look at your attacker while performing this and every other capoeira move!

When you are in position and ready to sweep away your opponent's leg using your hands, always be sure to have your extended leg behind his supporting leg and ready for a traditional *rasteira*, in case you change your mind while going for the *rasteira de mão*.

Keep your foot ready for an opportunistic *rasteira* at all times.

Keep looking at your opponent at all times.

Figure 39.22: The classic *rasteira de mão* and the *boca-de-calça* style. Always monitor your opponent.

Figure 39.22 shows the capoeirista using a *rasteira de mão* with his two hands on the inner side of the attacker's leg. He could have dodged down in the direction of the opponent's *armada* while sweeping his supporting leg with one hand, striking the leg from the outside.

If you want to use the same techniques against a *benção*, be sure to dodge out of the way of the capoeirista's (vertical) attacking leg. Be aware that the *benção* is a dangerous kick, which can get you before you accomplish your sidestep and get your head before you dodge down. A *negativa escala*, for example, would do the trick, but then you would be too far from his legs to execute a *rasteira de mão*.

The *boca de calça* can also be used as a surprise attack in different situations. In Figure 39.23 you can see the classic style, where you are just a couple of steps away from your potential attacker, who has stopped behind you.

Always dodge to the side to avoid his attacking foot.

If your opponent is moving, though, you will have to mislead him into a situation in which you will go along with the movement, pretending to execute a *meia-lua de compasso* or a *giro,* but will actually just bend in order to grab the hem of his trousers and pull him over.

I don't advise this in a *roda,* except if you do it slowly, allowing time for your partner to assimilate the idea and follow along in the flow of motion.

In a real-life situation, this technique really works well if your opponent has not noticed your intentions. Be aware that this is a dangerous fall that can cause your adversary severe injury!

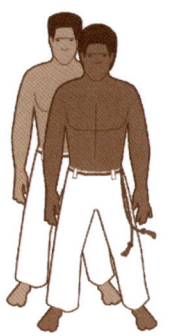 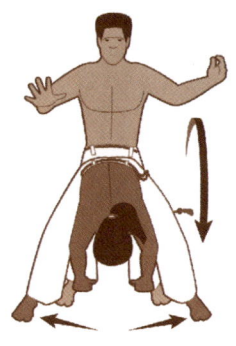 

Figure 39.23: Don't do it with someone you like!

Practicing Alone

Like with the *bloqueio* and with most takedown techniques, the *rasteira* is best practiced with a partner. Be careful with the *bandas* and with all effective moves, as you may end up hurting each other unnecessarily.

There is an interesting "individuality" in the practice of all takedown techniques, though – especially the *rasteiras* and *bandas*. When you practice with a partner, besides applying the *rasteira* and *banda* to his or her supporting leg, you also "absorb" the sense of power of the attacking *rasteira* or *banda* on your legs, and this is when you must concentrate on your sense of touch at the same time you compare your present partner's power to yesterday's partner's power and to their different body weight, strength, experience and so on. Later, you accumulate this important data in your "muscular memory," which is the capacity that most advanced athletes, especially those involved with acrobatic moves, develop for storing external and mostly interactive actions that are later recalled as known events, which can also be remembered bodily. That is my case, for instance. Today I am pretty sure I can do a *mortal de costas* from a table down to the floor. "I know how to do it and have done it many times!" Regretfully, this happens a lot with "bold" 60-year-old athletes who like to tell this kind of story from a hospital bed...

Therefore, seize the opportunity! Feel your partner's counterattacks, as well as your own attacks, and gather experience from each and every *jogo* that you play.

Defenses and Counterattacks

There are countless techniques that can be used against a capoeira takedown. Of course, the best is always to avoid putting yourself in such a fragile position as to open your guard. However, if you have been caught by a *rasteira* in a *jogo*, you can still try an *escapada da rasteira* (literally a "sweep escape"), a *negativa,* or even an *aú* or a *macaco;* in real fighting, though, there is little chance to escape once your opponent grabs your legs or sweeps you off the ground.

In this vein, if you are executing a *martelo,* be sure to do it quickly and precisely, and try not to open the angle too much to avoid an opportunistic *rasteira. That is*, make the most closed arch possible from the ground to your target, so that your opponent does not have too much space to execute his *rasteira*. Now, if you want to do an *armada* in real combat, make sure your opponent is slower than you, or that he has no idea you are going to come up with an outside crescent kick. The *armada* is a great move, but it is also a very "telegraphic" one, and a surprise *rasteira* or *banda* could cause you severe damage. Hence, it's better to try a *gancho* or a *chapa* instead, or possibly a *ponteira,* if you feel your adversary is able to try a *rasteira* against you. In other words, high spinning kicks and *rasteiras* are a bombastic combination, unless you execute these kicks in their jumping versions, out of a *rasteira* range.

For low, ground sweeps, if you are quick enough there is always the possibility of an aerial escape with a *mortal* or a *xangô*. However, I do not recommend these two techniques in real combat, unless you are sure you have plenty of space in which to execute one of them.

You can use the *escapada da rasteira* to escape a sweep in the *roda* or in real combat, if you have time to see your opponent's *rasteira* approaching. Escape by rolling away from the attacking *rasteira* foot the moment the opponent reaches your supporting foot; turn around, reaching for the ground with your two hands, and roll over, away from the *rasteira* and into a *negativa* or a *queda de rim*.

Remember, these are my personal choices out of hundreds of possibilities that are available when you have a good repertoire of capoeira moves. Also, bear in mind that I am always considering the point of view of real fighting events, which does not mean that you actually need to fight for real to acquire the skills discussed in this book. On the contrary, the idea is to explore the potential of the technique to your maximum level of achievement. Then, with your good capoeira under control, have fun and enjoy all the friendly *rodas* that you can.

> **ALWAYS PRACTICE UNDER PROFESSIONAL GUIDANCE AND IN AN ACCREDITED CAPOEIRA SCHOOL.**

Rolê

The roll. A deceptive move, generally done with the aid of an *esquiva* and a *negativa,* in which you move low to the ground from one side to another as a means of escape, to deceive your adversary, or simply to prepare for a new move. You can also choose to go halfway through the move and then return to the starting position, reversing the move. Here we are using an *esquiva* to the right, followed by a *negativa* and the *rolê*. Although the *rolê* has been proven in the *roda*, many capoeiristas at beginning and intermediate levels don't know how important and strategic this simple move is in real combat. It is just so great that it can be used in combat against, virtually, any type of martial artist. However, the perfect *rolê* is not as easy as it looks at first, and when I say "simple move" in the context of this book, I always mean "simple in someone else's eyes because you have certainly worked your guts out to make it perfect and *look* simple."

Objectives

The main objective is to remain protected while moving on the ground. It is a great technique for evasive directional movements in front of, or around, your adversary. It is also a very good time for considering the next strategy during combat, where you will have the choice to convert your *rolê* into other ground or even standing maneuvers.

The Point of Impact

There is no direct impact from a *rolê*. However, one can always consider the *psychological* impact of a well-executed, cunning capoeira maneuver. Believe me. In addition, from your *rolê* you will also be able to engage in several other moves that will eventually lead to a variety of kicks.

The Technique

The *rolê* forms what we can call a basic "mobility system" of capoeira, especially executed in the *roda* almost as a religious routine, together with the *ginga*, the classic *aú* and the smooth *negativa escala*. In real combat, though, both the system and the *rolê* itself are excellent tools for an inspired fighter.

Starting from the point of view of the *negativa*, lean quickly and smoothly to the side opposite the direction in which you're going to perform your *rolê*, with your supporting hand on that same side for further leverage. Continue the move by changing direction (and intention), and switch your supporting hands while extending the leg on that side. Start rotating along the axis of your first stretched leg until your chest is facing the ground. As you extend your other leg (once your chest is facing the ground), continue to roll, with your two hands on the ground, as if you were going to execute a *meia-lua presa*. While you are turning, watch your opponent from between your legs. Pull off your formerly bent leg and swing it around to complete the move as you make a 180° turn, placing that leg behind, so as to be able to create new leverage.

Throughout the move, keep your upper body low and in constant circular movement to protect yourself against attacking spinning kicks. Pay special attention to straight kicks, such as a low *ponteira* or *benção*, which could be delivered to your head – with harmful results.

There are several combinations that can be done from the *rolê*, such as a *martelo de chão*, a *meia-lua presa*, an *s-dobrado*, a *negativa* or a *queda de rim*, to mention the most efficient combos. You should guide your *rolê* into the style and distance you want, closing in on your adversary or moving away from him, depending on your next move.

ROLÊ

If you want to do the "bouncing," misleading reverse *rolê*, simply execute the same move to the rear when you have your two supporting hands on the ground and your chest facing the ground, instead of continuing to the other side. In this case, you will quickly return to the same position from where you started. Some advanced capoeiristas like to do this, and then engage in the complete *rolê*, causing extra confusion to their partners in a *roda* or to their opponents in real combat.

Rolê reverso.

Practicing Alone

The *rolê* is best practiced in the *roda*. However, a fixed object, such as a chair with a tall back, is an excellent "target" for practicing several *rolê* stances, closing in on and out, from and around your "opponent," trying to find all the possible combinations of moves that can derive naturally from each type of *rolê*.

Defenses and Counterattacks

Your own *rolê*, or the *giro*, is a great strategy if you don't want to be a victim of someone else's *rolê*, waiting for an efficient combo to get you. The problem is that, normally, you will not notice that your opponent is starting a *rolê* until he has begun to execute one! An *aú fechado* is also a great countermeasure against a *rolê*, but in both cases you will have to be pretty fast in order to perceive your rival's intention to do a *rolê*. If you are that fast, though, go around him, i.e., execute an *aú fechado* or a classic *aú* prone to *chibatas* in the same direction as his *rolê* – actually sort of following your opponent around his *rolê* path. This will confuse him exceedingly.

S-dobrado

The double "S." Another trademark of the capoeira repertoire of moves, the *s-dobrado* is a sweeping leg motion, originally created to help delivering a high *martelo* from a ground stance, such as a *negativa* or a *rasteira*. Do not confuse it with the *martelo de chão* (a ground *martelo*), which is done with one supporting leg. On the contrary, the mechanics of the *s-dobrado* allow you to "fly" off the ground, aiming to kick your opponent in the head with the top of the attacking foot, both laterally and vertically (through the *chapéu de couro*) at variable speeds.

Objectives

A good *s-dobrado* can help you to quickly recover from a *rasteira,* or other type of fall, and come back to your opponent with a powerful *martelo,* which – depending entirely on you – can be a fast, devastating move, or rather an elegantly slow warning move.

S-DOBRADO

The *s-dobrado* is a great technique to use against high crescent, spinning and rotating kicks, such as an *armada* (Fig. 41.1), when you can execute a *negativa* as a form of *esquiva lateral*, and then turn back to get your opponent before he can prepare a response, as long as he is not as good a capoeirista as you are!

Figure 41.1: Go down to your right, as in an *esquiva lateral*, but execute a *negativa* to thrust your *s-dobrado* after his *armada* leg.

The Point of Impact

Originally, the *s-dobrado* was usually used as a thrust for a *martelo* delivered on the opponent's face or the top of his head, coming down from an even higher *chapéu de couro*. However, the *s-dobrado* is frequently used as a *floreio* to engage in other movements, such as the *macaco*, the *bananeira*, or in several variations of the *aú*, to name the most common ones.

The Technique

You don't really get to execute a *rasteira* when you go down to the ground to start an *s-dobrado*, but the most common technique is exactly the combination of *rasteira* and *negativa* in one composite movement that should begin from a standing position, at *ginga* or zero stance.

Suppose you are going to kick your opponent's head with your right leg. From your standing stance, step forward with your right leg, diagonally to the right relative to your adversary, while starting to go down on your left leg, looking to do a *rasteira*. At this time, your *rasteira* leg is far from your diagonally extended right leg, still trying to sweep your opponent's right leg – but that is not what you really want this time.

You should continue to move your *rasteira* "form" downward, until you come to a *negativa* with your outstretched left leg encountering your bent right supporting leg, with your left supporting hand on the ground. You are still in motion and ready to let fly with your *s-dobrado*.

Continuing the flow of motion, swing your body back to the left while thrusting your supporting leg up, using the entire movement as a lever and all the power from your right bent supporting leg.

Keep your supporting hand on the ground and use all the strength you can muster from the muscles of your attacking right leg, to deliver a roundhouse kick all the way from your ground stance to the opponent's head, until your body has done a complete 360° rotation to end the movement.

Chapéu de couro.

For the *chapéu de couro* (the "leather hat," meaning the capoeirista's shoes on the opponent's head), use your right arm for executing a *macaco*-type move in order to fly more vertically, kicking your adversary's head from above, in a *chibata*-like technique.

Practicing Alone

Make sure you practice different speeds and degrees of power on the sandbag. Take advantage of the great reliability that this technique provides by doing elegant, slow and quick *martelos*. Here is a nice sequence you could try: from a *chapéu de couro*, stop in front of the bag and do some *chibatas*, interrupting your flow of motion to end on a *ponte*. Then, from the *ponte*, return to the bag with a couple of *chibatas* and continue the original flow of motion. Then, start all over again from the other side.

Defenses and Counterattacks

The *s-dobrado* brings much grace to the flow of motion in a capoeira *roda*. It offers a variety of countermeasures, which can be executed from ground navigation, most of them in the *floreio* class. However, the *s-dobrado* has proved highly efficient in real fighting, and if you are ever attacked by one, chances are you will be vulnerable to a *martelo* or a *chibata*. If you are on the ground, you can always do a *troca* and invert the path of your *negativa* to escape your opponent's attack. However, your own *s-dobrado* is a good strategy if you are quick enough to go down and start it before your adversary reaches you. Remember your *aú fechado*, which you can execute from your *s-dobrado* in order to use your feet as an extra defense. A mean and efficient counterattack would be a *rasteira giratória* on your opponent's supporting hand, delivered the moment he flies for his *martelo* from the *s-dobrado;* in that case, make sure you anticipate that he is really planning an *s-dobrado* against you, so that you execute a timely *rasteira giratória*.

Xangô

The back handspring. The *xangô* is a wonderful capoeira move. Similar to the back handspring done in Olympic gymnastics floor exercises, it is generally executed individually or in a pair, rather than in a series of tumbles. Some capoeiristas also call it *pulo do gato* (the jump of the cat) or simply *gato*; others call it *palhaço* (clown) or *macaco solto* (loose *macaco*). The *xangô* is a serious and very effective capoeira move, which can be used both in the *roda* and in real combat, and often even to avoid real combat!

Once I was leaving the YMCA school where I taught, in a public park not far from the school that I used to cross in order to catch the bus home, there was a gang of hostile guys smoking some strange things and messing with everyone passing by. Luckily, they messed with me too. There were maybe six or seven of them.

At first I pretended I hadn't heard their provocative noises, but they kept trying to get my attention anyway. I turned back and walked in their direction until I was close to one of them. I said: "This is not funny at all. You guys shouldn't be here in a public park messing with people. Go home! Find something better to do. I don't want to fight you guys, I just want to catch my bus and go home!" to which the alpha bozo replied: "Man... we don't think you're going to take this bus now..."

That did it! Suddenly I executed a quick, high *xangô* away from the group. At this time, two of my students who were going with me to the bus stop said: "Mestre, should we wait for you or what?"

Immediately the scoundrels realized I was the capoeira teacher at the nearby Y. The same guy who said I was not going to take my bus was now saying "sorry, man! We didn't know. It's not going to happen again!" And I replied: "No problem, my friend. Just remember that one day, instead of finding someone like me in this situation, you may find someone like yourself, and on that day, things may come out differently for both of you."

I was then a young and very devoted athlete and capoeira teacher. It took me one single back handspring to make them reflect on their virtues and faults, at least on that lucky Thursday night. Not one drop of blood, or one drop of sweat – either.

Yes, I was lucky. Who in the world could guarantee that I would come out the winner in a real fight? In fact, we were all winners that night: we all learned the meaning of the word "opportunity."

> **MESTRES, TEACH YOUR STUDENTS HOW TO FIGHT THEMSELVES FIRST, SO THAT THEY CAN BETTER COPE WITH THEIR DIFFICULTIES IN LIFE.**

Objectives

I believe most of the objectives of the *xangô* were summarized in the last section. It is a versatile move, which can be performed in a *roda* for both decorative and tactical purposes. In real combat, it provides an opportunity for a quick escape. I do not recommend it for attack, though, as when you start to jump back there is too much of a blind space before you land on the other side. During your jump, this blind space will not allow you to see your opponent as well (and as soon) as you should in order to aim an attack with your feet.

The Point of Impact

Unless you do a *chibata*-type kick over your opponent's head or back, or try to use the floor-exercise type on his chest, a *xangô* should not normally generate any impact. Instead, there is impact of your hands on your landing site, which could be a rough surface, a paved road, sand or even a surface located at a lower level than the one you jumped from. For this very reason you should take your time and practice, at least, a couple of times over different surfaces in order to get used to them while retaining control of your move.

Normally, the daily practice session is enough to harden the skin of our hands for ground movements. However, there are those radical practitioners who need extra protection if practicing on rough surfaces. Some athletes use alcohol (surgical spirit) to harden the skin, by soaking a cotton wool pad in it and then smearing it on their hands (and feet) every night before going to bed, for a couple of weeks.

Since chemistry and medicine are not my fields of expertise, I strongly recommend consulting your physician and your credentialed capoeira teacher before using any of these techniques.

Another point of impact worth noting is your back. If you are out of shape, overweight or somehow unprepared to tumble, don't use these techniques since you may hurt your backbone and get yourself a herniated disk.

NEVER PRACTICE CAPOEIRA WITHOUT A PROPER WARM-UP!

The Technique

The best way to learn how to do a *xangô* is with the help of a tumbling belt wrapped around your waist, with two straps on each side and a mat under you. Two partners then hold the straps and pull up when you jump back, so that you won't fall. This builds the confidence you need to do it by yourself.

If you don't know how to do the back handspring, then first of all don't try to do it at home or in your backyard! You'd better ask your capoeira teacher to help you out or go to a gym.

As with the *mortal,* there is one good basic training move you can do on your own, if you have a proper mat, as shown in Figure 42.1.

Practice the preparation jump. From your upright standing position, bend your knees and move your arms back and then forward and up, as a leverage to help you jump as high as possible, as if you were going to reach for a fruit hanging on a branch high above and slightly behind you. You must start at one point and end the move some three feet to the rear. This means you need to lean slightly backward when jumping.

Figure 42.1: Feel your jump before you tumble.

Another good training move is to turn a somersault on the floor in order to get used to the 360° movement of your head. "Looking at the sky" (Figure 42.2) is an important complement to learning and practicing the *xangô*.

Figure 42.2: Do back somersaults to "look at the sky."

Before you start, make sure to look at your landing spot. You don't want to jump right into an obstacle. Then, begin as if you were going to sit down on a chair, slightly bending your knees and leaning back before thrusting up and flying backward. To do this, as you sit back and feel you are about to fall down, jump vigorously high, with your arms straight and hands pointed backward, looking at the sky, as if you were going to dive into a swimming pool behind you. Push your arms and hands hard, as if you had to fly past an obstacle before reaching the imaginary pool. This is the feeling you must have when you are up in the air beginning the curve to reach for your imaginary pool.

Once you have jumped up and backward, think of landing in a handstand. At first these two different images I am suggesting – the swimming pool and the handstand – may seem awkward, especially when they are just written words, but you will get the grip if you practice in a real swimming pool before actually doing it on the floor alone.

When you throw your arms back and start flying, you should be high enough to make an arch before landing on the other side. Do this by lifting your chest while making the "aerial arch." This technique is important for your control over a *xangô* started from zero stance, as opposed to the back handsprings done at the Olympics when the athlete builds momentum while gaining speed for his thrust. Do not execute low *xangôs*. You need to feel that you are *flying* from one point to another and not trying to act like a contortionist.

You can land with both feet together, as in the floor-exercise back handspring, or with one foot behind the other, in *chibata* style.

The entire movement must be learned with the help of an accredited and specialized professional, such as a recognized capoeira Mestre or an Olympic gymnastics coach. Don't try this alone or in an amateur fashion!

Landing on both feet together.

Practicing Alone

Once you have mastered the technique, you can practice the *xangô* on the beach or on the floor, as long as you understand that you need to warm up adequately before tumbling. If you want to practice it on rough or irregular surfaces, you can do so, provided you have really mastered a perfect *xangô* and are able to tumble buoyantly and elegantly, so as to not hurt your hands and feet (as well as your head).

However, if you insist on practicing before you have been cleared for it by your capoeira Mestre or coach, which often happens when you are at least a fairly good student, make sure to do it on a resi-pit or a foam pit. This will guarantee you some safety and fun.

Defenses and Counterattacks

Since the *xangô* is not really supposed to be used as an attack technique, you wouldn't expect my recommendation of a specific counterattack, but there is at least one: the *tombo da ladeira*. However, be cautious about it because there are many capoeiristas who believe that performing a back handspring over your head is good for their strategy, and they may be right if you don't know how to act quickly!

In addition, you can always prepare a good old *meia-lua* right onto your rival's head (actually square on his face if you want) if you believe he deserves one. Just time your movement with his jump, get out of the way diagonally and thrust your *meia-lua* when he finishes landing. Optimize your success by delivering a *meia-lua pulada* or a *compasso pulado*, instead of the classic *meia-lua de compasso*, in case he finishes his *xangô* a little too far away.

Xangô de Frente

The forward handspring. The *xangô de frente* is the reverse of the classic *xangô*. A most unexpected move in the *roda* and specially in real fighting, the *xangô de frente* is an efficient resource. It is similar to the forward handspring done in Olympic gymnastics floor exercises, but without the running start the gymnasts do in order to gain more momentum.

The *xangô de frente* should be executed in a single move, or at most in a pair, rather than in a series of forward moves.

Objectives

Your goal is to take your opponent by surprise, by quickly jumping from one point to another and still remaining standing, or landing in a squat for an evasive move. You can also use the *xangô de frente* as preparation for a new strategy, such as a forward attack with your two feet or a ground technique.

The Point of Impact

Doing the standing *xangô de frente,* like in the classic gymnastics manner, is a possible strategy for surprising your adversary with a heavy kick delivered to his chest with both feet together (see also *vôo do morcego*), like an unexpected flying "double" *benção*. However, I prefer its use as an escape strategy instead, for the sake of motion and displacement in real combat.

The Technique

In contrast to the classic *xangô,* the *xangô de frente* does not require so much preparation, although its efficiency is quite the same, in a reverse fashion. You just lunge forward, as if you were going to do a *bananeira,* placing your hands on the ground. Then thrust your legs up quickly, one after the other, and then forward, in a powerful movement. Both legs must travel together at the peak, from this point to the landing position. While your legs are traveling over you, push off with your hands, with the additional aid of a spring effect created by all your fingers at the same time. Note that the detail of the "finger technique" is crucial, as you will be very light when doing the move correctly, and your fingers will play an important role by helping thrust your body up and forward in the air. With practice, you will be able to thrust your *xangô de frente* with both legs together.

Gymnasts land in a standing position, after making an arch with their body during the movement. Capoeiristas too! To do this, you will have to "fly" as high as you can, using the "finger effect," and create the arch as you travel through the air. Some capoeiristas prefer to land in a squatting position, with their hands lower to the ground, which is a way to connect the forward handspring to other low moves.

Practicing Alone

The best way for practicing your *xangô de frente* is on the floor of your gym or capoeira school. Look for the combinations of strength and at the same time lightness, so that you perform a vigorous but smooth and silent move – one of the important characteristics of capoeira. Think of yourself as a cat when moving.

Defenses and Counterattacks

The *xangô de frente* is seldom used as an attack technique. However, if you come upon such an attack in a real fight, your best defense would be to time your escape, getting out of the way while delivering a perfect and timely *meia-lua diagonal* right on your adversary's head as soon as he lands, or thrusting a *compasso pulado* similar to the counterattack against the classic *xangô* discussed in the *compasso* chapter.

The *compasso* and *the compasso pulado* are always excellent ways for you to get your opponent in most landing actions.

Unexpected Moves

There are several mixed techniques in capoeira, which originated from a variety of ancient and pre-colonial African sources. More recently, history showed us that Mestre Bimba learned a few jiu-jitsu, wrestling and boxing moves, and – together with techniques from the batuque, an old fighting style of African origin practiced in Bahia, of which his father was a known champion – were later incorporated into his Capoeira Regional.

Trying to locate the origin of each and every capoeira technique is not an easy task. Mostly, one relies on oral traditions or recent history covering roughly the last three centuries.

I believe in giving credit to those multitudes of unknown practitioners who incorporated their personal experience into the realm of capoeira throughout the years, and to all Mestres who were able to filter and balance the new implementations that were envisioned by these capoeiristas.

It is also important to emphasize the contribution of the new Brazilian social settings of the early twentieth century, which helped capoeira develop in the urban areas and was responsible for the rise of a cultural expression and the birth of a new (martial) art in Brazil.

Today we see capoeira valued all over the world for its essence and its principles, a renewed capoeira that blends its old foundations with a fresh and enthusiastic contemporary view. Yet it is the same capoeira – alive and evolving like everything else that surrounds us.

I have classified these "unexpected moves" as a set of self-defense techniques, most of which not usually used in a *roda* due to their traumatic effects or their lack of flow of motion, but all of them practiced regularly in most of the capoeira schools worlwide.

Objectives

The objective of these (normally traumatic) moves is to surprise your partner, opponent, or a common street assailant who will not anticipate them if you are a capoeirista – or if he is negligent in his initial approach.

The Point of Impact

These moves consist of attacks with the hands and head and are aimed at the nose, the eyes, the chin, the chest or the abdomen of the assailant. Unless you are in a *roda*, where you can "demonstrate" the move without further consequences for your partner, these techniques can be pretty aggressive and terminate a fight.

The Technique

The illustration that opens this chapter shows the *asfixiante*, a direct power punch delivered on the assailant's Adam's apple. Make sure you have a hard, tight fist. Do not loosen or bend it, or you will risk breaking your wrist! Execute a direct move with your firm arm, traveling quickly and decisively to the assailant's throat. If your life is at stake, make sure you use the "Towel Factor" described in the Introduction to this book.

For the *cabeçada* called *arpão de cabeça* (the head spear) and shown in Figure 44.1, leap onto your opponent's chest and fire a *cabeçada*, as hard and precise as you can, using either your forehead or the top of the head as a weapon. However, be very careful: most moves shown in this chapter can be lethal! Never execute a full move in the *roda*, but rather withdraw your move before completing it on your partner.

UNEXPECTED MOVES

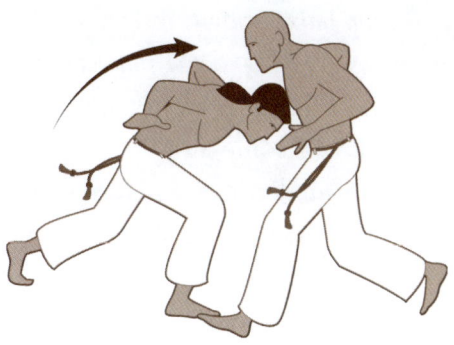

Figure 44.1: Make no mistake: the *arpão de cabeça* can be a lethal blow!

Note that you can use the *cabeçada* in different ways, according to the situation at hand, as shown in the three examples in Figure 44.2.

Figure 44.2: The *cabeçada* is a tactical, opportunistic move that can be done by surprise.

The *cabeçada* as shown in Figure 44.3 is called *escorumelo*. It can be done if you are closer to your opponent or if he is behind your back. Normally, you would come up from a *cocorinha* or other ground position, straight to his chin, using the top of your head. Here the attacker is completing his *armada* against the defending capoeirista who came from an innocent *cocorinha*.

Figure 44.3: The *escorumelo* can end a fight. Don't do it in the *roda*!

Figure 44.4: The *cabeçada* against an *aú*.

The *cabeçada baixa* shown in Figure 44.4 is normally executed in the *roda* though without the intention of hurting your partner. You can come at a 90° angle to intercept his *aú*, or at a 45° to parallel angle, using a sideways or a forward low *cabeçada*. The attacked capoeirista will be able to change his *aú* into an *aú dobrado* to avoid the fall, or use his knees against your head or a *chibata* against your back before you reach him. Therefore, you'd better think twice before trying a *cabeçada* attack against a good *aú*.

The *cabeçada de chão* (ground *cabeçada*) is another technique widely used among capoeiristas of all sorts.* It is a very cunning move, which can be executed in a *roda* by an apparently very slow capoeirista who, in a sudden change of attitude, can turn it into a quick and powerful blow to the his opponent doing the *aú*.

Going down for a *cabeçada de chão*.

The next three techniques are very common in real-life self-defense incidents. Together with the repertoire of *cabeçadas*, a capoeirista can avoid some unexpected and difficult situations.

---

* The terms "ground," "low," or "sideways" are all methodological constructions that I use in order to identify the same technique in different situations.

The *telefone* (literally the telephone) can be hazardous if applied correctly (Figure 44.5). **Do not** use your hands curved in a shell-like shape. This will not help you to get the most out of your attack. Instead, use your open hands as straight as possible, and hit as hard as you can on both ears of your opponent **at the same time**. Failure to do so will cause your adversary no damage at all, whereas if you do it right, chances are that the assailant will find himself in a big (and painful) trouble.

Figure 44.5: Applying the *telefone*.

Figure 44.6: Applying the *dedeira*.

The *dedeira* (Figure 44.6) is another handy move when done by surprise against a careless assailant. If you are being hugged, specially by a stronger assailant, or if he is too close, simply attack his eyes with your index and middle fingers at the same time (and then escape with a complementary *cabeçada* on his nose).

The palm heel strike called *escala* (not to be confused with the *negativa escala*) is also a direct blow launched with your arm on the assailant's head. Usually, this punch is fired under your opponent's nose (as shown in Figure 44.7), or chin in a quick, powerful movement.

Figure 44.7: Applying an *escala*.

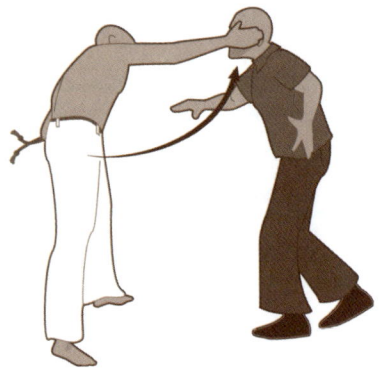

The *galopante* (Figure 44.8) should be done in a quick, sudden move. Actually, in real fighting all these techniques should be executed without the "telegraphing" aspect discussed in previous chapters; as a matter of fact, this applies to the *roda* as well.

Figure 44.8: The *galopante*.

While writing this book, I had some pleasant meetings with my friend Mestre Peixinho, who kindly helped me with the "curatorship" of those hundreds of drawings that I had created for the huge repertoire of capoeira techniques. With his well-known generosity, we engaged in some specific technical discussions.

Once we were discussing the best way to do a straighter *meia-lua de compasso*, with no delay, rather than doing it diagonally. Brilliantly, Peixinho came up with the *meia-lua na base* (the wheel kick over the same base, without further body displacement). Peixinho and I have not yet agreed on the move's name, but it is a very fast, dangerous and straightforward kick. I asked him if he would do it in a *roda*, with an advanced partner. He reminded me that we can do all movements in a *roda*, as long as we know how to do them – and how to "undo" them, i.e., stop the move every time we see that our partner is at risk.

IF YOU DO NOT HAVE FULL CONTROL OF A MOVE, DON'T EVER EXECUTE IT AGAINST YOUR PARTNER!

The back fist strike known as *godeme* (shown in Figure 44.9) can be fired to the side of the assailant's head or the bridge of his nose. You can use your ginga stance to fire most of these arm attacks; however, they are usually most effective if fired from zero stance.

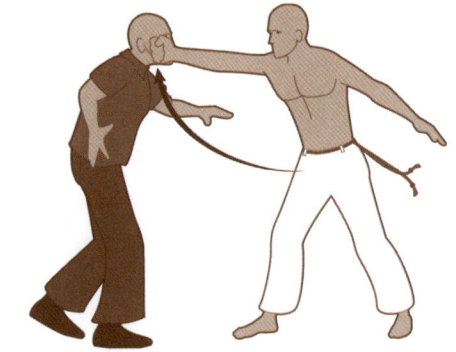

Figure 44.9: The *godeme*.

UNEXPECTED MOVES

To finalize these traumatic capoeira strikes, which, it is never too late to mention, are not as unusual as some practitioners may think, we still have the elbow strike called *cotovelada* (Figure 44.10), the knife hand attack called *cutelo* (Figure 44.11), and the *joelhada* (Figure 44.12).

The *cotovelada* can be done from inside to outside, but in capoeira we prefer to execute it from outside to inside, as in a backhand elbow strike to the adversary's jaw. If you are looking for more accuracy and power, try holding your forearm at wrist level and pulling it in your direction while at the same time, as in a lever, firing your elbow at the desired target.

Figure 44.10: The *cotovelada*.

The *cutelo* can be delivered from your *ginga* or from zero stance as in a "fake" *armada* (you rotate, but give up your *armada*, replacing it with the *cutelo* fired at the assailant's neck), which is the most efficient way. Alternatively, you may prefer to execute the *cutelo* from scratch, i.e., without faking a kick and with or without rotating your body.

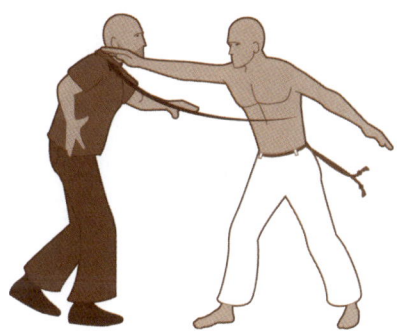

Figure 44.11: The *cutelo*.

The knee strike called *joelhada* (Figure 44.12) can often be executed against an attempted *arrastão* to your legs, just to mention a classic example. You may use your forward leg from your current stance, or retrieve your supporting leg to create more space before delivering the strike to your attacker's head.

Figure 44.12: The *joelhada*.

Practicing Alone

I advise you to practice the moves presented in this chapter **moderately** on your training bag. Never execute head butts without first discussing it with your physician and your Mestre or coach!

When doing the *galopante,* make sure to keep your attacking arm slightly bent at the elbow. If you hit the sandbag too hard with your attacking arm too straight, you may hurt your elbow joints and ligaments. Take this advice as an example for all the other hand attacks, and please, do not try hitting the sandbag with a *dedeira,* or else you might break your fingers!

Defenses and Counterattacks

In the *bloqueio* chapter, we saw a special defense against the *galopante*. For all the other hand attacks, your best choice is to use the opposite strategy, i.e., counterattack with your kicks. To do this you will have to retrieve your attacking leg, assuming you want to use a *meia-lua de compasso,* a *chapa giratória,* or an *armada,* for example. If you want to use a *martelo* or a *ponteira* (the best choices against hand attacks), retrieve your supporting, pivot leg and surprise your adversary with the *martelo,* or the *ponteira,* fired from the front leg.

Using the backward (retrieving) *negativa escala* is also a good defensive approach when you see that your adversary is going to use hand or head attacks. Ultimately, though, if you cannot avoid contact, try a crossed-arm blocking defense against any *cabeçada*. However, if you do have some space for action, you can still use several flying kicks, including some aerials like the *compasso pulado*.

If you happen to be in the situation of the bald-headed guy in Figure 44.12, try a crossed-arm defense or, ultimately, grab his *boca de calça* on his attacking leg and use a *passa-pé* on his supporting leg, while going down to a *negativa*. Keep hold of his pants!

Mestre Bimba's Sequences

In order to organize a method for teaching his Capoeira Regional, Mestre Bimba created eight sequences of attack and defense techniques to be practiced by the students in a capoeira school. These moves should be practiced until the capoeirista is proficient in all eight sequences. The Mestres should verify the quality of each move being performed and correct the moves along the way. However, capoeiristas should be often encouraged to participate and help correct his or her partner's moves as well. The sequences must be trained while alternating capoeiristas **(a)** and **(b)**, as well as left and right sides.

Each move must be followed by a return to the original *ginga* stance. In addition to the normal practice, I encourage all practitioners to perform the sequences all over again, returning to zero stance after each move. However, moves must follow the flow of motion, independently if you are practicing from a *ginga* or zero stance.

In the table below I used the "+" sign to propose a continuous flow of motion, i.e., when **capoeirista (a)** attacks **capoeirista (b)** with a *meia-lua de frente* executed with his left leg in the first sequence, he immediately follows his *meia-lua de frente* with an *armada* with his right leg, while **capoeirista (b)** executes the *cocorinha* to protect herself against his *meia-lua de frente,* and immediately follows it with a *negativa* to defend herself against his *armada*.

In addition to Bimba's eight sequences, many capoeira schools have their own proprietary sequences, which is always an excellent asset for any capoeirista.

First Sequence

Step	Capoeirista A	Step	Capoeirista B
1	*meia-lua de frente* with right leg	2	*cocorinha*
3	*meia-lua de frente* with left leg + *armada* with right leg	4	*cocorinha* + *negativa*
5	*aú*	6	*cabeçada*

Second Sequence

Step	Capoeirista A	Step	Capoeirista B
1	*queixada* with right leg	2	*cocorinha*
3	*queixada* with left leg	4	*cocorinha + armada* with right leg
5	*cocorinha + benção*	6	*negativa*
7	*aú*	8	*cabeçada*
9	*rolê*		

Third Sequence

Step	Capoeirista A	Step	Capoeirista B
1	*martelo* with right leg	2	*rasteira em pé* with left leg
3	*martelo* with left leg	4	*rasteira em pé* with right leg + *armada* with left leg
5	*cocorinha + benção*	6	*negativa*
7	*aú*	8	*cabeçada*
9	*rolê*		

Fourth Sequence

Step	Capoeirista A	Step	Capoeirista B
1	*godeme*	2	*bloqueio* with hands
3	*godeme*	4	*bloqueio* with hands
5	*galopante*	6	*arrastão*
7	*aú*	8	*negativa + cabeçada*
9	*rolê*		

Fifth Sequence

Step	Capoeirista A	Step	Capoeirista B
1	giro	2	cabeçada
3	joelhada	4	negativa
5	aú	6	cabeçada
7	rolê		

Sixth Sequence

Step	Capoeirista A	Step	Capoeirista B
1	meia-lua de compasso	2	cocorinha + meia-lua de compasso
3	cocorinha + joelhada	4	negativa
5	aú	6	cabeçada
7	rolê		

Seventh Sequence

Step	Capoeirista A	Step	Capoeirista B
1	armada with right leg	2	cocorinha
3	armada with left leg	4	cocorinha + armada
5	cocorinha + benção	6	negativa
7	aú	8	cabeçada
9	rolê		

Eighth Sequence

Step	Capoeirista A	Step	Capoeirista B
1	benção	2	negativa
3	aú	4	cabeçada
5	rolê		

Cintura Desprezada

Besides the eight sequences of moves, Mestre Bimba created the *cintura desprezada*, a sequence of throws executed from a series of connected techniques, where the capoeirista projects his partner up into the air and onto the ground in a way that he/she, can land on their feet, either standing or in a crouching position. These exercises were created in order to develop self-confidence and a sense of cooperation between capoeiristas, as well as to teach them to always fall on their feet. It is a training method designed to be practiced in a specific order. However, we often see small variations in the order – and sometimes in the style – in which the sequence is practiced. This does not compromise the quality of the method, as long as the practitioners perform at their best.

The leading capoeirista, normally an advanced student or a ranked instructor, should execute the throws in such a way as to avoid hurting his partner, but rather taking him or her through the intended pathway in a fluid combination of moves. The capoeirista who is projected over the leading capoeirista must touch the ground with the tip of the feet, with knees and upper body slightly bent, so as to be comfortable in the fall, just like a cat jumping from one point to another. As an example, following is a description of a common series of Mestre Bimba's sequence of throws.

The first of the sequence is the *cintura desprezada*. The two capoeiristas are in a *ginga* stance when **capoeirista (a)** executes an *aú* and stops in a *bananeira* in front of **capoeirista (b)**; **capoeirista (b)** approaches **capoeirista (a)** in a timely manner within the flow of motion, bending his head and torso to receive **capoeirista (a)** by his waist and belly over his shoulder; and then, with the help of his back, launches **capoeirista (a)** back over his shoulders.

Capoeirista (a) then touches the ground behind **capoeirista (b),** immediately grabbing him around his neck in a typical *gravata* (necktie), stepping forward to begin a *balão de lado* (lateral throw); **capoeirista (b)** uses his hands as support on the waist of **capoeirista (a)** who, using a leverage created with the aid of his hips and of his slightly bent legs, throws **capoeirista (b)** over his back as in a judo move. **Capoeirista (b)** should land smoothly on his feet and immediately execute a *tesoura de costas* (back scissors) toward **capoeirista (a),** as he quickly executes a timely and evasive *aú* over his *tesoura de costas* in order to escape and continue the *flow of throws* with the next move, which will be the *balão cinturado*.

As **capoeirista (a)** finishes his *aú* over the *tesoura de costas*, **capoeirista (b)** then tries to execute a *cabeçada* or a *boca de calça* on **capoeirista (a)**, but is caught on a *balão cinturado* (waist throw) by **capoeirista (a)** who bends over his back, grabs him by the waist and throws him back high over his shoulders. **Capoeirista (b)** should land smoothly on his feet, and both capoeiristas should recover their original *ginga* stance.

Following the flow of motion for just one or two *ginga* moves, **capoeirista (a)** starts the *balão em pé* (upright throw) by approaching and turning his back to **capoeirista (b)** and grabbing him around his neck with a *gravata alta* (high necktie); **capoeirista (b)** uses his hands as support on the waist of **capoeirista (a)** who, using leverage created with the aid of his hips and of slightly bent legs, throws **capoeirista (b)** over his back. **Capoeirista (b)** should land smoothly on his feet and start the sequence all over again, alternating the original lead.

The following table is a quick reminder of Mestre Bimba's sequence.

Step	Capoeirista A	Step	Capoeirista B
1	executes *aú* + *bananeira*	2	receives **(a)** by his waist and belly and launches him back over his shoulders
3	touches the ground behind **(b)**, grabs around his neck with a *gravata* and begins *balão de lado*	4	uses his hands as support on **(a)**'s waist to enhance the leverage for the throw, and lands smoothly
		5	executes a *tesoura de costas* toward **(a)**
6	executes an evading *aú*	7	tries a *cabeçada* or a *boca de calça* on **(a)**
8	executes a *balão cinturado* and goes back to *ginga* stance	9	lands smoothly on the ground and recover the *ginga* stance
10	starts the *balão em pé* with a *gravata alta*	11	uses his hands as support on the waist of **(a)** to help the lever for the throw, lands smoothl

Roda de Boca

I will never forget this wonderful day on Mestre Camisa's farm in upstate Rio de Janeiro. I had discussed my book project with my friends Mestre Paulo Siqueira and Mestre Peixinho, with whom I also had wonderful times on different occasions over lunch and dinner at my home.

With Paulo Siqueira, my colleague at the original *Grupo Bantus* in Rio de Janeiro, besides enjoying a great coconut manjar dessert, I revived good old memories from our capoeira school at Morro do Pavão & Pavãozinho.

With Peixinho, I brought back the good memories from the time we practiced Olympic gymnastics together, when he was a famous Mestre from the *Senzala* School of Capoeira and I was just a student on my way to becoming a teacher myself. He was one of my idols in capoeira at that time (though he hadn't known that until I met him over this book project). I also had the pleasure of having him as the "curator" of this book.

From Mestre Camisa, besides being introduced to the *ecological berimbau* (see Introduction) and to his amusing couple of (free) macaws over a delicious lunch at his farmhouse, I was introduced to what I named (with his blessings, I hope) the *"Roda de Boca,"* meaning the "Mouth *Roda*."

These three great characters have contributed in their own way to the international development of capoeira, and their generosity toward me personally and toward this book project was overwhelming and priceless. Three great friends, three great Mestres!

The Roda de Boca functions like a blind game of chess. It is, in fact, a blind game of capoeira. I must confess that I was surprised that I hadn't had the opportunity to play the Roda de Boca in my years of capoeira back in the 1970s.

When Camisa, out of nowhere, suddenly said *"armada!"* I just stared at him. I didn't know what he meant at first. Then he said *"meia-lua de compasso!"* – and I realized I was already dead! Next, we played a delicious Roda de Boca, to be repeated again over dinner at my home as a special "live" presentation to my wife, and here is my recommendation for a good Roda de Boca:

Beginners, Start with Bimba's Sequence

I suggest that all students of capoeira at beginner's level practice the Roda de Boca with the 8 sequences of Mestre Bimba first, followed by the Cintura Desprezada. Student **(a)** would say *"meia-lua de frente,"* and student **(b)** would quickly answer *"cocorinha,"* followed by student **(a)**'s *"meia-lua de frente and armada,"* to which student **(b)** would immediately answer *"cocorinha and negativa,"* followed again by student **(a)**'s *"aú"* and quickly finished by student **(b)**'s *"cabeçada."*

Mestres, Evaluate Your Students

It would be an excellent practice to have the students evaluated and corrected during the course of a Roda de Boca. The practice could include a beginner's level evaluation of the entire Bimba's sequence, followed by evaluation and/or contest between partners of the same level in a free Roda de Boca. This activity could be held publicly in the center of the *roda,* or as a more private evaluation in the presence of the Mestre and each pair of the same cord level.

The Roda de Boca is a great asset for the practice and evaluation of a capoeira repertoire. I humbly thank my friend Mestre Camisa for having introduced me to the game.

Mental rehearsal and visualization are great companions of the serious martial arts athlete. The Roda de Boca is one great way to motivate capoeiristas and give them confidence, which could activate the needed muscles to almost 20% of what is required for performing the techniques in reality!

In addition, practicing alone having in mind your opponent in a physical self-simulation from mentally visualized unprogrammed movements, conducted in response to your memory events, will complete your methods of mental skills and physical simulations, which could then activate not only the needed muscles to a higher response when performing the techniques against a real opponent, but also help stimulate a more constant search for techniques in the vast repertoire of capoeira moves.